*George Washington
and the Half-King
Chief Tanacharison*

ALSO BY PAUL R. MISENCIK

*The Original American Spies:
Seven Covert Agents of the Revolutionary War* (2014)

George Washington and the Half-King Chief Tanacharison

An Alliance That Began the French and Indian War

PAUL R. MISENCIK

McFarland & Company, Inc., Publishers
Jefferson, North Carolina

LIBRARY OF CONGRESS CATALOGUING-IN-PUBLICATION DATA

Misencik, Paul R., 1940–
　　George Washington and the Half-King Chief Tanacharison : an alliance that began the French and Indian War / Paul R. Misencik.
　　　p.　　cm.
　　Includes bibliographical references and index.

　　ISBN 978-0-7864-7950-4 (softcover : acid free paper) ∞
　　ISBN 978-1-4766-1540-0 (ebook)

　　1. United States—History—French and Indian War, 1754–1763—Causes.　2. Washington, George, 1732–1799—Relations with Indians.　3. Washington, George, 1732–1799—Military leadership.　4. Pennsylvania—History—French and Indian War, 1754–1763—Campaigns.　5. United States—History—French and Indian War, 1754–1763—Campaigns.　6. Mingo Indians—History—18th century.　I. Title.

E199.M67 2014
973.4'1092—dc23   2014014952

BRITISH LIBRARY CATALOGUING DATA ARE AVAILABLE

© 2014 Paul R. Misencik. All rights reserved

No part of this book may be reproduced or transmitted in any form or by any means, electronic or mechanical, including photocopying or recording, or by any information storage and retrieval system, without permission in writing from the publisher.

On the cover: *A Charming Field for an Encounter* by Robert Griffing (Paramount Press, Inc.)

Printed in the United States of America

McFarland & Company, Inc., Publishers
　Box 611, Jefferson, North Carolina 28640
　　www.mcfarlandpub.com

This book is dedicated to my family:
my wife, Sally, my daughter, Karen, and my son, Paul Jr.
Without their love, encouragement and
assistance this book would never have been written.

Table of Contents

Preface   1
Prologue. Tuesday, May 28, 1754—Jumonville Glen   7

1. Conflicting Claims   11
2. Céloron   21
3. Opening Moves   33
4. French Forts on the Allegheny   46
5. Washington Warns the French   57
6. The Race to the Forks   80
7. The Spark Is Struck   97
8. Rationalization and Justification   116
9. The Half-King Gets His War   121
10. Battle at Great Meadows   139

Epilogue   151
Chapter Notes   179
Bibliography   189
Index   195

Preface

The French and Indian War has captivated those with an interest in American history almost from the time it was fought. It contained all of the elements that typified the clichéd American romantic ideal: remote wilderness forts, resourceful frontiersmen, wild Indian tribes, and savage battles fought in the rugged mountains and primitive forests of a largely uninhabited continent.

Most students of history are aware of the significant facts and events of the French and Indian War in that it was primarily a wilderness war between England and France, and that it began with an early morning exchange of musketry in a very remote forest glen between troops under young George Washington and the French officer Ensign Jumonville, who was killed in that skirmish. Students of history also realize that the forests, which became battlefields in that war, were the homelands of American Indians who had lived there for centuries, and who found themselves caught up in the Anglo-French struggle for the continent. The war itself has been the subject of many scholarly works, which detail the basis of French and English claims to the territory, the campaigns, battles, and the major European and colonial personalities who took part in the war. However, little emphasis has been placed on the specific chain of events that led to the fatal confrontation at Jumonville Glen, or for that matter, the Indians' motivations and involvement in the cumulative occurrences that precipitated the French and Indian War. Along with the Indians' relationships and interactions with both European powers, this book explores some of the more significant reasons for their participation in those events.

There are a myriad of works on the life of George Washington, and while most detail his missions and accomplishments, few delve into the personality of young Washington during his first experiences as a military leader. This work examines Washington who, barely into his twenties, accepted incredibly daunting missions into the wilderness on behalf of the lieutenant governor of

Virginia, and how Washington faced the numerous challenges he was forced to address on his own. Among those challenges was the necessity of winning the friendship and support of the Ohio Indians, who were caught in the middle of the Anglo-French controversy. Washington's other more pressing challenge was to take command of a disparate force of colonial troops and somehow on his own, evict a larger, more powerful and veteran French army from the disputed area of the upper Ohio and Allegheny Rivers. With no one else to provide him with support and advice, Washington turned to the sage and wily Seneca half-king Tanacharison for assistance. However, Washington was not yet aware that Tanacharison had a mission of his own that required Washington's involvement in precipitating a war with France. This book studies the relationship between young Washington and Tanacharison and how each sought to influence the other to further their respective agendas.

It is well documented that the Indians were recruited by both sides prior to and during the conflict, but there are few studies that shed light on why the Indians were willing to join in a war between two European powers, or why they chose to ally themselves with one side over the other. Certainly there were ancient enmities between Indian nations, like the bitter hostility between the Huron and Iroquois confederacies, which some historians allude to as the definitive reason for those particular nations aligning themselves on opposite sides in the war. Those thoughts may be overly simplistic, but they have been reinforced for generations in all genres that pertained to the war. Even romanticized novels like James Fenimore Cooper's *The Last of the Mohicans* helped promulgate the notion that hereditary animosities were the overriding reasons for an Indian nation's particular allegiance. They convey the idea that, quite simply, the Indians chose a side because their ancient tribal enemies were associated with the other.

While the blood feud mentality that existed among some Indian societies may have had a significant impact on determining their alliances, those decisions were often arrived at because of more current situations that generally affected their economy or their way of life. The respective Indian nations and indeed the individual tribes who found themselves caught up in the prelude to the war between France and England were far more sophisticated and pragmatic regarding frontier diplomacy and how various alliances would affect them than most white people realized. White leaders on both sides considered the Indians as simple savages or, at best, as naïve children. They constantly used patronizing terms in communications with the Indians, referring to the Indians as "my children" and to themselves as "your father." For the most part, they believed that it was their trade goods, technological superiority, military power, and eloquence that brought the Indians over to their side. In reality, the reasons that the Indians allied themselves with either the French or the English were far more subtle and complex. These are the facets this work explores: primarily the relationships between the Indians and the French and the English, and indeed between the various Indian societies themselves. Not surprisingly, it provides another perspective in examining reasons for the Indians' direct and overt participation in events that led to a war that they knew would certainly encompass them and their families.

My interest in Native American history came naturally to me as a young person growing up in rural Ohio. The melodic Indian place names, beautiful petroglyphs, and the flint arrowheads that I found in the newly plowed fields behind our home were reminders of the Indians who once lived there. Those tantalizing mementos captured my interest to the point where I wanted to learn all I could about these vanished people and their way of life. As a student prior to and during high school, I was fortunate to have met several old-timers who were veterans of the Indian wars in the west, and the tales of their encounters with the western Indians were enthralling. However, the wild Indians of Ohio and the northeastern woodlands had vanished long before. There were no longer any living souls who could talk about encountering them in their natural state. The Ohio Indians left only their bones, their arrowheads, and their magnificent place names as reminders that they were once the masters there. The best I could do at the time was to visit the places where they once lived, hunted, traveled, or traded before they moved on or died. Among my most prized processions at the time was a signed edition of *Ohio Indian Trails* by Frank Wilcox, and from high school through university, I crisscrossed the state locating the sites of old Indian villages and following ancient aboriginal trails. Fortunately at that time, many of the traces could still be recognized and followed.

Through my studies of the history of Indian trading centers like Pickawillany, Lower Shawnee Town, Junundat, Conchaké, and white trading posts like those of François Saguin, John Croghan, and Fort Sandoski, I became increasingly familiar with the complexities and challenges of the Indian trade as it pertained to the European traders, but also from the perspective of the Indians. The French and English trade competition in Ohio and their respective efforts to exclusively control it impacted the Indians in the Ohio territory profoundly. The expanding spheres of influence into the area by both European powers not only affected the cost and availability of trade goods, but also initiated changes in the relationships between Indians and the French and English, and even more significantly, it impacted the relationships between the various Indian societies themselves. The Indians living in the area reacted out of necessity to the struggle between the French and the English, but their reactions were rarely in concert. Their courses of action depended on their particular and often personal circumstances and situations. One thing was certain, however; all were forced to choose a side. The Oneida half-king Scarouady once said, "You can't live in the woods and be neutral." Their rationale and the actions and initiatives the Indians and their leaders took in the face of the Anglo-French intrusion into their homeland is the basis for my book.

In this work I use the generic term "Indians" as a synonym for the indigenous peoples who inhabited the Americas prior to the coming of the Europeans. The term originated as early as 1492 when Christopher Columbus first thought he had found an alternate route to India and the natives he encountered were Indians. It wasn't long before that misconception was rectified, but his name for the people endured. Today, we tend to use more accurately descriptive or politically correct terms like "Native Americans" in the United States, or "First Nations" in Canada. However, throughout the eighteenth, nineteenth, and most of the twentieth centuries, the term Indian was in common use, even by Native Americans in reference to themselves. Most of the eighteenth-century documents cited as references in this work use the term "Indian," and I have continued to use the term for continuity.

My thanks to the many research sources I was able to access, and their incredibly helpful and knowledgeable staff without which this book would not have been possible. Those include the National Museum of the American Indian in Washington, D.C.; the Library of Congress in Washington, D.C.; George Washington's Mount Vernon Estate, Museum, and Gardens; the William L. Clements Library at the University of Michigan; the Fort Necessity National Battlefield at Fayette County, Pennsylvania; the Braddock's Field Historical Society in Braddock, Pennsylvania; The Fort Lebœuf Historical Society in Waterford, Pennsylvania; the Fort Ligonier Association; The Ohio Historical Society; The Historical Society of Pennsylvania; Fort Crown Point New York State Historical Site; the Washington County Historical Society at Fort Edward, New York; The Winchester-Frederick County Historical Society at Winchester, Virginia; The Fairfax County Historical Society; the Pickawillany Ohio State Historic Site near Piqua, Ohio; Fort Bedford Museum and Old Bedford Village, in Bedford, Pennsylvania; Fort Roberdeau at Altoona, Pennsylvania; my friends and colleagues of the First Virginia Regiment of the Continental Line; the magnificent archives and living history resources at Colonial Williamsburg; and the many others that I may have inadvertently omitted.

And finally, my love and thanks to my wife, Sally, my daughter, Karen, and my son, Paul Jr., for their unfailing support, great suggestions, and marvelous technical expertise. Sally is not only an enthusiastic, energetic, and fun-loving companion, but she is also a tireless researcher who loves the adventure and excitement of seeking out, visiting, and documenting sources and sites referenced in the book. Without her marvelous help, this book wouldn't be quite as complete and the experience wouldn't be nearly as much fun.

Prologue
Tuesday, May 28, 1754— Jumonville Glen

The volley fired by a young Virginian in the backwoods of America set the world on fire. —Horace Walpole

It was just past dawn on Tuesday, May 28, 1754, in a remote wilderness ravine, and the musket smoke from the early morning skirmish had hardly dissipated when twenty-two-year-old George Washington realized that he had just started another war between England and France. The two countries had held a tenuous peace for the past five years, but even so it seemed that England and France had been at war with one another for as long as anyone could remember. For the past 66 years, three generations of Englishmen both in Europe and in North America had battled Frenchmen almost continuously. Since 1689, the two nations had fought three long and bloody declared wars with only a few short pauses in between that allowed each side to regroup and rearm before once again hurling their armies at one another. King George's War, or the War of the Austrian Succession, had lasted eight years, from 1740 to 1748, and had ended less than five years previous. Before that, Queen Anne's War, or the War of the Spanish Succession, had raged for 11 years, from 1702 until 1713, and prior to that, England and France had battled in King William's War, or the War of the League of Augsburg, from 1689 through 1697.

The wars were devastating in North America. French and Indian raids destroyed several English villages in which the inhabitants were either massacred or carried off into captivity. Isolated homesteads were particularly vulnerable and hundreds of families were either killed or carried off as captives. Countless other families fearfully abandoned the smallholdings they had so laboriously carved out of the wilderness and returned to areas they hoped were beyond the range of hostile raiding parties. However, even the larger towns and villages were not immune to attacks, and several settlements with larger populations suffered devastating raids. These included the Massachusetts Bay Colony villages of Deerfield and Haverhill, the New York towns of Schenectady and Saratoga, and the hamlet of Falmouth in Maine. It wasn't all one-sided however. The English and their Iroquois allies launched their own attacks on villages and settlements in New France. As a defensive measure, communities on both sides sent out tough ranger units and Indian allies to take the war to the enemy. Villages continually sent rangers out to patrol the forests and intercept enemy raiders, or at least to provide sufficient warning of an imminent enemy attack. Around the time of King William's War, the Massachusetts Bay Colony went one step further when they offered bounties for Indian scalps. It was hoped that the program would result in more numerous and aggressive operations against the Indians. However, the French also began to pay bounties for English scalps and prisoners, and the attacks on small farms and tiny hamlets became bloodier and more frequent. Even during the short periods of supposed diplomatic peace between the wars, Indian raiding parties supported by both the French and English regularly struck, with deadly results, against the other's frontier settlements. This partisan warfare extended onto the sea, where privateers preyed on the other side's shipping and fishing fleets. The formally declared wars were certainly long and bloody, but the intervals between the wars were in many instances just as deadly. Hundreds of people in New France and the English colonies were killed or captured and their settlements were ravaged or destroyed by savage attacks during those periods of supposed peace.

Notwithstanding the long history of hostilities between the two nations, young Lieutenant Colonel Washington realized that he had been the one to break the current fragile peace between France and England. He was justifiably concerned about how his actions would be judged by his superiors, and especially by the king in England. Worse in Washington's mind than having drawn the English colonies and indeed the British Empire into another war with France, was how his actions would be judged by history, and whether his personal honor would survive intact. To young Washington, honor and integrity were the true measures of a man and how a person was judged by his peers and by society in general. From his early years, he had always tried to comport himself in a manner that was considered honorable and above reproach. As a youth, Washington had hand-copied the "110 Rules of Civility & Decent Behavior in Company and Conversation," based on rules composed by French Jesuits in 1595, and which he used as a guide for genteel and moral behavior. But now he found himself in a situation where his personal honor may have been compromised, and he must have pondered how that came to pass and wondered what would be the consequences.

As he walked among the 13 dead and 21 captive Frenchmen at the bottom of the small glen, Washington reflected on the missions he undertook on behalf of the Virginia lieutenant governor Robert Dinwiddie and how he had tried to complete them ably and honorably. His first undertaking, which was carried out the previous winter, had been to deliver a summons to the French commander on the upper Ohio directing him to withdraw his French troops from the area. Upon his return with the French officer's response, Washington received praise from Dinwiddie for his intrepidness in carrying out such an arduous and dangerous assignment. Soon after, the young Virginian was honored with a second mission for the lieutenant governor, which was to assist in the construction of a fortified post at the Forks of the Ohio (present Pittsburgh, Pennsylvania). However, this enterprise began to unravel almost from the very beginning. Washington first found it impossible to recruit the planned number of troops for the expedition, and worse, a superior French army had captured the strategic Forks of the Ohio while he and his Virginians were still en route. To complicate matters, Washington's commanding officer, Colonel Joshua Fry, who was to take overall command of the expedition, was accidently killed as a result of a fall from his horse. This event elevated the untested twenty-two-year-old Washington to the position of commander of the troops that were marching toward the Forks. However, now with the full responsibility of the expedition resting on his shoulders, he was in a quandary on how to salvage the mission, and he wondered if it even would be possible to do so.

With no one else to look to for advice, Washington formed a closer association with a comrade from the previous winter's expedition, the Seneca half-king Tanacharison,[1] who had allied himself with the English. The term "half-king" was essentially an English appellation applied to leaders or headmen who represented the Iroquois council. The half-kings supervised the subjugated tribes that were under the domination of the Iroquois and also the expatriate Iroquois who were referred to as "Mingos." It appeared to Washington that Tanacharison had the most stature and authority of the Indians in the area, and being alone in his wilderness command, Washington placed considerable reliance on Tanacharison for guidance and military intelligence. Indeed, Washington and Tanacharison formed a fairly close and personal relationship, but as Washington would soon discover, the half-king had an agenda of his own.

Surveying the carnage from the early morning fight, Washington almost certainly began to comprehend that he had been cleverly manipulated by the wily half-king into precipitating this bloody and consequential event.

Tanacharison had embellished the intentions and menace of a nearby bivouacked contingent of French troops and incited Washington and his Virginians to launch a dawn attack on them. The French survivors steadfastly maintained that they were peaceful diplomatic emissaries, and Washington was very concerned that he had not only begun a war, but had done so by attacking a party of French envoys. To make matters worse, the French commander had been brutally and cold-bloodedly murdered after the cease-fire and after the French had surrendered. Would that action forever taint Washington as having acted dishonorably? The young Virginian realized that the war was started, and all he could do now was make the best of it. He also hoped that in the process he would somehow be able to salvage his honor and reputation.

Hostilities would continue, major campaigns would be launched, and bloody battles would be fought even before France and England would formally declare war in May 1756. In North America, the English and American colonists would call it "the French and Indian War," while it was known as "la Guerre de la Conquéte" or "the War of Conquest" in Canada. The so-called "Seven-Years War" that young Washington and Tanacharison started would rage for almost nine years until 1763, and because it involved so many countries across the globe, it could justifiably be called "the First World War." This is the story of how it began.

1

Conflicting Claims

The French claim all the land on one side of the river, and the English claim all the land on the other side of the river. Where does the Indians' land lie?—Delaware[1] chief at the Logstown Council of 1752

During the first half of the eighteenth century, the land west of the Alleghenies, particularly the area drained by the Ohio River, was settled and populated by Native American tribes who had lived there for centuries. But the land was also claimed rather arrogantly by both England and France without regard to the people who inhabited the region. In 1748, there were perhaps six or more jurisdictional claims to the area around the Forks of the Ohio. The claimants included France, England, the Iroquois, Virginia, Pennsylvania, and of course the several Indian tribes that were indigenous to the area or had recently been driven there from their eastern homelands. The French claimed the territory primarily because of the explorations of René-Robert Cavelier, Sieur de La Salle (1643–1687), who in 1682 was the first European to travel the length of the Mississippi River. La Salle claimed the entire Mississippi basin for France on Sunday, April 9, 1682, and named the region "Louisiana" in honor of the French King Louis XIV. The French supported their claim by right of discovery and exploration by citing the explorations of several other noted Frenchmen who explored the interior of the North American continent from the early seventeenth century. The listing of illustrious French explorers included Jacques Cartier (1491–1557), Samuel de Champlain (ca. 1570–1635), Father Pierre François-Xavier de Charlevoix (1682–1761), Louis Joliet (1645–1700), Pierre Gaultier de Varennes, Sieur de la Vérendrye (1685–1749), Father Jacques Marquette (1637–1675), Jean Nicollet (ca. 1598–1642), and Pierre-Esprit Radisson (ca. 1640–1710). In addition, the French argued that their claim to the Ohio territory was affirmed by the treaties of Ryswick (1697), Utrecht (1713) and Aix-la-Chapelle (1748). Notwithstanding the documented history of French explorers, the French also based their claim on the natural boundaries and the routes of communication through the area. For more than a century, French-Canadian coureurs de bois and other entrepreneurial French and Canadian traders and trappers had penetrated deep into the interior of the continent, establishing trading posts northwest, west, south, and southwest of the Appalachians into the Great Plains and as far south as the Gulf of Mexico. Coureurs de bois, literally "runners of the woods," were independent entrepreneurial French-Canadian woodsmen, trappers, and traders who operated out of the mainstream of the fur-trading enterprise. Coming from every walk of life and social strata, they were drawn by the lure of the wilderness and the promise of adventure. They were hardy, resourceful, and fiercely independent, traveling the interior of North America and venturing deep into the wilderness to trap and trade for furs. Today we might describe them as having "gone native," which would be a very accurate description, because they generally went native in every sense of the term. Along their travels deep into the wilderness, the hardy coureurs de bois interacted with and developed an affinity with the Indians, often intermarrying with them "à la façon du pays" (literally, the way of the country, or according to local custom) and adopting their lifestyle. Since they generally went about their trapping and trading without obtaining the required permission from the French authorities, the coureurs de bois were sometimes considered as operating just outside the law. Aside from their rather dubious legal standing, the hardy coureurs de bois, along with other intrepid French and Canadian explorers and fur traders, were instrumental in expanding the borders of New France deep into the interior of the North American continent.

French forts and settlements stretched from north and west of Lake Superior, south along the Mississippi, Missouri, Wabash, Tennessee, Arkansas, and other rivers that drained into the Mississippi, and were established as far south as Le Nouvelle Orléans (New Orleans). French traders carried on a lucrative trade with the Indians, sending a steady stream of furs back to Montréal and Québec. Because they had established a very widespread network of habitations in the interior of the country that were tied to Montréal and Québec by navigable rivers, the French considered the Allegheny, Ohio, and Mississippi Rivers as normal and natural communication routes between Canada and the French outposts and settlements in the interior of the continent. At the same time, the French maintained that the Appalachian Mountains were a natural boundary that logically separated the British colonies from New France. It should be noted that the French did not consider the Allegheny as a separate river, but rather the upriver section of la Belle Rivière (the Beautiful River) or the Ohio River. Though the French referred to the Allegheny River as the

Ohio River, for clarity in this work, I shall continue to make the distinction between the Allegheny and Ohio Rivers.

The English claim to the Ohio territory was somewhat more tenuous. They based their claim to the area by declaring that John Cabot[2] (ca. 1450– ca. 1499) had reached the Atlantic coast of North America before anyone else. Interestingly, the British also referred to the treaty of Utrecht to support their claim, since one of the provisions was French recognition of British dominion over the Iroquois.[3] The British argued that the Iroquois had conquered the tribes in the Ohio region and therefore English jurisdiction logically extended to those lands by right of conquest.

While both the French and British monarchs claimed the Ohio territory, the colonists and royal representatives of New France and the British colonies were constantly creating friction in the area. Complicating the territorial border issue was the fact that the boundaries of the English colonies that bordered the Allegheny Mountains were not generally defined by a western limit. Virginia claimed that the dimensions of its colony was based on its charter of 1609, which imperiously defined Virginia's boundaries as 400 miles north and south along the Atlantic and from "sea to sea, west and northwest." Although the original Virginia charter was nullified and large segments of territory were carved off and given to Maryland in 1632, Carolina in 1663, New York and New Jersey in 1664, and Pennsylvania and Delaware in 1681, Virginia continued to base her western and northwestern claims on the earlier charter. To make matters more confusing, the individual colonial interpretations of their colonial boundaries overlapped or conflicted with their neighboring colonies' claims. For example, as late as 1783, Virginia was in possession of present Virginia, West Virginia and Kentucky, but still claimed the entire northwest area, including present Ohio, Indiana, Illinois, Michigan, Wisconsin and a large portion of Minnesota. Further complicating colonial relationships was Maryland's claim that its northern boundary was north of Philadelphia while Pennsylvania insisted that it ran south of Baltimore. Virginia, on the other hand, contended that Virginia was not bound by any agreement between the Penns and the Calverts and claimed all the land west "under the fortieth degree of northern latitude."[4]

Even though the Alleghenies were an intimidating 60-mile-wide barrier separating the English settlements on the east coast from the interior, the English colonists did not consider them to be a boundary defining the English colonies from New France by any means. As formidable as the Alleghenies were, they did not prevent a flood of English traders, trappers, settlers and land speculators from moving into the Ohio valley and beyond, much to the consternation of the French. French traders who had established trading centers in Ohio and had long enjoyed a virtual monopoly began to feel increased competition from their English counterparts, who were crossing the Alleghenies to take advantage of the lucrative Indian fur trade.

The period from about 1745 was notable in that despite controversial acquisition of Indian land by British colonists, the attitude of the Indians in the Ohio territory began to shift slightly in favor of the English. This was the result of an increased Indian dependence on European goods and an increasing number of English traders in the area who were able to supply trade merchandise. The burgeoning British industrial revolution and their resultant superior manufacturing capabilities allowed consumer goods, including trade articles, to be more plentiful and less costly than ever before. This certainly gave English merchants a distinct competitive edge. Nowhere was this commercial advantage more pronounced than in North America. The Ohio Indians were quick to realize that English traders had greater quantities of trade goods that were often superior in quality and less expensive than the French goods. Even before the end of King George's War in 1748, hardy entrepreneurial frontiersmen like George Croghan, John Fraser, and Conrad Weiser had penetrated into the Ohio valley, where they quickly established trade and good will between the English colonists and the tribes of the area.

George Croghan (ca. 1718–1782) emigrated from Dublin, Ireland, in 1741, but within a few years he was a very proficient frontiersman, fluent in Iroquois and Delaware dialects, and intimately knowledgeable of their habits and customs. He established several trading posts throughout the upper Ohio territory and was considered "the king of the Pennsylvania traders." Because of Croghan's recognized fair-dealing with the Indians and his respect for their culture, he was generally held in high esteem by the Indians of the Ohio and was extremely effective in spreading English influence throughout the area. The fact that English trade goods were better, cheaper, and more plentiful certainly helped Croghan win the loyalty of the Indians. The Ohio tribes were fully aware of the competition and how it benefitted them. A Wea[5] Indian chief at Fort Miamis[6] (present Fort Wayne, Indiana) complained to the French commander about the cost of French goods compared to those of the English: "You know well, my father, we pay for a wool blanket of 2 ½ points, 9 beavers; for one of cotton, 5 beavers; a pair of mitasses [leggings or gaiters], 3 beavers; a pound of powder, 3 beavers; 2 pounds of lead, a beaver. That is what rebuffs all our young men, and we are no longer able to keep them from going to the English, who give them everything very cheap."[7] French authorities were dismayed that English traders like Croghan were able to offer their goods to the Indians at about a fourth the price charged for comparable items by French traders, and the trade imbalance appeared to be getting worse. The industrious

Croghan set up trading locations throughout the Ohio territory as far afield as the mouth of the Cuyahoga River (present Cleveland, Ohio), the upper Great Miami River (present western Ohio), the Indian town of Pickawillany (present Piqua, Ohio), and as far down the Ohio River as the Shawnee villages near the Falls of the Ohio (present Louisville, Kentucky). Croghan's trading advantage was so one-sided that frustrated Indians often murdered French traders who were unable to compete and were perceived by the Indians as trying to cheat them. Because of his very successful trade in the Ohio territory at the expense of French traders, the French authorities soon realized they could no longer tolerate his blatantly criminal trespass and mercantile poaching without the French being viewed as weak and unable to maintain their sovereignty in the area. In an effort to curtail his activities and also to issue a stern warning to other potential English intruders, a bounty of approximately $1,000 or £225 was placed on Croghan's head. It was never collected.

John Fraser (1721–1773) was also a Pennsylvania trader and gunsmith who was cut from similar cloth as Croghan. He established a trading house near the mouth of French Creek on the Allegheny River near the Indian village of Venango (present Franklin, Pennsylvania). Fraser was a shrewd and successful trader, but was perceived as fair and honest in his dealings with the Indians. As a result, he was able to continue his business among the Indians, and was often protected by them while other traders were either killed or driven off.

The French and Canadians actually referred to French Creek as Rivière aux Bœufs, after the bison they found grazing there. There are several conflicting versions regarding the origin and the meaning of the name "Venango." The Indians originally referred to French Creek by the name Venango. It is thought to be a corruption of the Seneca or Delaware word for "mink" or "otter," by which they referred to the waterway. Interpretations of "Venango" have also included "crooked." The Indian village located near the mouth of French Creek also became known by the same name. For continuity in this work and to avoid confusion, I will endeavor to use the more common terms "Venango" for the village and "French Creek" for the waterway.

Johann Conrad Weiser (1696–1760) was born in Württemberg, Germany. After Conrad's mother died, his father and Conrad's siblings emigrated to North America in 1710 and settled in Schoharie, New York. Conrad, as he was called, spent most of his spare time with the Mohawk Indians. He lived with the Mohawks during the entire winter of 1713–14, where he learned their culture, customs and their language. When he returned home the following summer, Conrad had a series of quarrels with his new stepmother, and he packed up and left home for good. He lived among the Indians for about six years, where he farmed and also worked as an interpreter. By the time he married and moved his family to Tulpehocken, Pennsylvania, in 1720, Weiser had acquired a knowledge of Indian dialects, culture and customs unmatched by all but a few other colonists.

Weiser was one of the first to realize that the support of the Iroquois would be crucial to the English colonies in limiting French expansion. As a result, he became active in cementing relations between the Iroquois and the English and was instrumental in finalizing land purchase agreements and obtaining an alliance with the Iroquois at the Philadelphia treaty of 1742. However, Weiser had a more global view of Indian-colonial diplomacy. Rather than promoting agreements that only benefited one faction or the other, he generally urged for measures that were vital to the safety and security of Indians as well as the colonists. For example, in King George's War, Weiser supported the successful efforts of the Six Nations to remain neutral in spite of Sir William Johnson's powerful attempts to bring them into the war. In 1747, Weiser commented on the challenges he faced from white colonists in dealing with the Indians: "I shall be sick of Indian Affairs if no medium is found to do them justice.... I find it very hard sometimes to Excuse the Government.... The Indians have just reason to Complain at the behavior of some of our people."[8]

Weiser was instrumental in promoting the expansion of English colonial trade deep into French-claimed territory. He worked closely with George Croghan in negotiating provisions of the 1748 Treaty of Logstown, which facilitated Pennsylvania trade with the trans–Allegheny Indians as far west as the Mississippi River. Logstown was an important Indian village just north of present Ambridge, Pennsylvania, about 18 miles downriver from present Pittsburgh, Pennsylvania. It was called Shenango by the Indians and referred to as Chiningué by the French. Logstown was originally settled by the Shawnee around 1728, but later became a mixed village of several different tribes from the area. From 1743 to 1753, it was one of the most important Indian towns on the upper Ohio and the scene of several Indian councils.

While Weiser maintained extraordinarily good relations with the Iroquois, it was occasionally at the expense of other Indian tribes. In fact, some of his dealings that affected various eastern tribes, particularly the Delaware, served to alienate them against both the English and the Iroquois, and caused those tribes to gravitate toward the French for protection. For example, in 1736 at the treaty of Philadelphia, Weiser, with the aid of the Iroquois chief Shikellamy,[9] prompted the Iroquois league to sell land drained by the Delaware River to Pennsylvania. The dubious part of that deal was that the land in question belonged to the Delaware Indians, and the Iroquois had never laid claim to the land until they sold it to the Pennsylvanians. Though they protested, the Delaware realized they were not strong enough to defy either the powerful Iroquois or the Pennsylvanians, and they were forced to give up their land and move westward. The following year Weiser, again with the assistance of Shikellamy, was party to the infamous "walking purchase," in which Pennsylvania duped the Delaware Indians out of an additional 1.2 million acres (approximately 1,875 square miles) of land. While the two land deals served to cement good relations between the Iroquois and the English colonies, it created a lasting animosity on the part of the Delaware toward the English and the Iroquois,[10] which was advantageous to the French.

An interesting story regarding Conrad Weiser and Shikellamy illustrates the etiquette and diplomacy of the Iroquois and how well Conrad Weiser understood that aspect of Indian culture. One day they were travelling along the Susquehanna River opposite the Isle of Que (near present Selinsgrove, Pennsylvania), when Shikellamy pointed to Weiser's new rifle and said, "I have had a dream. I dreamed that you gave me a new rifle." Weiser, fully aware of Indian custom and etiquette, presented his rifle to Shikellamy, adding, "I too have had a dream. I dreamt that you gave me that island in the river." Shikellamy, the perfect diplomat, gave the island to Weiser, adding, "I will never dream with you again."[11]

Despite questionable acquisition of Indian lands and other mistreatment by the English, the French were finding it increasingly difficult to maintain their influence over the Indians in the area drained by the Ohio River. Quite simply, it was because they were losing the trade competition to the English. However, they were also faced with geographic, demographic, and political challenges, as well as industrial. As previously mentioned, French trade goods were generally of inferior quality and more expensive to manufacture, but to exacerbate the situation, the French had to cope with considerably longer supply lines in order to bring their products into New France.

The British industrial revolution gave the British a tremendous advantage over the French, and indeed, the British industrial and manufacturing capabilities were far beyond those of all of their European neighbors. English trade goods were produced faster, cheaper, and were generally of higher quality. As a result, English goods were more desirable to the Indians, because they were more plentiful, less expensive and therefore considered a much better bargain than French goods. In addition, the more plentiful English trade goods were transported a far less arduous and shorter distance than the French could transport theirs. Once French materiel, supplies and trade goods reached the Atlantic coast of North America, they had to be transported over 1,000 miles up the St. Lawrence River to Québec and Montréal, which could only be accomplished during the eight or so months when the St. Lawrence was not frozen over or filled with hazardous ice floes. The French goods then had to be transported over a grueling 600 mile route from Montréal, across the Niagara portages and over Lake Erie by canoe and batteau to Fort Detroit, from where they were painstakingly hauled by canoe or pack animal into the interior. A batteau was a shallow draft, flat-bottomed boat that was used extensively for transport during the colonial period. A batteau was traditionally pointed at both ends but they were built in a variety of sizes. The English, in contrast to the difficulties the French faced with supply logistics, had less of a challenge in bringing goods into North America. The English seaports were open year round, and roads and trails from English colonial cities into the interior were not only shorter, but also less arduous than the French routes from Montréal to the Ohio territory. Once English goods reached colonial ports like Alexandria, Annapolis, Baltimore, Philadelphia, and New York, the distance to transport the English trade goods into the Ohio territory was about a third the distance that the French travelled to convey their merchandise.

In addition to the other expenses regarding the transport of French goods to the North American interior, unscrupulous authorities often further inflated the costs. The commanders of the French forts generally controlled the trade goods that were so laboriously transported to their posts. In turn, the fort commanders supplied the trade goods to the fur traders who ventured out among the Indian towns and trading hubs. However, in addition to the already high cost of manufacture and transportation, greedy fort commanders often further raised the prices of the goods to line their own pockets, and the fur traders had no alternative but to pass those additional high costs on to the Indians.[12] This practice financially benefitted the corrupt officers, but undermined the French fur trade industry and exacerbated the trade advantage enjoyed by the English. The English traders by comparison were not tied to frontier outposts to replenish their supplies, and they obtained their stock at the towns and cities where prices were competitive and not controlled by a few unscrupulous officers. Unfortunately for the French, however, the high cost of manufacture and transportation of French trade goods alone was often enough to put the French traders at a disadvantage, without factoring in the avaricious practices of some of the frontier post commanders.

François Saguin[13] is a good example of the difficulties French traders encountered in their competition with the English. Around 1742, Saguin was licensed to establish a trading post in the Ohio area, and the French trader built what he hoped would be a permanent location at the mouth of Tinkers Creek on the Cuyahoga River (present Valley View, Ohio). François Saguin had come to stay, and that was borne out by the fact that he constructed at least two log buildings and had cleared and cultivated a large garden. His business initially thrived, but a short time later, around 1743 or 1744, the aggressive George Croghan built his trading post a mere 11 miles away at the mouth of the Cuyahoga River (present Cleveland, Ohio). While transient English traders coming into the Ohio territory presented somewhat of a challenge to Saguin, the competition from Croghan's nearby post was devastating. Saguin couldn't compete with Croghan's English trade goods, either in terms of quality, quantity or price. In an attempt to compete at least with a larger quantity and assortment of trade goods, the frustrated trader pleaded for additional French merchandise, and especially gunpowder, which the Indians needed. The authorities, however, apparently refused to continue in what they considered a losing venture, and they refused to support Saguin any further. Instead, sometime in 1744 or 1745, they ordered Saguin to abandon his trading post and return to Fort Detroit, where the French could concentrate on maintaining their still-lucrative trade with the northern Indians. So in the short period of two or three years, English competition caused the collapse of Saguin's initially successful trading venture.

Another advantage in favor of the English was the sheer weight of population. In 1740, excluding Indians, the population of New France was about 45,000, while the English colonies contained about one million people, of which approximately 940,000 were white and 63,000 were black. With a population of less than one twentieth of the white population of the English colonies, the French were hard pressed to counter the increasing influx of English traders and the resultant English influence among the Indians in the Ohio territory.

However, while the Indians appreciated the higher quality, cheaper, and more plentiful English trade goods, the Ohio tribes were also becoming aware of the disparity in population between the French and English in more ominous ways. In general the French presence in North America focused on exploitation through trade, primarily the fur trade. The French were not really concerned with eradicating, displacing or even changing the Indians or their culture. By contrast, the English were voraciously hungry for land. They considered America to be a vast empty wilderness that was theirs for the taking, even though savages rather inconveniently peopled it. In taking the land, the English policy was to displace the Indians to create English towns and villages, and failing that, the Indians would have to be eliminated.

In spite of the obvious English greed for land, most of the tribes were still somewhat ambivalent about whether to side with the French or the English. They generally preferred the French people, because there were fewer of them encroaching onto Indian lands. Compared to the English, the permanent French settlements were distant, and the French did not seem interested in carving out great areas of Indian lands for settlement. The French also appeared to respect Indian culture and customs more than the English, and were generally less disruptive of Indian society by their presence. However, this preference for the French people was more than offset by the Indians' preference for superior British trade goods. Driven by an increasing desire for European manufactured products, the Ohio Indians faced the difficult task of preventing British expansion while maintaining their lucrative trade for preferred British trade goods. Unfortunately, the Indians underestimated the power and determination of the English who coveted the lands in the Ohio territory, which they were determined to possess and open to speculation and settlement.

In 1747, a group of influential Virginians organized a land speculation venture, called the Ohio Company of Virginia. These major shareholders included Virginians Thomas Lee, president; Nathaniel Chapman, treasurer; John Mercer, secretary and general counsel; George Mercer; and two of George Washington's brothers, Lawrence Washington and Augustine Washington, Jr. Vested members of the company also included Virginia Lieutenant Governor Robert Dinwiddie, the Duke of Bedford, and John Hanbury, a wealthy London merchant. The Company intended to acquire deed to a portion of the lands west of the Appalachians that were claimed by Virginia in its colonial "sea to sea" charter. Once established, the Ohio Company planned to exploit the lucrative fur trade and also resell the land to immigrants for settlement. They petitioned for a grant of 500,000 acres, and in 1748, the British Crown approved a grant of 200,000 acres near the Forks of the Ohio (present Pittsburgh, Pennsylvania). The following year, the Virginia Crown Governor approved the grant on the condition that, within seven years, the Ohio Company of Virginia would settle 100 families near the Forks and erect a fort there to protect the settlements and enforce British authority in the area.

2

Céloron

All I can say is that the nations of these localities are very badly disposed towards the French, and are entirely devoted to the English. I do not know in what way they could be brought back. —Céloron

The French were concerned that within a few short years the British had gained the initiative in the Ohio territory through lucrative trade enterprises, and they were at a loss on how to reverse the British successes. They were also fully aware that English colonial land speculation and settlement ventures like the Ohio Company of Virginia posed the biggest threat to French sovereignty in the Ohio territory. Something would have to be done to regain control in the area, and it would likely take French troops to accomplish it. As a result, the governor-general of New France decided to send a military expedition to reaffirm French ownership and to reassert French authority and influence in the Ohio area. It was hoped that by marching a large, resolute military force through the Ohio territory, it would warn off the English interlopers and intimidate the Ohio Indians into maintaining their allegiance to France. In 1748, Governor-General Roland-Michel Barrin de La Galissonière, Marquis de la Galissonière (1693–1756), ordered Captain Pierre Joseph Céloron de Blainville (1693–1759) to lead a force of 216 French and Canadians and about 30 Indians[1] to penetrate the interior of the Ohio territory. They were to place markings at the mouths of several principal tributaries declaring France's claim of ownership of the Ohio region and to discourage English intrusions into the area.

Céloron departed La Chine (8 miles south of Montréal) on Thursday, June 15, 1749, in a flotilla of canoes and batteaux. On Sunday the 18th, only 20 or so miles into their journey, a canoe capsized in the Saint Lawrence River, and one of the men drowned. It was the only loss of life Céloron's expedition would experience. Along their route at certain principal tributaries, Céloron planned to nail to a tree a copper or tin plate bearing the French royal coat of

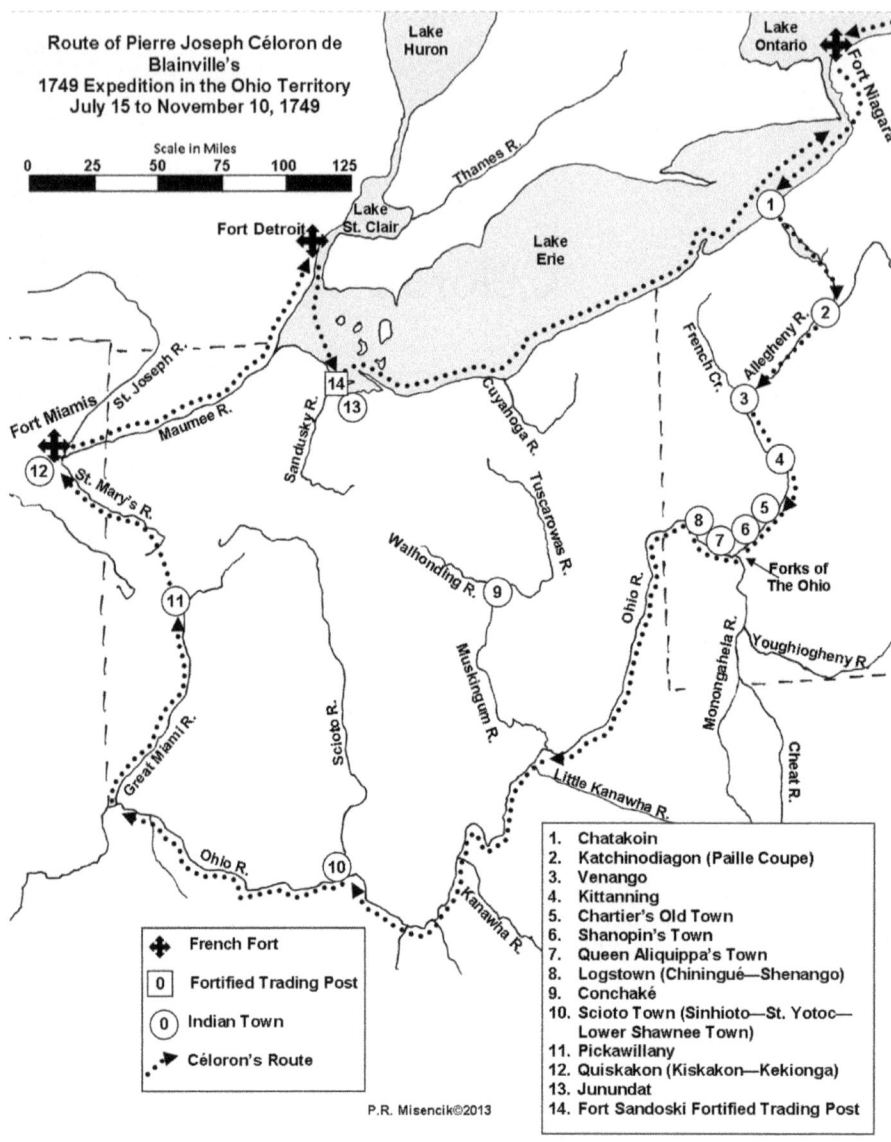

Figure 3. Céloron's 1749 expedition in the Ohio territory.

arms. Then he would order an inscribed lead plate declaring French ownership of the area to be buried beneath the tree. This was a time-honored European custom of proclaiming national ownership. Céloron conducted these formalities with appropriate Gallic military pomp and ceremony, with flags flying and officers and men drawn up in full martial parade. The lead plate containing the specific date and location was ceremoniously buried, after which the troops echoed their commander as he loudly proclaimed, "Vive le Roi!" Although placing markers may have been a standard method of designating territory in Europe, the observing Indians did not understand its significance. They were initially bemused by the French ceremony that centered around their nailing a piece of tin or copper to a tree and burying a slab of lead. It wasn't long, however, before the Indians learned the true significance of Céloron's ritual, in that he was arrogantly claiming ownership of their lands. Their amusement quickly turned to outrage. Where the English were biting off smaller chunks of Indian territory, the French were trying to swallow it whole. Céloron buried at least six lead plates along his route of march, but in most instances as soon as Céloron departed, the Indians tore the French coat of arms from the trees in disgust, and some of the lead plates were dug up and melted into bullets or were given to the English.

Céloron's force travelled via batteau and canoe to Chatakoin (present Barcelona, New York), which was the Lake Ontario terminus of the Chatakoin (or Chautauqua) portage to the Allegheny River. The portage trail led southeast to the northern end of Lake Chautauqua (present Mayville, New York) where the expedition launched their boats to travel the length of the lake. From the outlet of Lake Chautauqua (present Celoron, New York), Céloron's flotilla of canoes and batteaux were able to continue down the Chadakoin River to Conewango Creek, and thence to the Allegheny River where the Indian town of Conewango was located (present Warren, Pennsylvania). The first coat of arms was nailed to a tree and the first lead plate was buried there at the confluence of Conewango Creek and the Allegheny River on Saturday, July 29, 1749. The lead plate was inscribed as follows:

> L'an 1749 dv regne de Lovis XV Roy de France, novs Céloron, commandant d'vn detachment envoie par Monsievr le Mis. de la Galissoniére, Comandant General de la Nouvelle France povr retablir la tranquillite dans quelques villages Sauvages de ces cantons, avons Enterre cette plaque au confluent de l'Ohio et de Tchadakoin ce 29 jvillet, pres de la riviére Oyo autrement Belle Riviere, pour monument du renouvellement De possession que nous avons pris de la ditte riviére Oyo, et de toutes celle~qui y tombent, et de toutes les terres des deux cotes jvsqve avx sources des dittes riviéres ainsi qv'en ont jovy ou dv jovir les precedents rois de France, et qu'ils s'y sont maintenvs par les armes et par les traittes, specialement par cevx de Riswick d'Vtrecht et d'Aix la Chapelle.
>
> In the year 1749, of the reign of Louis the 15th, King of France, we Céloron, commander of a detachment sent by Monsieur the Marquis de la Galissonière, Governor of New France, to establish tranquility in some Indian villages of these cantons, have buried this plate of lead at the confluence of the Ohio and the Chautauqua,[2] this 29th day of July, near the river Ohio, otherwise Belle Riviere, as a monument of the renewal of the possession we have taken of the said river Ohio and of all those which empty into it, and of all the lands on both sides as

far as the sources of the said rivers, as enjoyed or ought to have been enjoyed by the kings of France preceding and as they have there maintained themselves by arms and by treaties, especially those of Ryswick, Utrecht and Aix la Chapelle.

With the coat of arms nailed to several trees and the lead plates buried beneath, the French overtly reaffirmed their possession of the Ohio territory with the type of martial ceremony that was familiar to Europeans since the Middle Ages. However, even Céloron realized that it was one thing for France to claim the territory, but it would take more than posted symbols and inscribed lead plates to hold it. He was certain that the French would need regular troops to enforce their claim.

Céloron's expedition continued down the Allegheny River, and the next day, Sunday, July 30, 1754, they reached the Seneca village of Kachinodiagon, which the French referred to as Paille Coupée (Cut Straw). This was an important Indian village at the meeting point of several major trails. As was fairly common, the town was known by different names. For example, the English called the village Buckaloons, which was a corruption of the Delaware name for the town, Paks-ka-lun-ska (Broken Straw). The village was located at the juncture where Broken Straw Creek enters the Allegheny River (at present Irvine, Pennsylvania). The Indians at Kachinodiagon welcomed the French commander, and as Céloron planned to do at every village, he held a council meeting with the Indians, during which he warned them against having any dealings with the English. He told them the English were evil and only wanted to steal their lands and open them to English settlement. He urged them to drive any English traders out of the area and promised that French traders with gifts and plentiful trade goods would take their place. The Indians listened respectfully and appeared to take Céloron's message to heart, but the French captain had yet to learn that most Indians found it easier to appear agreeable and mask their true feelings when dealing with an armed force of whites, rather than cause unnecessary confrontations.

Céloron planned to hold similar councils at each of the Indian villages along the way, but when he reached the Seneca village of Venango, his reception was quite different. The Pennsylvania trader-gunsmith John Fraser lived at Venango and maintained his trading house there. The Indians of the area, and particularly the Seneca who lived at Venango, held Fraser in high esteem. Warned of the French advance, Fraser was not at Venango when Céloron and his force arrived. The Pennsylvanian and most of the villagers had taken to the woods, leaving the village and Fraser's trading house in the care of several Seneca warriors who did not greet Céloron warmly at all. Céloron attempted to hold a council with the few braves who remained there, but it was apparent that they were not in the least receptive to Céloron's descriptions of the wickedness and duplicity of the English, which included the likes of their friend John Fraser. The surly demeanor of the Venango Seneca worried Céloron. Concerned that perhaps the rest of the villagers were planning a sneak attack on the French party, Céloron quickly departed Venango, not even taking time to bury one of his lead plates.

Apparently, the presence of Céloron's armed force caused more consternation among the Indians than his dire tales of English evilness. As he moved down river, Céloron found fewer and fewer Indians to hold council with. His journals states, "We had found the day before of several cabins abandoned with so much precipitation that the Indians had left behind a part of their utensils, their canoes, and even their provisions, to seek the woods. This action gave us proof of the terror of the Indians, and that they withdrew only through fear."[3]

On Sunday, August 6, 1749, the French party stopped at the Delaware Indian town of Kittanning, about 45 miles upstream from the Forks, but found that the inhabitants there had all fled. Céloron was disappointed at not finding any Indians at Kittanning, so he and his men continued down river and camped for the night at an abandoned Shawnee village called Chartier's Old Town (present Tarentum, Pennsylvania). Peter Chartier was half Indian, his mother being Shawnee and his father French. He had established a trading post there several years earlier, but abandoned it in 1744 or 1745 to take his Indian followers into what is now central Ohio. Chartier sided with the French, because he felt the French treated the Indians fairly and with respect. He later accepted a French military commission and participated in the French and Indian War, but no other significant information is known about him.

At the site of Chartier's Old Town, Céloron encountered six English traders passing through on their way back to Philadelphia with 50 horses and about 150 bales of furs. Céloron accused the traders of usurping French sovereignty, and before ordering them to leave the territory, he gave them a letter addressed to the English government that protested their trespass. Céloron released the traders with a stern warning never to return to the Ohio. His letter, translated, read:

> August 6, 1749—from the Old Town
>
> Sir: having been sent with a detachment into these parts by M. the Marquis de la Galissonière, Governor-General of New France, in order to reconcile with some Indian nations, which had fallen away on the occasion of the war that is just ended [King George's War], I have been very much surprised to find some merchants of your government in this country to which England has never had any pretensions. I have treated them with all possible mildness, though I had a right to look upon

them as intruders and mere vagrants, their traffic being contrary to the preliminaries of peace, signed more than fifteen months ago.

I hope, Sir, you will condescend to forbid this trade for the future, which is contrary to treaties; and that you will warn your traders not to return to these territories; for, if so, they can only impute to themselves the evils which might befall them. I know that our Governor-General would be very sorry to have to resort to violent measures, but he has received positive orders not to allow foreign merchants or traders in his government.

I am, etc.
Céloron[4]

On Tuesday, August 8, 1749, the party passed several recently deserted Indian towns, including the Delaware Indian village of Shannopin's Town, which was approximately two miles north of the Forks of the Ohio, (near present 40th St. and Foster St. in Pittsburgh). Again, it was apparent that the villagers had fled because of the approaching French force. Céloron passed the Forks of the Ohio that same day, and came ashore at Queen Aliquippa's Town at McKee's Rocks (present McKees Rocks, Pennsylvania), about three miles downriver from the Forks. At Queen Aliquippa's Town they once again found that almost all of the inhabitants had fled from Céloron's advance, and only the elderly female chief Queen Aliquippa[5] (ca. 1670–1754) and a few warriors were there to meet the French party. Céloron held a council with the Indians, and though Queen Aliquippa listened politely, it was very apparent to Céloron where her allegiances lay. The French commander described Queen Aliquippa in his journal: "She looks upon herself as a queen and is entirely devoted to the English."[6] The French also discovered six English traders camped near the old queen's town who claimed they were invited there by the Indians to trade. However, after being sternly admonished by Céloron, the traders agreed, most likely disingenuously, that they were intruders who had no right to be in French territory, and they promised they would leave, never to return.

The French party left Queen Aliquippa's Town that same day. Céloron and his men continued downriver to Logstown, where the French commander spent three days in council with leaders of the various tribes of the area. After his cool reception at Venango and the flight of inhabitants from subsequent villages, Céloron was not confident of the Indians' long-term loyalty toward the French or even their shorter-term peaceful intentions, particularly when large numbers of Indians were present as they were at Logstown. In fact, some members of Céloron's party claimed there were indications that the Indians were making preparations to attack the French. As a result, Céloron posted strong guard details round-the-clock and ordered his men to always be armed and extremely vigilant in case of confrontation. Whether his precautions deterred the Indians or he simply misread their intentions is not known, but the Indians remained peaceful and listened to him respectfully. In addition, they did not appear to resent his diatribes against the English or his warnings of their pervasive wickedness. The Indians even agreed, albeit with tongue in cheek, to deal exclusively with French traders and to expel the English. However, Céloron was no fool and had learned over the past weeks not to be taken in by the Indians' apparent acquiescence. He wrote, "This gathering forms a bad village, which is seduced by the allurements of cheap merchandise furnished by the English, which keeps them in very bad disposition toward us." He continued,

> There is little reliance to be placed in the promise of such people, and the more so, as I have just said, since their personal interests make them look with favorable eyes on the English, who give them their merchandise at one-fourth the price; hence there is reason to think the King of England or the country makes up the loss which the merchants sustain in their sales to draw the nations to them. It is true that the expenses of the English are not near so considerable as those which our merchants would be obliged to contract on account of the difficulty of the route. It is, however, certain that we can never regain the nations, except by furnishing them merchandise at the same price as the English; the difficulty is to find out the means?[7]

Leaving Logstown, on Saturday, August 12, 1749, Céloron and his party continued down the Ohio River and came ashore at present Portsmouth, Ohio, at what he referred to as the village of Saint Yotoc,[8] which was likely a corruption of Scioto. The village was mostly peopled with Shawnee Indians and was also known as Lower Shawnee Town. It was a populous village, and not having received advance word of the French force, the Indians were startled by the arrival of a large group of armed men. The inhabitants responded defensively and scores of Shawnee warriors swarmed forward and opened fire with arrows and muskets on Céloron's party. Fortunately, the fusillade did not cause any more damage than to pierce Céloron's flag in several places. Before anyone was harmed, the Indians attached to Céloron's party were able to communicate with the villagers and the situation was defused. However, although the firing stopped, the two sides continued to eye each other warily. Céloron and his men entered the village under a tacit and precarious condition of truce, but did not find the villagers to be welcoming in any sense. What might have contributed to the Indians' sullenness toward the French was the presence of a substantial number of English traders from North Carolina who were using the village as a trading hub, and who appeared to have been carrying on a thriving business during the previous spring and summer. Céloron sternly protested their presence as trespassers, but the traders made it clear that they were not inclined to leave until they chose to do so. Irked by their intractable attitude and behavior, Céloron contemplated plundering the traders' goods, but ultimately decided against it. It was obvious that the Indians were on good terms with the English traders, and Céloron did not want to unnecessarily alienate the Indians by taking forceful measures against their guests. More pragmatically, Céloron realized that he did not have sufficient superiority to do so without a fight that would likely result in unacceptable casualties and Indian animosity. The traders were tough, well armed, numerous and appeared to be well established with the Indians. Also, Céloron was fairly certain that the Indians would support the English traders if a battle started. The French commander felt his only option was to move on after giving the traders a letter, addressed to the Governor of North Carolina, in which he protested the traders' illegal intrusion into French territory.

Leaving the village, the French continued down the Ohio to the Great Miami River (present Cincinnati, Ohio), and there they turned north up the Great Miami toward Fort Miamis and Fort Detroit. They continued to nail their coat of arms to trees, bury lead plates and hold councils with whatever Indians they could find, and on Wednesday, September 13, 1749, they reached the large Miami[9] Indian village of Pickawillany. The Miamis had traditionally been on close and friendly terms with the French, but during the past several years, bands of Miami Indians broke away from their central villages in Indiana to establish settlements in Ohio where they could more easily come in contact with English traders and take advantage of the cheaper and more plentiful English trade goods. The Miami Indians were not the first to break away from French control by resettling in Ohio. Around 1739, a band of Wyandot Indians led by Nicolas Orontony[10] (ca. 1695–1750) left the Fort Detroit area and resettled at the southeastern shore of Sandoski (Sandusky) Bay. The Wyandots were Huron Indians or members of the Huron Confederacy who migrated from their homeland in Canada. The Huron referred to themselves as Wendat or "Dwellers of the Peninsula," and Wyandot or Wynadotte was a corruption of that term. They called their settlement on Sandoski Bay "Junundat," which was also a corruption of the word Wyandot.

At Fort Detroit, French trade was the only source of European goods for the Wyandots, but at Junundat, Orontony's band came in contact with the occasional English trader. This provided the Wyandots the opportunity to experience the growing trade competition between the French and the English. However Junundat was still near enough to Fort Detroit for the French to attempt force in order to coerce the Wyandots back into the French fold. Orontony responded to their intimidation by fighting back. He fortified his village and engaged in retaliatory hostilities against the French, during which his warriors killed several traders and destroyed a French trading post. Rather than continue a prolonged adversarial relationship with the nearby French at Fort Detroit, Orontony decided to leave the area. In 1748 he and several of his band resettled at the confluence of the Tuscarawas and Walhonding Rivers in present southeastern Ohio where they established the Wyandot village of Conchaké (present Coshocton, Ohio). Nicholas Orontony died at Conchaké in 1750, presumably a victim of smallpox.

When Céloron arrived at Pickawillany, he was aware of the split in allegiance among the Miamis, and was particularly cognizant of the pro–English leanings of the Indians at the Miami trading hub. The chief of the Pickawillany Miamis was Memeskia, who for some unknown reason was called La Demoiselle (young lady) by the French. The English, on the other hand, named him Old Briton, because of his staunch British loyalty. Memeskia had been inspired by Nicolas Orontony's example, which resulted in Memeskia also breaking away from French influence and resettling his band of Miamis on the Great Miami River near present Piqua, Ohio. The French, including Céloron, were well aware of Memeskia's loyalty to the British, and the French commander was not certain of how he would be received at Pickawillany. However, Céloron was somewhat heartened when he and his force were welcomed into the village, albeit not as cordially as hoped. He was invited to council with Memeskia and other Miami leaders, but before that could happen, suitable interpreters had to be found, which took a few extra days. In the meantime, Céloron learned that like Saint Yotoc, Pickawillany served as a large English trading center, and though the majority of the Englishmen who had spent the summer trading there had since departed, a few whom he referred to as "English soldiers" were still in the village. Encouraged by the Indians' lack of hostility, Céloron sent the remaining Englishmen away before he met with the Indians in council.

The council took place on Sunday, September 17, 1749, during which Céloron offered Memeskia and the other Indian leaders gifts and several belts of wampum.[11] He gave his usual speech describing English perfidy along with an exhortation that the Miamis break off all trade with the English and expel all Englishmen from the Ohio territory. The Miamis listened politely and even appeared to endorse his criticism of the English, but by now Céloron was fully aware that Memeskia was called Old Briton for a reason, and that he and the other tribal leaders were almost certainly being disingenuous. Nevertheless, hoping for a breakthrough in bringing the Pickawillany Miamis back into the French fold, Céloron asked Memeskia and the other village leaders to accompany his party on the 80-mile trek northwest to Quiskakon, the major town of the Miamis whose inhabitants were regarded as pro–French. Quiskakon, or Kiskakon (cut tail), also sometimes referred to as Kekionga (blackberry patch), was the central village of the Miamis located near the confluence of the Saint Joseph, Saint Mary's and Maumee rivers at present Fort Wayne, Indiana. In 1722, the French built Fort Miamis near Quiskakon for protection of the local French, to serve as a trading center, and to maintain French influence over the Indians in the area. By the mid to late 1740s, several of the Miami Indians began to rebel against French control of the fur trade in the western Great Lakes area. The French monopoly resulted in lower barter prices for Indian furs and consequently higher prices for French trade goods. Around 1747 to 1748, Memeskia and other Miami villagers left Quiskakon to establish a trading center at Pickawillany where English traders would also compete for their furs to the advantage of the Miamis. In the short time they had been there, Pickawillany had grown quickly and prospered as a result of the English trade. Now Céloron was asking Memeskia to abandon Pickawillany and return to the French-controlled Quiskakon, where the pro–British Memeskia and his followers would be subject to the influence and supervision of the French at Fort Miamis. The chief did not relish that situation at all, but rather than reject Céloron's suggestion outright, Memeskia said that he would adjourn the council until the following day and would give Céloron his response at that time.

The following day in council, Céloron pressed Memeskia to take his tribe to Quiskakon, where they would be afforded French protection, be closer to French trade at Fort Miamis, and escape the evilness of the English. Memeskia thanked Céloron for his kind words and his concern for the well-being of the Miamis, but said that he and the village leaders decided that they would reflect on Céloron's words during the coming winter and would return to Quiskakon in the spring. He added that the season was too far advanced for all of the inhabitants to leave Pickawillany, and he was concerned that when they arrived at Quiskakon there would not be sufficient lodging for his people. Céloron countered that his men would assist in constructing houses if there weren't enough, but Memeskia was adamant; they would wait until spring before leaving Pickawillany. To make matters worse, the Miamis somewhat insultingly returned the gifts Céloron had given them the previous day, refusing to accept them. Dejected, Céloron planned to depart the Miami village. Since there was no practical water route to Quiskakon, he ordered that the expedition's canoes and batteaux be burned. He apparently was unwilling to make a gift of the serviceable watercraft to the intransigent Miamis. On Tuesday, September 19, 1749, he and his men left Pickawillany and marched overland to Quiskakon. Before leaving, he tried one last time to convince the Miamis to accompany him, but Memeskia remained steadfast in his refusal to leave. However, to keep the French force peaceful and to hasten their departure, Memeskia assured

Céloron that he and his people would be in Quiskakon in the spring, and all that was keeping them from doing so now was the lack of sufficient cabins to accommodate them there.

Céloron and his party arrived at Quiskakon on Monday, September 25, 1749, where they found that a rebuilt Fort Miamis was just completed during the past summer. The old dilapidated and undermanned fort had been briefly captured and then burned by Indians in 1747 during the fighting between Orontony's rebellious Wyandots from Junundat and the French who were trying to force them back into the fold. Indians from Memeskia's band at Pickawillany had supported the Wyandots during the attack on Fort Miamis, and that was even more disconcerting to the French. It was yet another sign of the eroding French influence among the Ohio Indians.

Céloron had hoped to obtain provisions along with canoes and batteaux at Fort Miamis with which to complete his journey to Montréal but was unable to get sufficient watercraft to accommodate his entire force. As a result, he decided to split his force, and he, along with as many as could be accommodated in the available canoes and batteaux, planned to descend the Maumee River while the rest of his force would march overland.

While at Quiskakon, Céloron met with the village chief Wis-e-kau-kautshe, whom the French called Pied Froid (Cold Foot) (?–ca. 1751–52). Céloron told Pied Froid of his council with Memeskia and the Pickawillany Miamis. When he mentioned La Demoiselle's promise to return to Quiskakon in the spring, Pied Froid responded, "I hope I am deceived, but I am sufficiently attached to the interests of the French to say that the Demoiselle is a liar. It is the source of all my grief to be the only one who loves you, and to see all the nations of the south let loose against the French."[12]

After leaving Quiskakon, Céloron and his group stopped at Fort Detroit before rejoining the rest of his force at Lake Erie. Acquiring additional canoes and batteaux along the way, Céloron's force now had sufficient watercraft to accommodate everyone in order to complete their journey to Montréal, where they finally arrived on Friday, November 10, 1749. Leaving his troops in Montréal, Céloron continued on to Québec to report to Jacques-Pierre de Taffanel de la Jonquière Marquis de la Jonquière (1685–1752), who had recently arrived in Québec to succeed Galissonière as the governor-general of New France.[13]

By his reckoning, Céloron's journey had taken him about 1,200 leagues[14] or about 3,000 miles, and he had lost only one man who had drowned early in the expedition. His report to Jonquière was frank, honest and pessimistic concerning the challenges of maintaining French sovereignty in the Ohio region. He made it clear that his expedition alone was not sufficient to secure the exclusive allegiance of the Indians nor deter the flood of Englishmen into the Ohio area. He reported that even the once loyal Miamis were being won over by the British and were influencing neighboring tribes, including the traditionally loyal Wyandots[15] of the Huron Confederacy, who for the previous century and a half had steadfastly allied themselves with the French. He told Jonquière that the pervasiveness of English traders in the Ohio territory was truly surprising, and worse, they were winning over the Indians of the area with their inexpensive and plentiful trade goods. Céloron wrote, "All I can say is that the nations of these localities are very badly disposed towards the French, and are entirely devoted to the English. I do not know in what way they could be brought back." He continued, "If our traders were sent there for traffic, they could not sell their merchandise at the same price as the English sell theirs, on account of the many expenses they would be obliged to incur." He ended his journal with a subtle suggestion for Jonquière to take action that would reestablish French preeminence in Ohio: "I feel myself obliged on account of the knowledge I have acquired of all these places, to put these reflections at the end of my journal, so that one may make use of them as he shall judge proper."[16]

3

Opening Moves

I shall send from Montréal 300 soldiers, 1700 habitants, and about 200 Indians whom I am assigning to go and establish themselves on the Belle Rivière, which we are on the verge of losing if I do not make this hasty but indispensible effort. —Duquesne

Although he exhibited exceptional courage and skill as a naval officer during King George's War and was considered a fairly good administrator as governor-general of New France, by 1749 Jonquière was worn out and not inclined to take aggressive action. He was 67 years old, in failing health and would not live another three years. His bold decisiveness was a thing of the past. Even before Céloron returned from his expedition, Governor-General Jonquière was advised by his departing predecessor, Galissonière, to take action and establish a chain of fortified posts along the Ohio River and its headwaters, because if the French didn't, the English certainly would. Galissonière warned that if the British established forts along the Ohio, they would sever French communications with Louisiana, isolate the existing French posts west of the Appalachians, and prevent future establishments. Unfortunately, Galissonière's warnings fell on deaf ears. While Jonquière's failure to heed Galissonière's advice could be blamed on age and lack of initiative, there were no directives from Versailles to take military action to secure New France or even Canada from the English. In fact, most of King Louis XV's closest advisors did not believe that Canada was worth the effort or the cost to occupy and defend. Even Frenchmen not associated with the French government questioned the economic and strategic value of Canada. The popular writer Voltaire criticized any and all initiatives to defend Canada against the British. His three main points were

1. that "Canada is a country covered with snows and ices eight months of the year, inhabited by barbarians, bears and beavers"[1] and almost all of Canada is an unproductive and useless frozen wasteland;

2. Great Britain has an overwhelming advantage in population in North America, has better control of the maritime routes between Europe and North America, and therefore will inevitably prevail;
3. An effective defense of Canada requires an extraordinarily large commitment of money and resources in comparison to the scant economic value in return.

In a letter to his friend and fellow writer François-Augustin Paradis de Moncrif (1687–1770), Voltaire wrote, "One pities that poor human race that slits its throat on our continent about a few acres of ice in Canada."[2] Then again in his 1758 novel *Candide,* Voltaire commented on the struggle for Canada: "You know that these two nations are at war for a few acres of snow in Canada, and that they spend over this beautiful war more than Canada is worth."[3]

Before he left the Governor's Palace in Québec, Galissonière argued passionately that the loss of Canada would cause the collapse of France's overseas empire, which would create a great negative impact on France's economy. However, Jonquière vacillated for the almost three years he was governor-general without taking any meaningful decisive action to reclaim preeminence in the Ohio territory, to strengthen French influence and authority, or to militarily oppose English incursions there. The only actions he took were half-hearted and accomplished little more than to add impetus to the English efforts in the Ohio region.

The loss of French authority over the Indians in Ohio was even worse than Céloron had described. In fact, in 1747, Memeskia not only had supported Orontony's feud with the French, but the Miami chief had also made overtures to the Iroquois asking them to arrange a general council with Pennsylvania commissioners to facilitate trade. As a result of his request, a council was held at Lancaster, Pennsylvania, where a treaty was signed on Saturday, July 20, 1748, in which the English promised to send traders among the western Indians if the Indians would provide protection for them. Memeskia did not personally attend the council, but sent three Miami chiefs from Pickawillany who joined with a Seneca, two Oneidas, two Mohawks, and three Shawnee Indians. At the council, the Miami chiefs announced that twelve other Wabash and Illinois tribes were also interested in being included in the treaty alliance. To make matters worse for the French, bands of Indians from present Illinois and Indiana began to join the Miamis at Pickawillany. In 1750, in spite of Pied Froid's pleading, most of the Miamis at Quiskakon abandoned their homes to resettle at Pickawillany, making Pickawillany's importance as a major Indian village superior to that of Quiskakon. Remaining steadfastly loyal to the French, Pied

Froid and his family remained at Quiskakon, where that winter Pied Froid died from smallpox.

Instead of acting to seal off the Ohio territory to prevent English encroachment, Jonquière's first initiative was an attempt to coerce the Ohio Indians back into the fold by chastising and making an example of the more flagrant of the Ohio tribes who were trading with the English. That certainly included the Pickawillany Miamis. In 1751 after learning of recent visits by George Croghan and Christopher Gist to Pickawillany, Jonquière ordered Céloron, who was now the commander at Fort Detroit, to punish the wayward Pickawillany Miamis. Céloron tried to gather a force of friendly Indians, but after more than 20 days of unsuccessful talks with the Ottawa, Chippewa, and Adirondack Indians in the Detroit area, he abandoned the punitive expedition. Further, when several Adirondack warriors decided to go it alone, they were warned off and turned back by Ottawas who were friendly with the Miamis. Another attempt to punish the Pickawillany Miamis was launched that summer of 1751. About 50 Nippissings and a few other Indian warriors from other tribes led by François-Marie Picoté, sieur de Belestre II (1716–1793) started off for Memeskia's village, but when the war party reached Fort Sandoski[4] (south of present Port Clinton, Ohio), most of Belestre's force deserted when the Ottawa and Chippewa Indians there threatened them if they harmed the Miamis. The greatly reduced war party did reach Pickawillany. However, an Ottawa woman had raced ahead and warned the Miamis of Belestre's approach. When the raiders got there, they found the town almost deserted. To vent their frustration, the Nippissings killed and scalped a Miami man and woman before they headed back to Fort Detroit. In retaliation the angered Miamis killed and scalped two unfortunate French traders who happened to be in the vicinity.

Jonquière's other half-hearted effort in trying to win back the Ohio Indians was his licensing of several French traders to conduct business in the Ohio area. One of the traders, Phillipe-Thomas Chaubert de Joncaire, who had been on Céloron's expedition, was sent in 1750 to establish a French trading post at Logstown. In an attempt to make a strong impression on the Indians, he arrived with five canoe-loads of goods, which he lavishly gave as gifts to the tribal leaders. However, he also incensed the Indians when he said he intended to build a fort at Logstown. In spite of his abundant gifts, Joncaire was not warmly welcomed at Logstown, because the town's inhabitants tended to lean toward the British. In fact, in May 1751, Joncaire was tersely advised by the Iroquois half-king Tanacharison to "go home directly off our lands."[5] Joncaire stayed in the area, but his reports to Jonquière echoed Céloron's comments in describing the difficulties of competition with the English traders. The harsh truth was that the French were losing the trade war, and it was trade that had a significant influence on the loyalties of the Indians. Governor-General Jonquière continued to do nothing, and it would take almost three years before his successors, Charles Le Moyne de Longueuil (1687–1755) and Michel-Ange Duquesne de Menneville, Marquis Duquesne (ca. 1700–1778), would finally take action in an attempt to regain and preserve French control of the Ohio area. By then, however, the English had made significant inroads and were actively and overtly challenging French influence and authority in the Ohio territory.

While the French were squandering their opportunities to reassert themselves in the Ohio area, the English were beginning to take advantage of the French lack of initiative. The English colonists, particularly the Virginians, were quick to interpret Céloron's 1749 expedition as one of the opening moves in the struggle for control of the vast, rich territory west of the Appalachian Mountains. Almost immediately in 1749, the Ohio Company of Virginia made its first overt efforts to penetrate the Ohio territory by establishing a permanent, fortified depot referred to as Wills Creek at the confluence of Wills Creek and the Potomac River (present Cumberland, Maryland). The Wills Creek settlement was only 114 miles from the strategic Forks of the Ohio, almost 500 miles closer than Montréal was to the Ohio territory. That same year, 1749, Maryland frontiersman Thomas Cresap (1702–1790) and the Delaware Indian Nemacolin, acting for the Ohio Company of Virginia, blazed and mapped a route over an ancient Indian trail from Wills Creek across the Allegheny Mountains to Red Stone Old Fort (present Brownsville, Pennsylvania) at the mouth of Red Stone Creek on the Monongahela River. They were instructed to find the most direct route, which they did, but portions of the trail later proved difficult or impossible to convey wagons or artillery over. Later expeditions would generally follow the Nemacolin trail, but in some areas detours would have to be carved out to facilitate wagon traffic. While the blazed route was generally called the Nemacolin Trail or Nemacolin's Path, it was also sometimes referred to as Dunlaps Path after a trader named William Dunlap who was in the area from about 1730. There is a Dunlap's Creek, named after the trader, that empties into the Monongahela River near Red Stone Old Fort. Later, after Fort Cumberland was established at Wills Creek, the trail began to be referred to as "the Cumberland Road."

The company planned to establish a storehouse at Red Stone Old Fort, which was only 37 miles from the Forks. The site was referred to as Red Stone Old Fort, because of the ancient mound builder earthworks in the immediate area that resembled an old fortification. The Indian earthworks were circular in nature and were located on a hill that overlooks present Brownsville, Penn-

3. *Opening Moves* 37

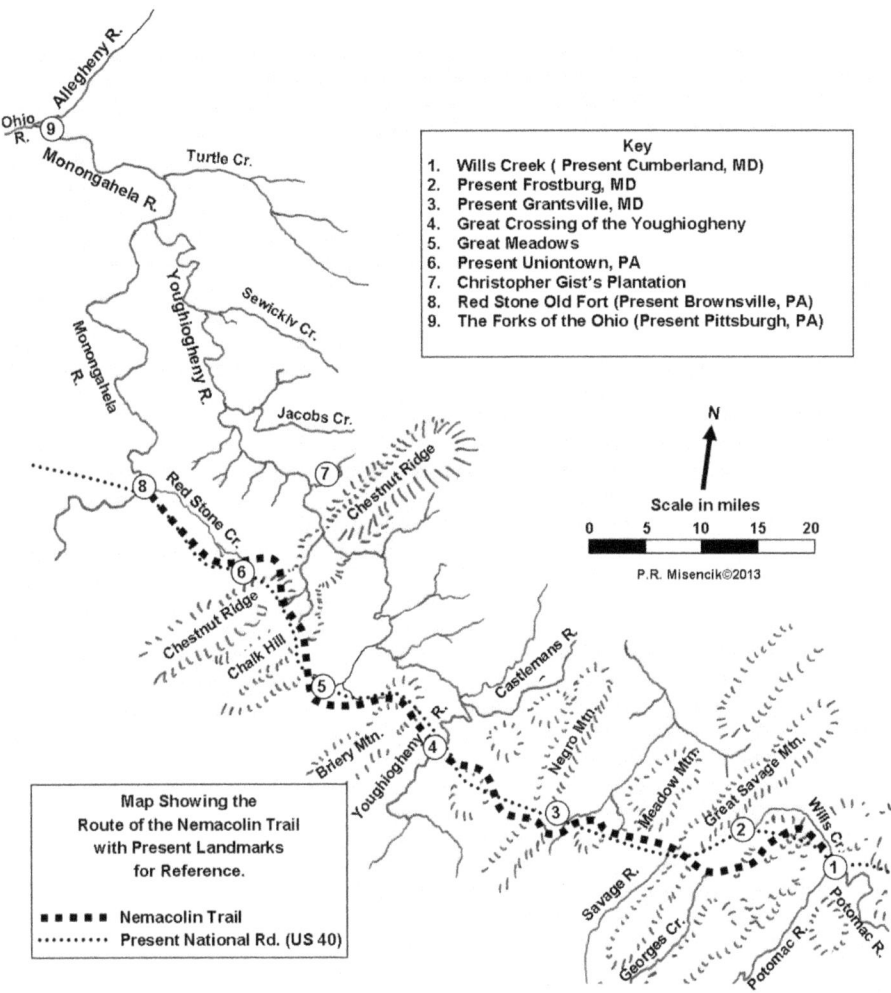

Figure 4. Nemacolin Trail.

sylvania. In spite of the location's name, neither the English nor the French ever built a conventional fort at the site.

The following year, 1750, the Ohio Company of Virginia hired the experienced frontiersman and surveyor Christopher Gist (1706–ca. 1759) to explore the Ohio Valley area as far west as the Falls of the Ohio. At Logstown, the Indians correctly assessed his motives and initially received him with coolness. They told him they knew he had come to settle the Indians' land and threatened that he would not go home safely. The fact that Gist came to no harm was undoubtedly due to his tact, diplomacy, and his knowledge of Indian customs. Indeed, he got on well in the Ohio territory and actually promoted good will between the English and the tribes of the area. Gist spent the following two years surveying far into the interior for the Ohio Company of Virginia. His reports to his employers described the broad meadows, oak forests, and fertile bottomland. He reported salt licks and sent back samples of coal and fossils, including four-pound molars from fossilized mammoth remains. Interestingly, as a result of Gist's survey, the Ohio Company of Virginia had a more detailed description of the Ohio territory than did the French who claimed ownership of the area.

Governor-General Jonquière died on Tuesday, March 17, 1752, after a month-long illness, and Charles Le Moyne de Longueuil became the acting governor-general until the new Governor-General Duquesne took office. Longueuil, born in Canada, had a distinguished military career and also served ably as governor of Trois-Rivières and Montréal. He was understandably chagrined when he was not appointed governor-general. However, while he held the office as acting governor-general, Longueuil was determined that he would reassert French authority in the Ohio territory. Longueuil was well aware that the growing English influence in the Ohio area was causing a serious erosion of French authority and trade among the Indians. He recalled that within the past dozen or so years, significant Indian defections from the French sphere of influence had occurred. The most notable were Nicholas Orontony's Wyandots and Memeskia's Miamis who severed their ties with the French and reestablished themselves in the Ohio area. The French tried every means to bring the Indians back under their control, eventually resorting to armed coercion. The Indians responded to force with force and by April of 1752, hostilities occurred frequently between the French and the English-leaning Ohio Indians. Five French scalps were taken near the Vermillion River, and Memeskia's warriors killed two Frenchmen near Fort Miami. The French responded by killing at least thirty Miamis. In the later part of 1750, a smallpox epidemic swept the Indian villages in Indiana, killing scores of Indians, including Pied Froid at Quiskakon. Longueuil hoped in vain that the epidemic would spread to the Ohio Indians, where it would curb their desire and ability to wage war against the French. However, the Ohio Indians were largely spared the disease. Now that Longueuil read Céloron and Jonquière's reports regarding the further estrangement of the Indians of the Miami River valley, and of the pro–British attitude that was spreading to other tribes in Ohio, the acting governor-general directed Céloron, who was still the commander of Fort Detroit, to take decisive action to chastise the recalcitrant Miamis and curtail British influence among the Ohio Indians. Longueuil's plan was to make an example of the Pickawillany Miamis, who at that time represented the most flagrant and militant defection from the French. Longueuil was certain that a strong punitive demonstration against the rebellious Miamis at Pickawillany would intimidate the wayward tribes back into the fold. It would serve as an unmistakable warning that the French would not tolerate any shift in allegiance away from the French toward the English in the Ohio territory.

Céloron selected Charles Michel Langlade (1729–1802) to lead the force that would chastise the Pickawillany Miamis and particularly their leader Memeskia or Old Briton. Langlade was a good choice for the assignment. He was a very effective leader and had strong ties to the Ottawa Indians who had thwarted the previous punitive expeditions against the Miamis. Langlade's father, Augustin, was a French fur trader, and his mother, Domitilde, was an Ottawa woman who was also the sister of Nissowaquet, a noted Ottawa war chief, called La Fourche (The Fork) by the French. Domitilde was the widow of Daniel Villeneuve, another French trapper and trader, and she had six children by Villeneuve when she married Augustin. However Augustin and Domitilde only had only one child, Charles. Charles was educated by the Jesuits and may also have been sent to school at Montréal, but it was his mother's Indian culture that Charles Langlade more readily absorbed.

When Langlade was ten, his uncle Nissowaquet took him as a member of an Ottawa war party against the Chickasaw. Before leaving, Langlade's father told his ten-year-old son, "You must go with your uncles, but never let me hear of your showing any marks of cowardice."[6] Apparently young Langlade acquitted himself admirably and earned the respect of the Ottawa war chiefs, who gave him the title Auke-wing-eke-taw-so (defender of his country).[7] Langlade embraced the Ottawa culture and way of life and was highly respected as a leader and an exceptionally brave and fierce warrior. Various writings described Langlade as honest, ambitious, diplomatic, charming, and courageous. Some descriptions also portrayed him as being egocentric, self-seeking, and possessing a cruel streak. Around 1750, Langlade married an Ottawa woman named Agathe, and they had a son, Charles Jr. Langlade later left Agathe, but remained in contact with his son, who first settled at La Baye (present Green Bay, Wisconsin), and later at Michilimackinac.

On Sunday morning, June 21, 1752, just at sunrise, Langlade and his friend, the Ottawa war chief Pontiac, with a strong force of over 250 Ottawa and Chippewa Indians and some Canadian militia, struck Pickawillany. At the time of the attack, most of the defenders were away hunting, and the invaders swept through the town without much opposition. Many of the inhabitants were killed before they could escape into the woods and a large number were wounded or captured, including Old Briton and five English traders who were also in the village. Thirteen of Old Briton's warriors were killed and scalped after they were captured, and Old Briton and one of the English traders were ritually killed, boiled and eaten. It's not certain whether Memeskia was ritually cannibalized as a sign of respect for his personal qualities, or whether Langlade's raiders meant to shock the Ohio Indians with a horrific example of what could happen to other defectors from French allegiance.

The assault on Pickawillany completely eliminated the village as an English trading center and convinced the Miami Indians of French military superiority in the area. More importantly it showed the surviving Indians in the Ohio territory how ruthlessly the French would deal with Indian attempts to transfer their trade to the English. Many survivors of Langlade's attack meekly moved back to French-dominated Quiskakon only a few years after they had left there to take advantage of the English trade at Pickawillany. Not all of the Miamis returned to French control however. A number of the Miami Indians and their allies began to attack French targets of opportunity to avenge the attack on Pickawillany. In August 1752, Céloron at Fort Detroit reported that the Indians had killed and scalped several French soldiers, civilians and slaves, and the Miami were becoming even more hostile and dangerous.

The destruction of Pickawillany caught the English off guard. They sent gifts and other expressions of sympathy to try to regain their standing among the Indians, but otherwise they were at a loss regarding an appropriate response. Though the destruction of Pickawillany may have forced the English trading activities to be somewhat surreptitious in avoiding French military patrols, the English traders aggressively continued to ply their trade among the Ohio Indians. The new governor-general who had just taken office decided it was time to end English trespass once and for all.

On July 1, 1752,[8] a week and a half after the destruction of Pickawillany, Duquesne took office as governor-general. He was described as arrogant, stubborn, self-important and one who acted aggressively and was more than willing to use force to support his initiatives. Almost immediately, following the Pickawillany raid, the new governor-general began to formulate measures to restore French influence and authority in the Ohio territory by force of arms and to interdict English encroachment into the area. He was angered that despite a presence of French troops, repeated warnings to the Indians, and French efforts to increase trade, English incursions into the Ohio territory continued to increase. It was frustrating to the French that in spite of Langlade's punitive attack on Picawillany, the aggressiveness of English traders continued to erode French influence among the Indians. The English incursions were damaging French trade, their control of the Ohio Indians, and worst of all, they were threatening French sovereignty.

In the spring of 1752, just a few months before Duquesne took office, the Ohio Company of Virginia, under the authority of Virginia Lieutenant Governor Dinwiddie, held a council at Logstown to reaffirm Virginia's claim to the land west of the Alleghenies. It's important to remember that Dinwiddie was a major shareholder in the Ohio Company and stood to profit greatly from the venture. The land claim benefitting the company stemmed from the Treaty of Lancaster in 1744, where the Iroquois had ceded the land to the English for a paltry £400. The agreement contained the curious wording "as far as it is settled, & back from thence to the sun setting."[9] To the Iroquois, that phrase simply meant from the land already settled by the English to the crest of the Alleghenies, behind which the sun disappeared in the evening. However, the English chose to interpret the phrase as "from sea to sea." As a further inducement to the Indians and to convince them to accept the English interpretation of the Treaty of Lancaster boundaries, the Virginians at the Logstown Council included the vague promise to further compensate the Indians greatly. They assured the Indians that English trade goods would be cheaper and more plentiful, and grandly pledged that the Indians would have protection from the French. In addition, they ironically promised to protect the Indians from unscrupulous traders and speculators, and duplicitously guaranteed that the Ohio Indians' status and way of life would not be jeopardized.

Whether or not the Indians fully understood the Virginians' interpretation of the land boundaries or even the agreement in general, they reaffirmed the 1744 Lancaster Treaty, and received a promise from the Virginians to build a "strong house" for trade and protection at the Forks of the Ohio. However, when the Virginians implied that the strong house would be accompanied by settlement so that those stationed there would be able to grow their own food, Tanacharison flatly refused. A trading house and small garrison was one thing, but white homesteads were another. The half-king would not allow white settlements of any kind on Indian land. He said that the Indians would supply the food for the strong house and that "there would be no scarcity of that kind."[10]

Even before Duquesne learned of Dinwiddie's plan to fortify the Forks, he reasoned that the surest way to curtail English activities in the Ohio area would be to eliminate English bases of operations there, and also prevent further English encroachment into the area. He believed that a strong French military presence and a chain of forts would best encourage the English to abandon their pretentious claim to the Ohio territory. However, at the time of Duquesne's accession, there were no French troops or French forts in what is now western Pennsylvania or eastern Ohio. The nearest French military outposts to the Ohio territory were Fort Niagara (present Youngstown, New

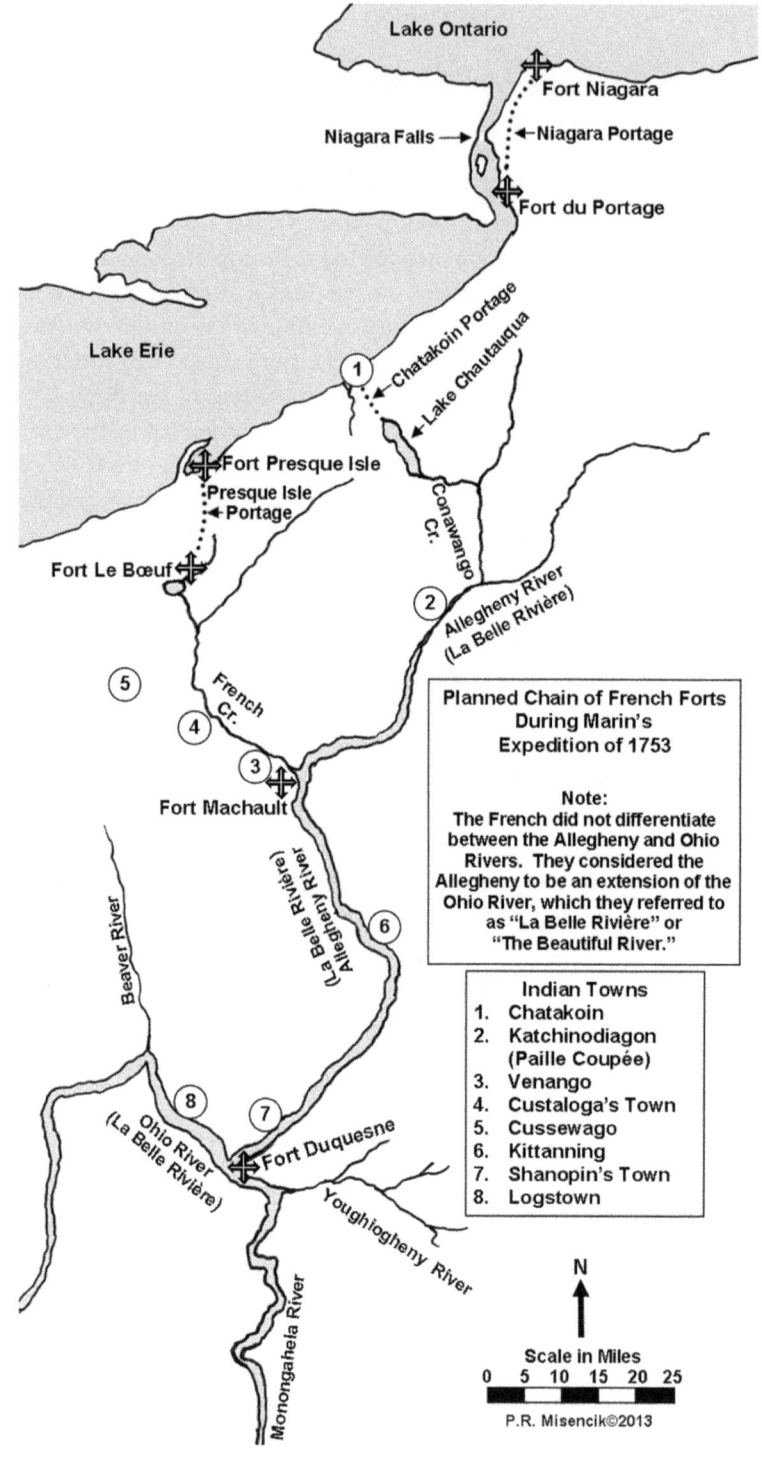

York) and Fort Detroit. Since most of the English incursions were from the east along the Allegheny and Monongahela Rivers to the Forks of the Ohio and downstream beyond Logstown, neither Fort Niagara, which was about 260 miles from the Forks, nor Fort Detroit, about 410 miles away,[11] were situated for a rapid military response, and therefore provided little deterrence to English incursions.

It's important to understand the unusual governing structure of New France, in which responsibilities were shared between the governor-general and the "intendant." Duquesne as governor-general was the king's representative and also the commander-in-chief of the military in New France. The intendant was a civil administrator whose primary responsibilities included finance, procurement of supplies, economic development, taxes, and the administration of justice. The two heads were intended to be a check and balance for each other, but the blurred or overlapping areas of authority and responsibility often resulted in jurisdictional disputes between the governor-general and the intendant. While the governor-general was the more prestigious position, it could easily be argued that the intendant was the more powerful office.

The intendant at the time was François Bigot (1703–1778), who had also recently taken office. Bigot was described as exceptionally able, but unfortunately he was also unscrupulously greedy and dishonest. His talents were primarily used to amass wealth, and his term was marked by patronage, commodity manipulation and outright theft. His corrupt behavior created widespread hunger and hardship among the populace, deprived the troops of necessary supplies and brought New France to financial ruin. During his tenure, government expenses for New France rose fivefold, with Bigot and his cronies stealing most of the money.

Bigot was enthusiastic about Duquesne's plans to send troops to the Ohio territory, because it was up to Bigot to find the resources and money to make it happen. Bigot looked at the venture as a new opportunity for profiteering from furnishing supplies at grossly inflated costs and by skimming from the additional taxes and levies that would have to be implemented. On October 26, 1752, Intendant Bigot summarized Duquesne's plan in a letter to the Minister:

> When we received your last letters on the 8th of this month, the general [Duquesne] was already informed concerning matters relating to the Belle Riviere [Beautiful River—the Ohio River], and his plans were already made to chase away the English.
> To accomplish this, it is necessary to send 2000 Frenchmen with 200 of our domiciliated savages to this river [the Ohio River] by way of the Chatakoui

Opposite: **Figure 5. Planned chain of French forts.**

[Chautauqua] portage in the spring; to build a store house at the lower end of this portage on the shore of Lake Erie, and another at the end of this same portage on Lake Chatakoüin [Chautauqua]; likewise, to make a fort at La Paille Coupée [present Irvine, Pennsylvania] where M. Joncaire is located, another at the Written Rock [McKees Rocks, Pennsylvania] or at Chiningué [Shenango or Logstown, present Ambridge, Pennsylvania], and a third at Sonhioto [Scioto Town, present Portsmouth, Ohio]. The garrisons of these forts will be taken from the 2,000 men; the remainder will go to spend the winter with the Illinois, if they see they will be unable to reach Montréal in the fall, which seemingly will not be possible, since the 200 men who made this same journey 3 years ago, and who had no fort to build, had great difficulty reaching Montréal in the first days of November.[12]

While Céloron's march through the Ohio territory in 1749 was meant to reinforce French claims to the territory by awing the Indians and expelling any English traders that were encountered, this new expedition was something more. It was an indisputable military invasion to seize, hold and defend the area against English incursions, and to intimidate the Ohio Indians by force of arms to maintain their political and economic allegiance to the French. For this purpose, Duquesne selected the crusty, 61-year-old Captain Paul Marin de la Malgue (1693–1753), to head the expeditionary force. Marin had a distinguished military career and was described as an officer who was both feared and respected by the Indians. He had a reputation of bravery, ruthlessness and of always being willing to risk his life for the French cause. During King George's War, he led troops in Acadia and commanded the French and Indian force that ravaged the New York frontier, destroying Saratoga (present Schuylerville, New York) and several other English settlements. His orders were to establish a fortified post at Chatakoin on the south shore of Lake Erie, which was the northern terminus of the Chatakoin[13] or Chautauqua portage. The nine-and-a-quarter-mile portage from the Indian Village of Chatakoin to Lake Chautauqua was the same route Céloron had used in 1749. Marin was ordered to improve the route along the Chatakoin portage and to construct a road to the headwaters of the Allegheny River near present Coudersport, Pennsylvania. They were then ordered to make the waterways along the route navigable for batteau transport and to construct and garrison a chain of forts down the Allegheny to the Forks of the Ohio.

At the same time, the commander of Fort Niagara, Captain Claude-Pierre Pécaudy de Contrecœur (1705–1775), who had been second-in-command of Céloron's 1749 expedition, received orders to complete a portage road from Fort Niagara to Fort du Portage about one mile above the Niagara Falls. Contrecœur was furnished with craftsmen to construct boats that would be used to supply Marin's expedition via the Niagara Portage route, and on October

5, 1752, Duquesne wrote to Contrecœur, informing him "in the greatest secrecy" that in the spring of 1753, 2,000 men would be travelling to the Ohio territory "to reestablish a communication which we would soon lose without this step."[14] Duquesne added in a letter dated Wednesday, October 18, 1752, again in the greatest of secrecy, that "in the course of May, I shall send from Montréal 300 soldiers, 1,700 habitants, and about 200 Indians whom I am assigning to go and establish themselves on the Belle Riviere, which we are on the verge of losing if I do not make this hasty but indispensible effort."[15] Duquesne also said that he was sending workmen to Chatakoin to improve the portage route via Lake Chautauqua, which was the original planned route of Marin's expedition. But the route was soon changed.

The first detachment of 250 troops under the command of Lieutenant Charles de Deschamps de Boishébert et de Raffetot (1727–1797) set out from Montréal on Thursday, February 1, 1753. However, their orders now directed them to establish a base at Presque Isle (present Erie, Pennsylvania) rather than at Chatakoin on the Chautauqua portage, because it was decided that the route down French Creek to the Allegheny River would be faster and less costly than via the Lake Chautauqua route. Presque Isle also had the advantage of an excellent harbor on Lake Erie. However, the following year, the Chatakoin Portage route was revived and used along with the Preque Isle Portage during the time the French army remained on the Allegheny and Ohio Rivers.

Boishébert's detachment arrived at Presque Isle on or about Thursday, May 3, 1753, where they prepared for the arrival of the rest of the expeditionary force. The next detachment of troops departed Montréal on Sunday, April 15, 1753, under the command of Captain François-Marc-Antoine Le Mercier (1722-ca. 1798), an artillerist and also a military engineer. Le Mercier's group arrived at Presque Isle about a month after they left Montréal, and they immediately began construction of Fort de la Presqu'isle, the first French fort located within the present boundaries of Pennsylvania.

4

French Forts on the Allegheny

This Wampum I do not know, which you have discharged me off the Land with: But you need not put yourself to the Trouble of speaking, for I will not hear you. I am not afraid of Flies, or Mosquitos, for the Indians are such as those.—Captain Paul Marin de la Malgue

The arrival of French military detachments at Presque Isle and start of construction on a military fort there was noted by the Indians, who quickly spread the word of the French activities. Within a short time, the news was conveyed to Sir William Johnson (1715–1774), the former British Indian Commissioner who had very close ties to the Iroquois, particularly with the Mohawk nation. Johnson had resigned as Indian Commissioner in 1751 because of pressure from his political adversaries; however, the Iroquois held him in high regard and were steadfastly loyal to him. Johnson spoke the Mohawk language, was familiar with Iroquois customs and was recognized by them as someone who would advocate for their interests in the British political system.[1] The Iroquois called him Warraghiyagey (a man who undertakes great things). Around 1742, he was adopted by the Mohawks and elevated to sachem or civil chief status. After the death of his first wife, the German immigrant Catherine Weisenberg, Johnson's next two wives were Mohawk women. After Catherine died about 1749, he took Caroline Hendrick as a wife. Caroline was the daughter of the Mohawk Chief Abraham and niece of the famous Mohawk Chief Tiyanoga, who was called King Hendrick by the British. Caroline died around 1752 and Johnson next took Molly Brant as his wife. Molly Brant was the sister of Thayendanegea (1743–1807), who was also known as Joseph Brant, the renowned Mohawk war chief and political leader. Interestingly, there is no extant documentation indicating that Johnson ever formally married any of the women with whom he lived and who bore him children.

Because of his close connection with the Iroquois, William Johnson was likely one of the first English white men to receive word of Marin's expedition.

Johnson immediately sent word to Lieutenant Governor James Hamilton (1710–1783) of Pennsylvania, and Hamilton in turn relayed the message to Provincial Governor Horatio Sharpe (1710–1790) of Maryland, and Lieutenant Governor Robert Dinwiddie of Virginia. Hamilton also sent messengers to the traders on the Allegheny and Ohio Rivers regarding the French military force that had landed at Presque Isle. The traders, however, had already received word from their own friendly Indians who were observing the French activities, and they in turn passed the news from one to another. In this way, the news of the French advance spread very rapidly across the frontier. For example, the first French detachment came ashore at Presque Isle on Thursday, May 3, and by Monday, May 7, 1753, word reached George Croghan about 115 miles away at his Pine Creek storehouse near present Etna, Pennsylvania, just north of the Forks of the Ohio. Crogan had received the message from an Indian runner who was sent by John Fraser at Venango. Fraser had included details that the French force included eight brass cannon and was equipped with ammunition and stores. The following day, two messengers from the central Iroquois village at Onondaga (present Syracuse, New York) arrived with the news of the French incursion. The system of runners the Indians used to disseminate information was obviously very effective. Lieutenant Governor Hamilton's warnings sent by dispatch riders did not reach Croghan until Saturday, May 12, 1753, five days after Indian runners had given him the same information.

Two Indians that happened to be at Croghan's Pine Creek post were Tanacharison and Scarouady,[2] who were both half-kings of the Iroquois. Historians are not in complete agreement regarding the nature of the title "half-king" and the authority that may be associated with it. The title appears to have been an English designation that recognized certain individuals as representatives of the Iroquois Council at Onondaga. French sources use the term *le demi roi*[3] (the half-king) in the same context. As such, half-kings were responsible for maintaining Iroquois authority and influence over the Mingos, who were expatriate Iroquois in the Ohio country, and also over the other Indian nations who had been conquered by the Iroquois and who were now considered subservient to them. In the Ohio region those dominated nations included the Wyandot, Delaware and Shawnee. It's not known whether the half-kings had been sent to the Ohio territory by the Iroquois Council, or had migrated there with the other expatriate Iroquois and had subsequently been accepted as prominent village leaders, rather than having been appointed by the Iroquois Council. Regardless, the Iroquois Council recognized them as their agents in the Ohio territory. Even though the Mingos were recognized by the Council at Onondaga as Iroquois relatives, those expatriate Iroquois tribes in Ohio were regarded as "hunters," without authority to hold formal councils. The Iroquois Council obviously found it convenient to have representatives in the Ohio territory that could supervise the Ohio Indians, monitor the French and English activities in the area and gauge the effect that the Europeans might have on the Ohio tribes. As a result, it became expedient for them as well as the Mingos and other tribes who were subservient to the Iroquois to be represented by resident half-kings like Tanacharison and Scarouady. However, the half-kings were limited in what they could do. The Iroquois Council only permitted the half-kings to engage in minor negotiations and exchange diplomatic gifts. The half-kings were not authorized to speak for the Iroquois Council or make binding treaties, which were solely the prerogatives of the Iroquois Council. The Iroquois Council also insisted that those activities be conducted at Onondaga. When the Iroquois were invited to participate in a Council at Logstown, they haughtily replied, "It is not our custom to meet to treat affairs in the woods and weeds."[4] While it appeared on the surface that the half-kings had powers similar to a European feudal lord, in reality the half-kings' authority and influence depended for the most part on the willingness of their member tribes to comply. The half-kings technically represented the grand Iroquois Council, but neither they nor the Ohio tribes they supervised always agreed with the diktats of the Iroquois Council. In those cases, the pragmatic half-kings often found it more expedient to administer by compromise, diplomacy and what appeared to be best for themselves and the Ohio tribes, which often placed the half-kings in a divergent position to that of the Grand Council. It appears that whether or not the British were fully cognizant of the limited authority, responsibilities and diplomatic capabilities of the half-kings as representatives of the Iroquois Council at Onondaga, the British and the half-kings to some extent merely chose to exceed the authority of the half-kings for expediency of local affairs or in negotiating local alliances. At any rate, the English found it more convenient to deal with the half-kings as sort of viceroys who represented the Iroquois Council. Virginia's interests in particular in obtaining land for settlement and speculation encouraged direct dealings with the Ohio Indians rather than the Iroquois Council. In fact, both Pennsylvania and Virginia preferred to deal directly with the Ohio Indians and their half-kings, rather than with the more remote and aloof Iroquois overlords at Onondaga.

Little is known of Tanacharison prior to 1747. Most sources indicate he was a Catawba[5] Indian, and according to some sources he was born near present Buffalo, New York. However, the Catawba were indigenous to North and South Carolina, so it is likely that he was born somewhere in the Carolinas around 1700. When he was a child, both he and his mother were captured by a Seneca war party and taken north, where they were adopted into the Seneca nation. It was a common practice for tribes to adopt captives into their societies to introduce new bloodlines and to replace deceased members of the tribe. Often newly adopted captives would be given the name of a deceased person and be granted similar status in the tribe. As an adopted Seneca, Tanacharison evidently showed promise as a leader, rising in stature and influence within the Seneca nation and also within the Iroquois Confederation. Sometime prior to 1747, Tanacharison was recognized by the Iroquois Grand Council as their representative or half-king to provide administrative oversight over the Mingos and subservient Wyandot and Delaware tribes of the Ohio region. Tanacharison lived in the area of the Forks of the Ohio, taking residence at different times either at Logstown or Sauconk. Sauconk was sometimes referred to as Shingas's Town (present Beaver, Pennsylvania), which was located at the mouth of the Beaver River about 15 miles downstream from Logstown. The first document that mentions Tanacharison was dated Thursday, April 20, 1747, when he and other Indian leaders wrote to Deputy Governor George Thomas of Pennsylvania on behalf of Memeskia's rebelling Miamis and Orontony's Wyandots who were attempting to break away from French control. They were requesting a council between the English, Iroquois, Ohio Miamis, and other Ohio tribes who had previously been inclined toward the French. The intended goal of the council was to secure protection and friendly relations between the English and the breakaway Ohio Indians. One of the other signers of the 1747 letter was Scarouady, who was perhaps Tanacharison's closest associate. Scarouady was occasionally referred to by the local Indians, traders, and even George Washington as Monacatootha. He was a half-king, recognized by the Iroquois Council to primarily supervise the Shawnee Indians in the Ohio region.

By 1749, Tanacharison was recognized as a dominant figure in the area of the Forks of the Ohio and was protective of Indian autonomy in the Ohio territory. As such, he was mistrustful of any uninvited forts or white settlements in the area, regardless of whether they were French or English. Both he and Scarouady were concerned that an increased military presence of either white power in the Ohio area would erode the authority of the half-kings and the influence of the Iroquois, but they realized that the Indians were not powerful enough on their own to prevent, much less evict a strong force of European troops. However, Tanacharison and Scarouady sided with the British in their struggle for influence in the Ohio territory, even though the official Iroquois stance was to remain neutral. Both half-kings were aware that friction between the French and English would likely erupt into a full-blown conflict in which the Ohio tribes would be compelled to take sides. Scarouady once said, "You can't live in the woods and be neutral."[6] The fact that both half-kings preferred to support the British side begs the question why. Why would they choose sides so early in the affair when their superiors at the Iroquois Council advocated neutrality for the Six Nations, especially when backing the eventual loser could be disastrous? The most common answer is that the Iroquois had traditionally allied with the English against the French ever since the summer of 1609, when Samuel Champlain and two French soldiers and a group of about 60 Huron warriors encountered a war party of about 200 Iroquois near the southern end of Lake Champlain. Instead of the easy victory the Iroquois expected, Champlain fired his matchlock musket called an arquebus and killed two of the three Iroquois chiefs. One of the other French soldiers shot and killed the third Iroquois chief. The unexpected gunfire and the loss of their leaders unnerved the Iroquois, causing them to flee. The Iroquois, however, had long memories, and they never forgot that event and they never forgave the French. Unfortunately for the French, that small skirmish in 1609 affected French and Iroquois relations for well over a century.

Champlain's involvement in the 1609 encounter with the Iroquois certainly precipitated a long-term animosity between the Iroquois and the French. However, the Huron-Iroquois acrimony stemmed from a series of seventeenth century conflicts in North America called the Beaver Wars, which were fought for control of the fur trade. With the arrival of Europeans, the fur trade was a lucrative commercial enterprise for the Indians who were becoming increasingly dependent on European manufactured articles. Indians wanted the full gamut of trade merchandise, including trinkets, beads, clothing, fabric, cooking utensils, tools, knives, tomahawks, firearms, powder, lead, and almost anything else that a trader could pack into the forest. At the same time, the European demand for beaver fur for hats, clothing and fashion was increasing, and the fur trade soon became a flourishing industry in the new world. Supplied with modern weapons by the Dutch, the aggressive and highly organized Iroquois confederacy sought to expand their traditional territories to facilitate their control, if not their monopoly, of the fur trade. They encroached on neighboring tribes in all directions from their homeland in present northern New York and Pennsylvania, but their primary and most aggressive thrusts were north against the Huron Confederacy and west against the Ohio Indians that included the powerful Erie nation. The Iroquois wars of conquest were brutal and bloody efforts to eliminate competition through the simple expedient of destroying their competitors. The Beaver Wars were perhaps the most savage wars ever fought in North America. In the end, the Erie nation was almost totally annihilated, and the mighty Huron Confederation was decimated. The remaining Ohio Indians fled farther west, and the surviving Huron moved beyond the reach of the Iroquois, and relied on their old allies the French for protection. The all-out warfare only subsided when the Dutch, who had been allies of the Iroquois, lost their colony of New Netherlands to the English. The English promptly renamed the colony New York. By that time, however, the Iroquois who had achieved dominance among the northeast Indians began to exploit their newly won power and stature. With the Dutch gone, the Iroquois gravitated toward the English as allies and trading partners, but they also conducted a lucrative commerce with the French. Interestingly, because of this trade partnership with the Iroquois, England based its tenuous claim to the Ohio territory on the Iroquois conquest of the area's tribes during the Beaver Wars.

Notwithstanding Champlain's 1609 fight against the Iroquois or the lingering hostilities resulting from the Beaver Wars, the six nations were very astute in attempting to maintain a balance of power between the French and the English. They realized early on that they were not strong enough to stand alone against either power, but instead they tried to use each of the European powers as a counterweight to keep the other at bay. The French wanted a monopoly on the Indian trade and the English wanted Indian land. Both concepts were disadvantageous to the Six Nations, so the Iroquois tried to keep either European power from gaining a distinct advantage over the other. At the Montréal Treaty of 1701, the Iroquois allied themselves to a certain extent with the French, promising neutrality in the event of a Franco-British war, but they also demanded that France respect Iroquois neutrality. Interestingly, while one group of Iroquois was agreeing to the Montréal Treaty of 1701, another group was in Albany renewing the chain of friendship with the British. The Iroquois hoped that these two treaties based on armed neutrality would maintain the balance of power between the French and the English.

However, Tanacharison and Scarouady most likely based their early affinity toward the British on more personally pragmatic grounds than Champlain's ancient battle or even on Iroquois diplomacy. Tanacharison claimed that he hated the French, because they had killed, boiled and eaten his father, which would certainly be sufficient grounds for hatred, but there is no other evidence to support that allegation. The half-king may have been symbolically referring to the fate of the Miami chief Memeskia at Pickawillany. Most likely the half-kings' support for the British involved the preservation of their personal stature and authority as half-kings. The French military show of strength associated with Marin's mission certainly caught the attention of the tribes in the Ohio territory who had been subjugated by the Iroquois, and as a result were under the control of the Six Nations. Those tribes now looked upon the French as a means of escaping Iroquois domination. In particular, tribes like the Delaware who had been victimized by both the Iroquois and the English seized upon any chance to distance themselves from them both. Quite simply, the French provided those tribes with the attractive opportunity to once again be their own people.

Tanacharison realized that French protection of the Ohio Indians would erode the authority of the half-kings over the Iroquois-dominated tribes. That would certainly come to the attention of the Onondaga Council as a weakening of the Six Nation's power and prestige, and worse, they would likely consider it as a personal failure of their respective half-kings. Tanacharison realized that as long as the Ohio Indians had the alternative of French protection in the Ohio territory, the half-kings' authority and influence over the Ohio Indians would continue to diminish. It would be best to eliminate the French alternative for the Ohio Indians, but he knew that it would take British assistance to accomplish that.

The French in the meantime continued their advance into the Ohio territory. While the fort at Presque Isle was still under construction, the French commander Marin turned his attention toward the next phase of the expedition; clearing the portage route to French Creek, which flowed into the Allegheny River. The Presque Isle Portage route to French Creek was recorded as seven leagues or about 17.5 statute miles. It crossed relatively flat but often wet and soggy ground, and its course often varied as travelers sought firmer and drier ground. Though it could be readily negotiated on foot and with pack horses, it was extremely difficult to traverse with wagons except in the driest weather. After clearing and improving the route, Marin was ordered to build a fort at the end of the Presque Isle Portage. The work was incredibly arduous, and although the troops increasingly suffered from sickness and exhaustion, Marin would not allow the pace to slacken. He continued to drive himself and his men unmercifully, and any troops who appeared to be shirking were severely punished. Officers who exhibited the slightest lack of enthusiasm or zeal were threatened with being immediately cashiered from the service.

Fort de la Rivière au Bœuf (present Waterford, Pennsylvania), more commonly called "Fort Le Bœuf," was begun on Thursday, July 12, 1753. It was situated on a small hill on the west fork of French Creek (that west branch is now called Le Bœuf Creek), about two and a half miles north of the main branch of French Creek. Because of its size, French Creek has often been referred to as a river. Even though the Presque Isle Portage could be difficult at times, the French Creek waterway was an important link between Lake Erie and the Allegheny River.

The construction of Fort Le Bœuf, though difficult, was only a small part of the obstacles and challenges facing Marin. Aside from the sickness and fatigue that were plaguing the French force, the troops lacked sufficient horse transport and adequate forage. In addition, Marin discovered that his provisions had been short-weighted by profiteering supply contractors. On Sunday, July 15, 1753, Marin wrote to Contrecœur at Niagara:

> All the barrels which have come to us, as well as the goods, are in very good condition, but they lack much more than they should of the weight they are supposed to have. I have had a number weighed in my presence, and one after the other they lacked at least seven pounds which was replaced with salt, and that cannot take the place of salt pork in the rations. I told M. Le Mercier to send a report on it to the General, and omit no details. I am advising him also, Sir, that I am asking you in this to please send him a report on the barrels of salt pork which you have both at Niagara and at the little fort, to make mention of everything which is spoiled, and to02 take about ten by chance from those that seem to be in good condition, and have them weighed, after removing the salt, so that he can see what our subsistence amounts to. Please also have the barrels in poor condition evaluated, so that the storekeeper can have them put in shape when he sends them here. I realize, Sir, the work that is going to give you, but even on this new task depends the success of the King's arms.[7]

In another undated letter Marin wrote, "Not a package, or at least very few of them, contains what is marked on the invoice. I am having note kept about them as they are opened."[8]

Already faced with a myriad of problems, insects plagued the troops and the late summer drought dried the streams to a mere trickle, making the movement of men and supplies by batteaux difficult if not impossible. Irascible by nature, the mounting difficulties, which included exhaustion, illness and a lack of provisions, vexed Marin to the point where he responded with ferociousness to anything perceived as interfering or impeding his mission. Adding to Marin's difficulties were the alarmed Indians along the Allegheny and Ohio who viewed the French expedition with an increasing amount of trepidation. The French army that was penetrating straight into their territory was of an unprecedented and overwhelming size. It was a considerably larger armed force than most of the Indians had ever seen before. In 1749, Céloron's troops awed the Indians with its size and power, but Marin's present force was about ten times larger and better armed than Céloron's. One Indian reported that "the earth was trembling from the multitude of French who were at Rivière au Bœuf, and beside that ... [t]hey are holding hands from Presquisle to La Chine."[9] Not knowing the reasons for the invasion of the French army, the Indians first sent emissaries to determine French intentions and later to attempt to dissuade the French from advancing. Unfortunately, it was a matter of bad timing that they encountered Marin as his anxiety and agitation were escalating toward the boiling point.

In May or June of 1753, the Iroquois Council at Onondaga took the unusual step of sending a group of women to meet with the French at Presque Isle to ask the reason for the military incursion into Indian territory, and whether the French army came with hatchet uplifted, or to establish tranquility. The implication of the Council sending a delegation of matriarchs was that the Council itself, which debated matters of war and peace, wished to avoid any situation that could be considered confrontational. This was a polite and diplomatic means of expressing Iroquois displeasure with the French incursion. Marin fully understood the significance of the matriarchal delegation, but his response was anything but diplomatic. Marin told the astonished women that "when he marched with the hatchet, he bore it aloft, in order that no person should be ignorant of the fact."[10] The French commander reported the episode to Duquesne, who endorsed Marin's response to "the trembling speeches of the Ladies of the Council," and for having responded "like a brave warrior to the lifted hatchet when at war." [11]

Although they were justifiably alarmed by Marin's breech of diplomatic protocol, the Iroquois did not immediately resort to warfare. Instead, they presented three separate ritual protests to the French commander, each stronger than the previous. It is certain that Tanacharison led the third delegation, but it is also likely that he was present when the previous two protests were delivered to the French. These were the strongest measures the Iroquois could take short of a declaration of war.[12] The first protest was delivered in July of 1753, directing the French not to proceed any farther, which Marin bluntly and summarily rebuffed. The second was delivered at French Creek where the construction of Fort Machault was in progress. The Iroquois message stated: "Your children on Ohio are alarmed to hear your coming so far this way. We at first heard that you came to destroy us. Our women left off planting, and our warriors prepared for war. We have since heard that you come to visit us as friends without design to hurt us, but then we wondered you came with so strong a body. If you had any cause of complaint, you might have spoken to Onas [Proprietary Governor Horatio Sharpe of Maryland] or Corlear [Royal Governor George Clinton of New York], and not come to disturb us here. We have a [council] Fire at Logstown, where are the Delawares and Shawonese, and Brother Onas; you might have sent deputies there and said openly what you came about, if you had thought amiss of the English being there, and we invite you to do it now, before you proceed any further."[13]

Marin, already frustrated by the innumerable vexing problems that were delaying his expedition, was rapidly losing patience with the constant complaints and demands of the Indians. He was barely able to keep his temper in check when he bluntly told the Indian emissaries that he had no intention of attending a council at Logstown to obtain permission to proceed into the area.

He said his authority came directly from the king of France who commanded him to occupy the Ohio territory and build forts at Presque Isle, Le Bœuf, Venango, the Forks of the Ohio, Logstown, and on Beaver Creek. The stunned Iroquois, who were initially frustrated by Marin's disregard for their concerns, or his lack of a reasonably diplomatic response to their protests, were now alarmed by his declaration that the French army intended to enter their territory uninvited and build a chain of forts along the Ohio Valley. The Iroquois hurriedly held another conference and sent Tanacharison with a third, more strident notice that lacked the customary diplomatic tenor. The Iroquois message bluntly forbade the French from progressing any farther and directed them to turn back and return to the place from whence they came.[14] Tanacharison's speech was unequivocal and was in essence an ultimatum to a declaration of war.

> Now Fathers, it is you who are the Disturbers in this Land, by coming and building your Towns; and taking it away unknown to us, and by Force.
> Fathers, We kindled a Fire a long Time ago, at a Place called Montréal, where we desired you to stay, and not come and intrude upon our Land. I now desire you may dispatch to that Place; for be it known to you, Fathers, that this is our Land, and not yours.
> Fathers, I desire you may hear me in Civilness; if not, we must handle that Rod which was laid down for the Use of the obstreperous. If you had come in a peaceable Manner, like our Brothers the English, we should not have been against your trading with us, as they do; BUT TO COME, FATHERS, AND BUILD HOUSES UPON OUR LAND, AND TO TAKE IT BY FORCE, IS WHAT WE CANNOT SUBMIT TO.
> Fathers, Both you and the English are white, we live in a Country between; therefore the Land belongs to neither one nor t'other: But the Great Being above allow'd it to be a Place of Residence for us; so Fathers, I desire you to withdraw, as I have done our Brothers the English: For I will keep you at Arms length. I lay this down as a Trial for both, to see which have the greatest Regard to it, and that Side we will stand by, and make equal shares with us. Our Brothers the English have heard this, and I come now to tell it to you; for I am not afraid to discharge you off this Land.[15]

For the irritable and cantankerous French commander, this was too much. Marin completely lost his temper and threw Tanacharison's proffered goodwill wampum belt to the ground shouting that he despised all the stupid things the chief had said. He added that he was not afraid of flies or mosquitoes, which he likened the Indians to and that he had sufficient numbers to crush any opposition and tread under his feet anyone who would oppose him. He insultingly added that the Indians foolishly claim that it is their land, but they don't even own land equal to the dirt under Marin's fingernails.[16]

Although Marin was by nature a blunt and autocratic officer, it must be stated that by the summer of 1753, he had already contracted the illness that would kill him just three months later. Throughout the spring and summer of 1753, Marin drove his troops mercilessly, but he drove himself no less. Many of his troops collapsed and died from lack of adequate food, from overwork and from exhaustion, but Marin shared those same brutal conditions, which destroyed the health of the 61-year-old French commander. Sickness and fatigue only made the irascible and abrasive Marin even more so.

Marin's complete response to Tanacharison as the chief reported to Washington was as follows:

> Now my child, I have heard your Speech: You spoke first, but it is my Time to speak now. Where is my Wampum that you took away, with the Marks of Towns in it? This Wampum I do not know, which you have discharged me off the Land with: But you need not put yourself to the Trouble of speaking, for I will not hear you. I am not afraid of Flies, or Mosquitos, for the Indians are such as those. I tell you, down that River I will go, and will build upon it, according to my Command. If the River was block'd up, I have Forces sufficient to burst it open, and tread under my Feet all that stand in Opposition, together with their Alliances; for my Force is as the Sand upon the Sea Shore: Therefore, here is your Wampum, I fling it at you. Child, you talk foolish; you say this Land belongs to you, but there is not the Black of my Nail yours. I saw that Land sooner than you did, before the Shannoahs and you were at War: Lead was the Man who went down, and took Possession of that River: It is my Land, and I will have it, let who will stand-up for, or say-against, it. I'll buy and sell with the English, (mockingly). If People will be rul'd by me, they may expect Kindness, but not else.[17]

Marin's belligerent and insulting rejection of Tanacharison's protest was an incredible breach of diplomatic protocol, and if it was meant to browbeat the Iroquois chief, it had exactly the opposite effect. Tanacharison was able to maintain his composure while he was with Marin, but the half-king was so outraged by the French commander's contemptuous manner, he returned to Logstown with tears in his eyes.[18] However, in spite of Marin's demeaning insults, Tanacharison was more concerned about the effect that French bellicosity would have on the Ohio Indians who were under the domination of the Iroquois. The Iroquois chief realized that Marin's belligerent attitude would likely impress the subjugated Ohio tribes and entice them to side with the French. The half-king knew that to maintain Iroquois supremacy and personally preserve his stature as half-king, French influence over the Ohio tribes would have to be eliminated, but he also realized that he needed the help of the English army to accomplish that.

5

Washington Warns the French

Sir, in Obedience to my Instructions, it becomes my Duty to require your peaceable Departure—Washington to the French commander on the Allegheny

Until February of 1753, neither Virginia Lieutenant Governor Dinwiddie nor, in fact, most of the other English colonial governors believed there was an imminent threat of a French military invasion of the upper Ohio Valley. The only recent overt actions in Ohio were Céloron's expedition four years prior and the French punitive raid on Pickiwillany the previous year. While those events served to alert the English of an increasing French bellicosity in defense of their claim to the Ohio territory, there still didn't seem to be any great cause for immediate alarm. Certainly the burying of lead plates and posting proclamations of French ownership, along with the destruction of the English trading hub at Pickawillany, were serious enough and signaled French intentions, but the French presence in the area was still minimal, and no fortifications containing French troops existed closer than Forts Niagara and Detroit. All in all, the status quo existed, which greatly favored English interests and gave the impression that the Ohio territory was England's for the taking whenever they were ready to act. English traders, primarily because of their cheaper and more plentiful trade goods, were still reaping the benefits of trade with the Ohio Indians. It appeared that the only people who were somewhat eager to begin settlements in the Ohio were the land speculators of the Ohio Company of Virginia, and they didn't seem to have any great urgency. At the treaty of Lancaster in 1744, the Virginians made a half-hearted promise to build a "strong house" at the Forks of the Ohio to facilitate trade with the Indians, and on Saturday, June 13, 1752, the Indians reaffirmed the agreement, promising that a strong house at the Forks would not be molested by them. However, the Virginians were in no apparent hurry to build their strong house or to fortify the Forks. In general, not much was being accomplished toward that end other than to send occasional emissaries and gifts to the Ohio Indians.

As a result, English colonial apathy was severely shaken by the arrival of an overwhelming French force on the Allegheny River. Marin's expedition signaled in no uncertain terms that it was France's intention to fortify and defend the territories west of the Allegheny Mountains, and to repel any and all English traders, settlers, and British military intrusions into the area. Nowhere did the French invasion cause greater alarm than in Virginia. Lieutenant Governor Dinwiddie in Williamsburg was frantic over the French incursion, but his concerns were more financial than patriotic. He and his fellow investors in the Ohio Company of Virginia faced serious financial losses if the French were able to enforce their claim to the Ohio territory and prevent the Ohio Company of Virginia from expanding into the area. Dinwiddie was determined to do all that was possible to prevent that from happening.

When Tanacharison, on behalf of the Iroquois, warned the French not to proceed into the Ohio territory, both the half-king and the Iroquois fully expected support from the English, at least in the form of a "strong house" at the Forks. The strong house was promised them in 1744 and reaffirmed again the previous June. Now that a French army had sent troops to occupy the area, the English colonial governors, particularly those of Virginia, Pennsylvania, and Maryland, were caught off guard and had no practical, collective idea about how to respond to the French incursion. The Ohio Company of Virginia certainly had authorization from the Indians to build a trading house at the Forks, but since the Ohio Company was essentially a trading company and land speculation endeavor, the Company was not strong enough to challenge the well-equipped and formidable French army. In addition, neither Dinwiddie nor the other colonial governors felt inclined to initiate military action without specific authorization and support from the king. They hurriedly sent messages that sought advice from the crown, and hoped the king would send an army powerful enough to challenge the French, but the response from London was somewhat less than they desired. That fall, letters dated Tuesday, August 28, 1753, and addressed to all the colonial governors arrived from secretary of state Robert Darcy, 4th Earl of Holderness. The message specified that before any hostilities could be initiated, the French must formally be requested to withdraw from the area, and if they refused to comply, the colonies were given a vague authorization to use force. The full text of Holderness's message follows:

> Sir—
> His majesty having received information of the march of a considerable number of Indians not in alliance with the King, supported by some regular European troops, intending, as it is apprehended, to commit some hostilities in parts of his majesty's

dominions in North America, I have the King's command to send you this intelligence and to direct you to use your utmost diligence to learn how far the same may be well grounded, and to put you upon your guard that you may be at all events in a condition to resist any hostile attempt that may be made upon any parts of his majesty's dominions within your government; and to direct you in the King's name, that in case the subjects of any foreign prince or state should presume to make any encroachment on the limits of his majesty's dominion or to erect forts on his majesty's lands, or commit any other act of hostility, you are immediately to represent the injustice of such proceeding, and to require them forthwith to desist from any such unlawful undertaking. But if, notwithstanding your requisition, they should still persist, you are then to draw forth the armed force of the province, and to use your best endeavors to repel force by force. But as it is his majesty's determination not to be the aggressor. I have the King's command most strictly to enjoin you not to make use of the armed force under your direction, excepting within the undoubted limits of his majesty's dominions. And whereas it may be greatly conducive to his majesty's service, that all his provinces in America should be aiding and assisting each other in case of invasion. I have it particularly in charge from his majesty to acquaint you, that it is his royal will and pleasure, that you should keep up an exact correspondence with all his majesty's governors on the Continent, and in case you shall be informed by any of them of any hostile attempts, you are immediately to summons the General Assembly within your government, and lay before them the necessity of mutual assistance and engage them to grant such supplies as the exigency of affairs may require. I have wrote by this conveyance to all his majesty's Governors to the same purpose.[1]

British troops were not on their way, and even worse, the king did not seem to have any intention of sending an army to expel the French. The colonies would have to do the best they could on their own. The message inferred that the colonies had the authority to use force against force, but there were required protocols that would have to be conformed to before any military action could be taken against the French. For example, the French first had to be asked to desist their objectionable activity so that the English colonial troops could not be viewed as the aggressor. In addition, it was stipulated that any action against the French could only be undertaken in areas that were unquestionably within the limits of the king's dominion. To further frustrate Dinwiddie, the Pennsylvanians believed the Ohio territory belonged to Pennsylvania and were not inclined to support Virginia. The Maryland colonial legislature was also apathetic about supporting Virginia's presumptive claim, and New York's royal governor was miffed by Dinwiddie's meddling with "their Iroquois." Even influential Virginians who were not a part of the Ohio Company of Virginia's land speculation scheme did not wish to throw their support behind what they considered Dinwiddie's business venture, especially when there was no apparent gain in it for them.

In the meantime, the French expedition had penetrated as far south as the Indian Village of Venango near the confluence of French Creek and the Allegheny River, where they built Fort Machault. The fort was named after Jean-Baptiste Machault d'Arnouville (1701–1794), who was the French Comptroller General for Finance. At Venango the French advance was halted by a combination of the approaching winter season and the physical deterioration of the troops. Since leaving Montréal, over 400 of Marin's men had perished from overwork, exhaustion, bad food, and sickness. Twenty percent of the original force was dead, and the majority of the surviving troops were decimated by fatigue, injuries, and illness. By the time they reached the Allegheny River at French Creek, less than 800 of the more than 2,000 men that left Montréal earlier that year were scarcely able to walk, much less work. The severity of the ailments plaguing the officers, troops and even Marin was staggering. The men's afflictions included fever, bloody flux,[2] pneumonia, spitting blood, lung diseases, and hemorrhaging caused primarily by exhaustion and a deficient diet. The troops desperately needed rest and recuperation. Fortunately, reason prevailed. Leaving only minimal garrisons at Forts Machault, Le Bœuf, and Presque Isle, the remaining troops were sent back to Montréal to rest and recover. When the wretched and totally exhausted troops staggered into Montréal, they were reviewed by a horrified Governor-General Duquesne. He wrote: "I reviewed them, and could not help being touched by the pitiable state to which fatigues and exposure had reduced them. Past all doubt, if these emaciated figures had gone down the Ohio as intended, the river would have been strewn with corpses, and the evil-disposed savages would not have failed to attack the survivors, seeing that they were but specters."[3] Ironically, in June a few months earlier, Duquesne had written to Marin regarding rumors that Marin was "living as magnificently as a Marshal of France in command of an army."[4] Nothing could be further from the truth. Marin shared the same sparse diet as the troops and drove himself as brutally as he drove his men, with the result that by the time they reached Venango, he was so sick and exhausted that he was bedridden. Marin had been ordered to return to Montréal to recuperate, but refused, preferring to die like a soldier in the field on active service. He got his wish. Marin died at the age of 61 at Fort Le Bœuf on Monday, October 29, 1753. In September, the month previous, he had been awarded the Royal and Military Order of Saint Louis, but notification of the honor did not reach Fort Machault until after his death. The Military Order of Saint Louis was a military order of chivalry founded on April 5, 1693, by King Louis XIV and named after Saint Louis. It was a reward for exceptional officers and was the first to be awarded to non-nobles. The award was the predecessor of the French Ordre national de la Légion d'honneur (National order of the Legion of Honor).

Upon receipt of the message from the Earl of Holderness, Lieutenant

Governor Dinwiddie realized there would no military help from England, and that he would have to take the initiative in response to the French incursion. The Virginia lieutenant governor took action almost immediately, and in doing so he used brazen patronage. Mixing the power of his position as lieutenant governor with his financial interest in the Ohio Company land speculation venture, Dinwiddie conferred military commissions on key members of the company and began to recruit militia to reinforce the company's claim to the Ohio territory. His first move was to draft a formal message dated Wednesday, October 31, 1753, to the French commander, demanding an answer to why the French army had occupied land that was "so notoriously known to be the Property of the Crown of Great Britain."

George Washington, who was 21 years old, had upon the death of his elder half-brother Lawrence, been commissioned by Dinwiddie as adjutant general in charge of militia in one of Virginia's four districts.[5] The young Virginian happened to be in Williamsburg at the time, and it's not known whether Washington was first approached by the lieutenant governor or whether he volunteered to deliver Dinwiddie's message to the French commander. At any rate, Dinwiddie's selection of Washington for the mission was likely influenced by the fact that Washington's family members were also shareholders in the Ohio Company of Virginia, and therefore Washington could be relied upon to look after Ohio Company interests. Dinwiddie's message read:

SIR,
The lands upon the River Ohio, in the Western Parts of the Colony of Virginia, are so notoriously known to be the Property of the Crown of Great-Britain, that it is a Matter of equal Concern and Surprize to me, to hear that a Body of French Forces are erecting Fortresses, and making Settlements upon that River, within his Majesty's Dominions.

The Many and repeated Complaints I have received of these Acts of Hostility, lay me under the Necessity, of sending, in the Name of the King my Master, the Bearor hereof, George Washington, Esq; one of the Adjutants General of the Forces of the Dominion, to complain to you of the Encroachments thus made, and of the Injuries done to the Subjects of Great-Britain, in open Violation of the Law of Nations, and the Treaties now subsisting between the two Crowns.

If these facts are true, and you shall think fit to justify your Proceedings, I must desire you to acquaint me, by whose Authority and Instructions you have lately marched from Canada, with an armed Force, and invaded the King of Great-Britain's Territories, in the Manner complained of; that according to the Purport and resolution of your Answer, I may agreably to the Commission I am honored with, from the King, my Master.

However Sir, in Obedience to my Instructions, it becomes my Duty to require your peaceable Departure; and that you would forbear prosecuting a Purpose so interruptive of the Harmony and good Understanding, which his Majesty is desirous to continue and cultivate with the most Christian King.

I persuade myself you will receive and entertain Major Washington with the Candour and Politeness natural to your Nation; and it will give me the greatest Satisfaction, if you return him with an Answer suitable to my Wishes for a very long and lasting Peace between us.

I have the Honour to subscribe myself,
    SIR,

                Your most obedient,
                      Humble Servant,
                          Robert Dinwiddie

Williamsburg, in Virginia
October 31st, 1753[6]

Washington departed Williamsburg that same day, Wednesday, October 31, on a more than 1,000 mile round-trip winter trek to and from the French forts on the Allegheny. The majority of the journey was through a wintertime mountainous wilderness. On Thursday, November 1, 1753, Washington arrived in Fredericksburg, Virginia, where he hired Jacob Van Braam (1727–?), a Dutch sword master and mercenary who served in the British navy with Lawrence Washington under Admiral Edward Vernon (1684–1757).[7] Recently, Van Braam had tutored young George Washington in sword exercise and military science, and while the Dutchman was an old family friend, his greatest asset to Washington on this mission was Van Braam's ability to communicate in French. In actuality, Van Braam's abilities as a translator would prove to be rather tenuous. His native language was Dutch, and while he was conversant in both English and French, any translations from English to French or vice-versa would mentally be first translated through Dutch, occasionally losing something in translation. This language anomaly would prove to be an issue the following year.

Washington and Van Braam travelled via Alexandria and Winchester to Wills Creek, and arrived there on Wednesday, November 14, 1753. At Wills Creek, Washington engaged the frontiersman Christopher Gist (1706–1759) to guide them through the wilderness. Gist was an explorer, surveyor, scout, and frontiersman. He was one the first white explorers of the Ohio Country, including present western Pennsylvania, northwestern West Virginia, northern Kentucky, Ohio, and eastern Indiana. He provided detailed information on the Ohio Country to Great Britain and the English colonies. His plantation near present Uniontown, Pennsylvania, was the first English settlement west of the Alleghenies. In addition to Gist, Washington also hired four other men: Barnaby Curran and John McGuire, who were experienced and savvy Indian traders; and Henry Stewart and William Jenkins, who were hired as general assistants.

Washington and his party left Wills Creek on Thursday, November 15,

5. Washington Warns the French

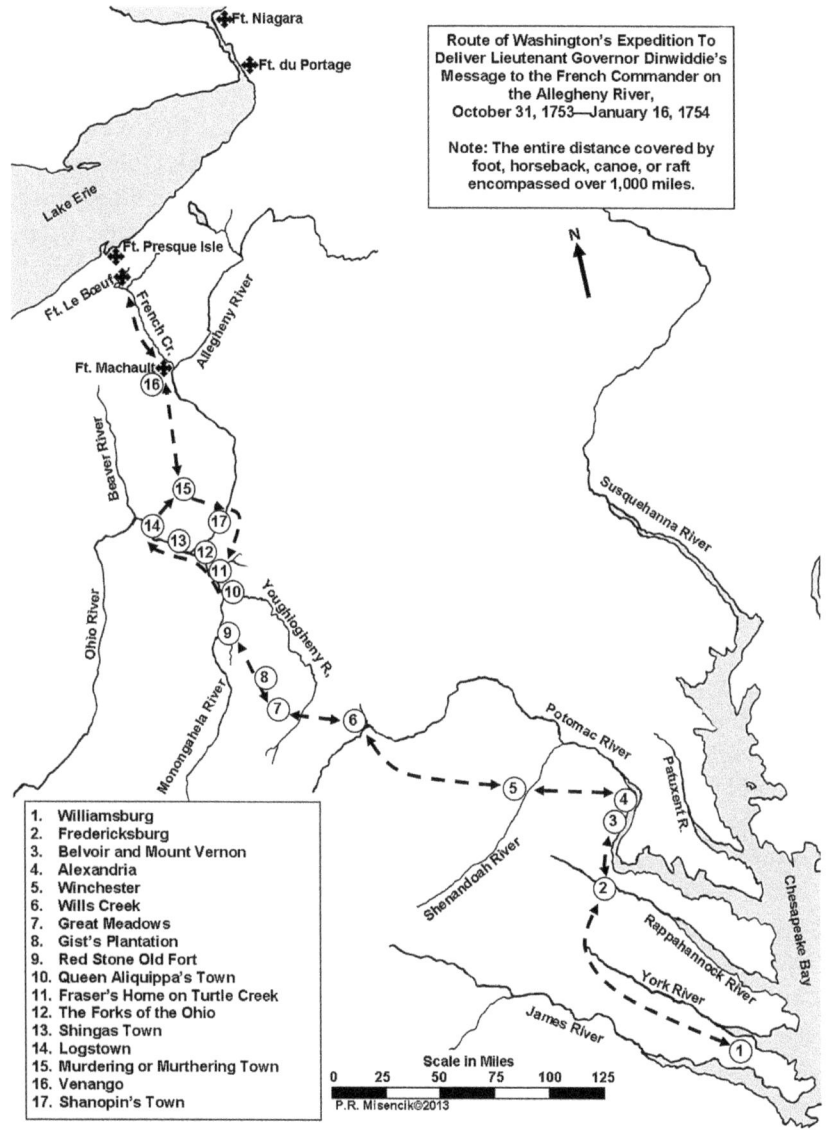

Figure 6. Washington's 1753–54 expedition to the Ohio territory.

and traveled over the so-called Nemacolin Trail that had been mapped and blazed in 1749 by the frontiersman Thomas Cresap and the Delaware Chief Nemacolin.[8] The party stopped to rest at the cabin of the trader and gunsmith John Frazer who now lived at the mouth of Turtle Creek on the Monongahela (near present Braddock, Pennsylvania). Frazer moved to Turtle Creek after having been driven away from his trading post at Venango earlier that year by the French. Washington's party reached the Forks of the Ohio on Friday, November 23, 1753. Eyeing the junction of the Allegheny and Monongahela Rivers, Washington wrote in his journal, "As I got down before the Canoe, I spent some time in viewing the Rivers, and the Land in the Fork, which I think extremely well situated for a Fort, as it has the absolute Command of both Rivers."[9]

Leaving the Forks, Washington and his small delegation met the Delaware chief Shingas[10] at his town about two miles below the Forks on the Ohio, near the mouth of Chartier's Creek. Shingas agreed to accompany them to Logstown where they hoped to meet with Tanacharison. They arrived at Logstown the evening of Saturday, November 24, where they met the Oneida half-king Scarouady and learned that the other half-king, Tanacharison, was at his cabin on the Beaver River some 15 miles away. The following morning, Scarouady sent a messenger to Tanacharison, asking him to come to Logstown. Tanacharison arrived that afternoon and met Washington with the aid of interpreter John Davidson, who happened to be at Logstown. Impressed with Davidson's knowledge of Indian dialects, Washington hired the interpreter to accompany him on the mission to the French forts.

This was Washington's first encounter with Tanacharison, and both men certainly wished to gauge the measure of the other and ascertain how much they could be relied upon. Both were self-serving to an extent. Washington's aim was to gain Indian support for his mission to ask the French to depart from what he considered to be Ohio Company of Virginia land. Tanacharison at the same time was trying to gain English support to eliminate French influence in the Ohio territory and negate the possibility of the Ohio tribes escaping Iroquois control by allying themselves with the French. Since the Iroquois half-kings like Tanacharison and Scarouady were responsible for supervising the Ohio tribes, both chiefs were certain their standing with the Iroquois Council depended on their ability to maintain control of the Ohio tribes. The goals of both Washington and Tanacharison were somewhat complimentary, but each man's personality led them to try to exert their influence over the other in their opening discussion. The talks with Tanacharison were somewhat disquieting to Washington when the Seneca began to control the conversation with probing questions regarding, among other things, Washington's motives, his mission to the French, and exactly in whose interest he was acting. This certainly was not the backward savage that Washington had expected to easily influence and gain support from in evicting the French from the upper Ohio. In fact, Tanacharison was a very intelligent and savvy diplomat. The half-king not only spoke several Indian dialects, but also was fluent in French as well as English. Washington, on the other hand only spoke and understood English.

Tanacharison was very unimpressed with Dinwiddie's inexperienced 21-year-old emissary and his handful of companions. With a powerful French army advancing on the Forks, the half-king was disappointed that Washington's small party was all that comprised Dinwiddie's initial response. The old chief told Washington that he had seen firsthand the might of the French army that was occupying the Ohio, and he bluntly asked Washington what he was going to do about it. Tanacharison was undoubtedly even more distressed when the young Virginian told him his mission was only to deliver a letter of very great importance to the French commandant, and then return to Dinwiddie with the French officer's response. Washington was astute enough not to mention that he was sent to warn the French off land that Virginia and the Ohio Company claimed as its own. He sensed that any mention of English ownership, much less the planned exploitation and settlement of the Ohio territory, would undoubtedly outrage Tanacharison, not to mention the Ohio Indians and also the Six Nations. He only commented on the obvious greed that the French had for the Indians' land, that they were sending a large army to take it for their own. Washington told the half-king that support of the English against the French were the Indians' best hope of preventing a French conquest of Indian territory.

Schooled in frontier diplomacy and having taken part in many councils with both the French and the English, the half-king was more than proficient in discerning motives. The chief was no fool and did not believe for a minute that Washington, Dinwiddie, or the English were acting solely in support of or even in the best interests of the Indians. The half-king knew that the English wanted the Indians as allies in support of their own agendas. Tanacharison, however, had his own priorities, which were to keep the Ohio tribes from defecting to the French, and right now Washington's feeble party was all he had in the face of the French juggernaut. The half-king realized that he would have to make the best of it in hopes of drawing the British army into the contest. He knew that in the long-term, the English desire for the Ohio territory was not in the best interest of the Indians, but in the short-term, the half-king needed the English army to help the Iroquois maintain authority over the Ohio Indians, which was in Tanacharison's personal interest. Keeping the English colonists from occupying and establishing settlements in the Ohio territory would have to be dealt with after the French were removed.

With Washington representing the English colonies, Tanacharison sensed an opportunity to regain a bargaining position to affect the balance of power between the French and the English. But to do so, he would first have to try to make Washington's feeble delegation somewhat more impressive to the French than it actually was. The half-king told Washington that he would accompany him to deliver Dinwiddie's letter to the French and that he would supply a guard of Mingo, Shawnee, and Delaware, so that the French would see the love and loyalty the Indians had for the English. This would require a delay of about three days to allow Tanacharison to assemble his "guard" for Washington's group and also retrieve the "French speech belt" from his hunting cabin. The weaving of wampum belts was a means of record keeping, and the pattern of the belt was associated with an agreement of friendship, a treaty, a transaction, or as mutual acknowledgment of some other event that the parties wished to document. The French had presented speech belts to the Delaware Indians, to Scarouady, who was half-king of the Shawnees, and to Tanacharison, the half-king of the Mingos and Wyandots. The decorative speech belts were accepted by the Indians in a spirit of friendship and cooperation at the time. They were large white belts, thirteen rows deep with "four Towns and Forts worked in it with black Wampum."[11] This was the belt that Marin referred to during his tirade against Tanacharison. Returning a speech belt was a sign of rejection of friendship and a repudiation of the agreements associated with the belt. The half-king was trying to assemble a show of force, and planned to return the French wampum belt to demonstrate to the French that not only the Iroquois but also the Ohio tribes would back the side that was most aligned with their interest, and that after Marin's unbelievably insensitive outburst to Tanacharison that summer, the French had some diplomatic ground to make up.

Washington was not inclined to wait three days to continue his mission. He would have preferred that Tanacharison accompany him, but if necessary they would go without the chief. Washington told Tanacharison that his orders were to proceed with all possible dispatch, which meant without delay, but the half-king was having none of it. Tanacharison showed his displeasure at having his plans summarily rejected, and remained adamant that he would not consent to Washington's leaving without a suitable guard. He claimed that he wanted to prevent Washington's party from experiencing some accident that would reflect poorly on Tanacharison or the Indians. The half-king reiterated that he intended to return the French speech belt, and he would require the Shawnees and Delawares to do the same. Washington stated in his journal, "As I found it impossible to get off without affronting them in the most egregious manner, I consented to stay."[12]

Unfortunately, the half-king was not able to deliver on his promise of a large guard composed of members of several of the Ohio Indian tribes. Worse yet, the Ohio Indians refused to return their wampum belts to the French. The Indians realized that the half-king was trying to show strength in support of the English and defiance to the French, but the Ohio tribes who smarted under Iroquois domination were not ready to give up the possibility of French protection. Returning the speech belts to the French would unequivocally state that they were abolishing all agreements and rejecting all dependence on the French. This was something they were not inclined to do. One chief, Custaloga[13] of the Delaware, was evasive in his refusal to return his nation's speech belt, claiming that he couldn't return it since Shingas had sent no speech for the occasion. The Ohio Indian chiefs also told Tanacharison that they were reluctant to send a large party of warriors to accompany Washington, because that might make the French mistrustful of their intentions and cause the Indians to be treated rudely. As a result, they only agreed to send three men to accompany Tanacharison and Washington's party. Those that were selected to accompany the party were two old chiefs, Jeskakake and Kaghswaghtaniunt[14] (White Thunder), and a younger warrior called Guyasuta (Hunter). Tanacharison was surprised, dismayed and embarrassed by the open rebelliousness on the part of the Ohio tribes, especially those that he was supposedly responsible for. The half-king asked Washington to delay his departure for one more day in hopes that he could still convince the Ohio chiefs to support him on their mission to the French. It was to no avail. Even Shingas said he could not muster any Delaware warriors to accompany Washington, and added that he would not personally escort the delegation either, ostensibly because of his wife's illness. Shingas's reticence was more likely due to his initial desire to stay neutral, but later he sided with the French and waged an aggressive war against the English colonists. Tanacharison's inability to raise a respectable group of Indians to accompany Washington was definitely a loss of face for the old chief, but he resolved to stay with the Virginian, and continue to work to get British and colonial help to counter the influence of the French on the Ohio Indians.

On Friday, November 30, 1753, Washington's party set out for Fort Machault at Venango, which was the most recently constructed French fortification on the Allegheny. The straight-line distance from Logstown to Fort Machault was about 60 miles, but by Washington's reckoning "more than seventy miles the way we were obliged to go."[15] The late autumn was unseasonably wet. Heavy rains swelled the waterways and flooded the low-lying fields. Tanacharison had warned Washington that because of the weather and the season the shortest and most level route was impassable, so the higher and drier route to Venango would have to be taken, even though it was longer. The first day they travelled about 15 miles to the vicinity of Murdering Town, sometimes referred to as Murthering Town (near present Harmony and Evans City, Pennsylvania).[16] They covered approximately 30 miles on the second day and about 22 miles on the third day. On the fourth day, they traveled 15 miles, bringing them to the vicinity of Fort Machault at Venango. By Gist's reckoning, they had trekked over 80 arduous miles since leaving Logstown.

The delegation arrived at Fort Machault on Tuesday, December 4, 1753, and was hospitably received by the French commander, Captain Phillippe-Thomas Chabert de Joncaire, who had previously marched with Céloron in 1749. He had also been the French officer sent by Governor-General Jonquière to establish the French trading post at Logstown in 1751. Joncaire was a seasoned veteran of frontier diplomacy and was very familiar with the various Indian tribal cultures. He had carried on effective negotiations and trade with the Indians since 1735. Surprisingly, he had even been successful in his dealings with the Iroquois, who had traditionally been ill-disposed toward the French. For example, in 1743, he had persuaded the Seneca to supply fresh game to the French garrison at Fort Niagara. Joncaire was so adept in dealing with the Indians that in 1744, the British offered a reward for him dead or alive, and Royal Governor Clinton of New York had once hoped that Joncaire might be persuaded to switch allegiance and join the British service, if he were offered sufficient inducement. The main reason for Joncaire's latest posting to Fort Machault was to conduct delicate diplomacy in an attempt to secure the support and goodwill of the Delaware, Shawnee and Wyandot tribes. The French were aware of the Ohio tribes' desire to break away from the dominant Iroquois, and Joncaire's mission was to woo the subjugated Ohio Indians to the side of the French. That would effectively neutralize the opposition of the Iroquois and their half-kings, primarily Tanacharison, who was the most outspoken opponent to the construction of French forts. Joncaire's mission was made easier by the fact that the Ohio tribes were awed by the powerful French army and were generally in favor of having Iroquois influence in the area challenged. Joncaire was familiar with Tanacharison, and he had previously warned Marin about the half-king, which may have influenced Marin to take a hard line with the chief. Joncaire had written to Marin that "the man named Thaninhison [sic] is the one who is to speak in the council which is to be held at your place. He was formerly inclined to the French, but at the present he is more English than the English, working only against the French by continually saying foolish things. In a word, he is no good, and it is he who sold the lands to the English. This man is from the Lake of Two Mountains, and wants to manage everything in his own way, listening to no one."[17] The Lake of the Two Mountains was formed by the widening of the Ottawa River at its mouth above the Island of Montréal. A Christianized Indian village was founded on the shore of the lake by the French Sulpician order. The community contained members of several tribes, but the majority were Mohawk Iroquois. It was called Oka (pickerel) by the Nipissing and Algonkin inhabitants, while the Mohawks called it Kan-es-ta-ke (sandy place). Mentioning that Tanacharison was from there was essentially implying that the half-king was a defector who was once one of "our people." However, there is no evidence that Tanacharison was ever a member of the community at the Lake of the Two Mountains, or that he was ever inclined toward the French. It's not known why Joncaire included those comments in his criticism of Tanacharison.

At Fort Machault, Washington and his small delegation met Joncaire in the former home of the trader-gunsmith John Fraser, from which Fraser had been driven the previous summer. Washington's group consisted of Tanacharison; Christopher Gist; Jacob Van Braam, who was the French interpreter; John Davidson, who was the Indian interpreter; the helpers Barnaby Curran, John McGuire, Henry Stewart, William Jenkins; and the Indians Jeskakake, Kaghswaghtaniunt, and Guyasuta. Joncaire treated his visitors in a kindly and hospitable manner, offering them as fine a dinner as could be provided on the frontier, which was accompanied by his best wine. However, the French officer told Washington that he could not accept Dinwiddie's letter. Joncaire admitted that he was in command of the fort, but he was under the command of Marin's successor Jacques Legardeur de Saint-Pierre (1701–1755) at Fort Le Bœuf, and Dinwiddie's message would have to be delivered to him. Initially Washington tried to keep his Indians away from Joncaire, but on Wednesday, December 5, the French commander asked to see the Indians and wanted to know why they had not been brought in. Washington said that he didn't think their presence would be agreeable to Joncaire since he had heard the French commander speak in "dispraise of Indians in general."[18] Washington added in his journal that "another motive prevented me from bringing them into his company; I knew that he was an interpreter, and a person of very great influence among the Indians, and had lately used all possible means to draw them over to his interest; therefore, I was desirous of giving him no opportunity that could be avoided."[19] Washington was correct in his assessment of Joncaire. During the visit at Fort Machault, the French there used every effort and intrigue to suborn the Indians away from their English companions.

Joncaire expressed great pleasure at seeing the Indians and presented them with gifts, along with a steady and plentiful supply of rum, which kept Washington and Gist constantly on alert. Washington wrote that the French "applied Liquor so fast, that they [the Indians] were soon rendered incapable of the Business they came about, Notwithstanding the Caution that was given."[20] The wine and the rum that the French drank as energetically as the Indians also caused their own tongues to loosen, and provided Washington with insight into the overall French strategy. Washington wrote, "That it was their absolute Design to take Possession of the Ohio, and by G— they would do it; For that altho' they were sensible the English could raise two Men for their one; yet they knew, their [the English] Motions were too slow and dilatory to prevent any undertaking of theirs. They pretend to have an undoubted Right to the River, from a Discovery made by one La Solle [sic] 60 Years ago; and the Rise of this Expedition is, to prevent our settling on the River or Waters of it, as they had heard from some Families moving-out in Order thereto. From the best Intelligence I could get, there have been 1,500 Men this side of Ontario Lake; But upon the Death of the General all were recalled to about 6 [600] or 700, who were left to garrison four Forts."[21]

On Thursday, December 6, Tanacharison held a council with Joncaire during which the half-king reiterated much of the same concerns that he had previously expressed to Marin. Washington had tried to dissuade the half-king from holding a council at Fort Machault, but Tanacharison was adamant. He said that his council with Marin had taken place here and since this is where the council fire had been kindled, it was to be where his business with "these people" should be transacted. Joncaire listened politely and respectfully, but when Tanacharison attempted to return the French speech belt, Joncaire refused to accept it, saying he was under the direct authority of Captain Jacques Legardeur de Saint-Pierre at Fort Le Bœuf. Legardeur was the successor to Marin and the present commander of French forces along the Ohio, so the speech belt would have to be given to him. There was no alternative for Washington but to continue on to Fort Le Bœuf to deliver the message to Legardeur.

The next day, Friday, December 7, Washington and his party set off for Fort Le Bœuf accompanied by one Monsieur René-Hippolyte LaForce[22] and three other French soldiers. LaForce was ostensibly the Commissary of the French Stores, but as subsequent events would indicate, he may have had a more significant role in the French military command. Even as Washington's small delegation prepared to depart Fort Machault, the French exerted and intensified every effort to sway the Indians away from Washington. Washington wrote: "We found it extremely difficult to get the Indians off today, as every stratagem had been used to prevent their going up with me. I had last night left John Davidson whom I had brought with me from town, and strictly charged him not to be out of their company, as I could not get them over to my tent."[23] Washington and his group were finally able to get under way, but the excessive rain and snow made travelling very difficult. The route from Fort Machault to Fort Le Bœuf essentially followed French Creek, with the trail to the east of the waterway. The heavy rains made many of the lower areas impassable, forcing the party to deviate off the trail for considerable distances and abandoning it altogether for the latter portion of the trip.

5. Washington Warns the French

The trip from Fort Machault was considerably more challenging than the route from Logstown to Venango. Many of the smaller streams could not be crossed at their normal fords, which required the party to swim the horses across, while the men floated their baggage across on hastily constructed log rafts. They passed Custaloga's Town at the confluence of Deer Creek and French Creek (near present Carlton, Pennsylvania), and reached Cussewago on Saturday, December 8. Cussewago was a Delaware village located at present Meadville, Pennsylvania. At Cussewago, Washington had to leave one of the horses that was too worn out to continue. From Cussewago, the group was forced to make an approximately eight-mile detour to the southeast to locate a safe crossing over Muddy Creek. From there they were finally able to proceed directly to the French fort. The trail between the two forts was approximately 47 miles in length, but because of the numerous detours, Washington's group travelled about 20 miles farther. It took the party over five unpleasant and arduous days to reach Fort Le Bœuf, near Rivière au Bœuf, which Washington renamed "French Creek" in his diary.

On December 12, 1753, Washington arrived at the French fort, where he was greeted by the garrison's second in command. Washington was eager to complete his mission and begin the long journey back to Williamsburg, but he was perhaps more anxious to get his Indians away from French influence and the intense and flagrant attempts to sway the Indians toward the French. He hurriedly acquainted the officer who greeted him with his mission and tried to give him the letter from Dinwiddie. However, that officer politely refused to take the letter, saying it would have to be given to the Fort's commander, Captain Legardeur. Legardeur was a formidable person coming from a very prominent family. In 1718, his father, who was an officer in the French army, had founded the post at Chagouamigon (present Ashland, Wisconsin). Young Jacques Legardeur, having grown up on the frontier, quickly acquired a comprehensive expertise and knowledge of Indian life, customs and language. In 1732, Governor-General Charles de la Boische, Marquis de Beauharnois claimed that Jacques Legardeur "knows the savage language better than the savages, as they themselves admit."[24] Upon Marin's death in October, Legardeur was sent to take over Marin's command, and had arrived at Fort Le Bœuf only seven days prior to Washington's arrival.

Legardeur greeted Washington cordially and Washington was impressed with the 52-year-old French commander, writing, "This Commander is a Knight of the military Order of St. Lewis, and named Legardeur de St. Piere. He is an elderly Gentleman, and has much the Air of a Soldier."[25] The French commander listened politely as the young Virginian major described his mission and handed him the message from Lieutenant Governor Dinwiddie. The

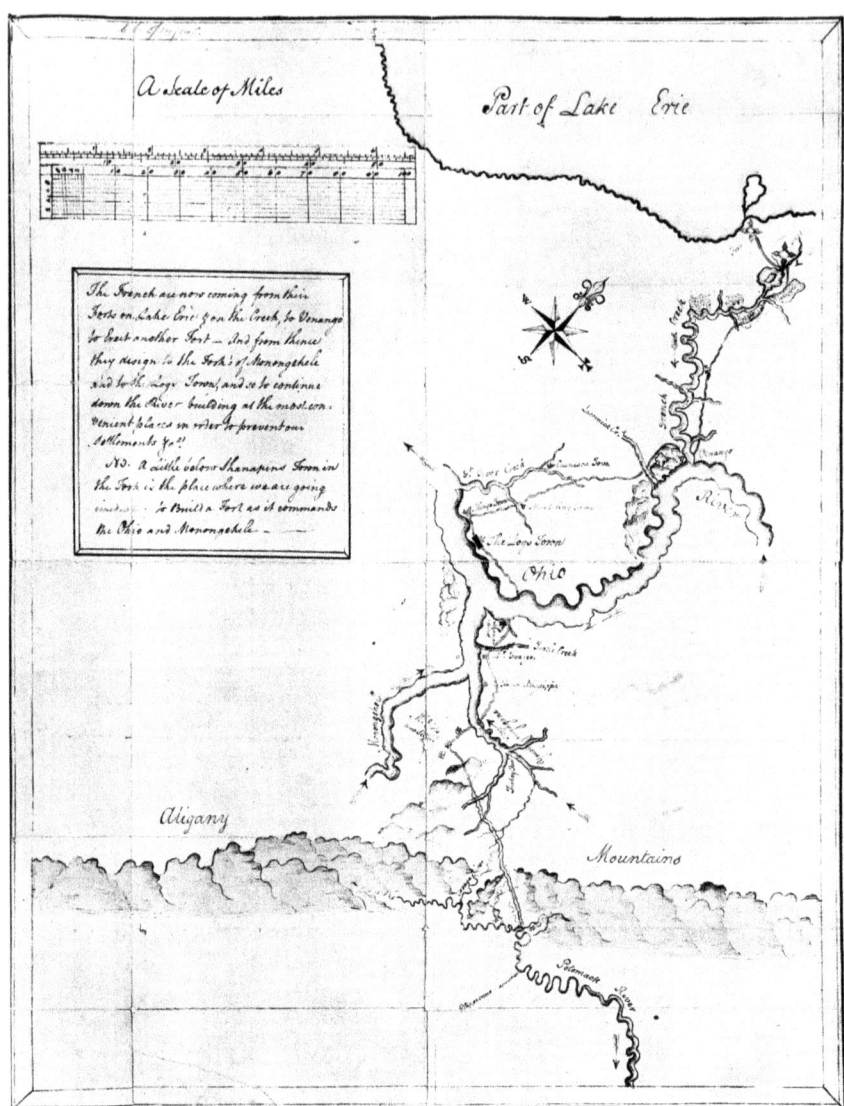

Figure 7. George Washington's 1754 map of the upper Ohio and Allegheny Rivers. Library of Congress—G3820 1754 .W3 1927 TIL.

seasoned, military professional Legardeur was undoubtedly more amused than impressed with the 21-year-old major and his motley delegation who had come to evict him from the Ohio territory. Ever the gentleman, however, Legardeur treated Washington and his party cordially and graciously. To Washington's vexation, the French commander was especially hospitable to the Indians in

Washington's delegation. Legardeur accepted the letter and said he would adjourn to his private quarters to have the message translated and carefully considered before offering a response. A few hours later, the French commander summoned Washington and Van Braam to examine the translation and make any necessary corrections. Then for the next two days, Washington and his party enjoyed the hospitality of the French at Fort Le Bœuf while Legardeur composed his response to Dinwiddie.

Washington spent those days carefully studying and taking notes on the fort's construction, disposition of troops, and French armament. Washington noted that Fort Le Bœuf was garrisoned by over 100 officers and men, and that there were 50 birch canoes and 170 pine canoes, some unfinished, that would all be available to the garrison in the spring. He noted that the fort was located on the south or west fork of French Creek and was almost surrounded by streams. The bastions were constructed of upright posts, sharpened at the top and standing more than 12 feet high. The bastions were pierced for cannon and also to allow small arms fire. Each bastion mounted eight six-pounder cannons. A four-pounder cannon was positioned to guard the gate. The four sides of the fort were composed of houses, guardhouse, chapel, doctor's residence, and a commander's stores building that were all inside the fort itself. Outside the fort were several log buildings, including a stable and blacksmith shop.[26]

On Friday, December 14, 1753, Legardeur met with Washington and explained that he was only a subordinate acting under the direct orders of Governor-General Duquesne in Québec and the governor-general would be the more appropriate recipient of Dinwiddie's letter. The French commander invited Washington to continue on to Québec to deliver the letter personally to Duquesne, but Washington demurred. Nevertheless, Legardeur assured Washington that he would forward the letter to Duquesne, whose answer would govern Legardeur's actions in response to Dinwiddie's demands. Meanwhile, the French commander politely, but firmly stated that in the meantime, he could not acquiesce to Dinwiddie's order to withdraw from the Ohio. In return, Legardeur gave Washington a letter for Dinwiddie, which strongly reaffirmed his resolve not to leave unless ordered by Duquesne:

> SIR,
>
> As I have the Honour of commanding here in Chief, Mr. Washington delivered me the Letter which you wrote to the Commandant of the French Troops.
> I should have been glad that you had given him Orders, or that he had been inclined to proceed to Canada, to see our General; to whom it better belongs than to me to set-forth the Evidence and Reality of the Rights of the King, my Master, upon the Lands situated along the River Ohio, and to contest the Pretensions of the King of Great-Britain thereto.

I shall transmit your Letter to the Marquis Duquesne. His Answer will be a Law to me; and if he shall order me to communicate it to you, Sir, you may be assured I shall not fail to dispatch it to you forthwith.

As to the Summons you send me to retire, I do not think myself obliged to obey it. Whatever may be your Instructions, I am here by Virtue of the Orders of my General; and I entreat you, Sir, not to doubt one Moment, but that I am determin'd to conform myself to them with all the Exactness and Resolution which can be expected from the best Officer.

I don't know that in the Progress of this Campaign any Thing has passed which can be reputed an act of Hostility, or that is contrary to the Treaties which subsist between the two Crowns; the Continuation whereof as much interests, and is pleasing to us, as the English. Had you been pleased Sir, to have descended to particularize the Facts which occasioned your Complaint, I should have had the Honour of answering you in the fullest, and, I am persuaded, most satisfactory Manner.

I made it my particular Care to receive Mr. Washington, with a Distinction suitable to your Dignity, as well as his own Quality and great merit. I flatter myself that he will do me this Justice before you, Sir; and that he will signify to you in the Manner I do myself, the profound Respect with which I am,
SIR,
Your most humble, and
Most obedient Servant,
Legardeur De St. Piere.

From the Fort sur La Rivière au Beuf
The 15th of December 1753[27]

With Legardeur's refusal of Dinwiddie's demands, Washington had no other orders but to return to Williamsburg to deliver the French commander's response to the lieutenant governor. In spite of Legardeur's refusal to withdraw, Washington was pleased that he had completed his mission and was now in a hurry to begin his return trip. Before his departure however, Washington had to deal with Legardeur's renowned capabilities in Indian relations and his attempts to sway Tanacharison and his Indians away from the English. Washington wrote of the difficulties he had in extricating the Indians away from Legardeur.

> Dec. 15th. The commandant ordered a plentiful store of liquor, provisions, &c. to be put on board our canoes, and appeared to be extremely complaisant, though he was exerting every artifice which he could invent to set our Indians at variance with us, to prevent their going until after our departure; presents, rewards, and everything which could be suggested by him or his officers. I cannot say that ever in my life I suffered so much anxiety as I did in this affair. I saw that every stratagem, which the most fruitful brain could invent, was practiced to win the Half King to their interest; and that leaving him there was giving them the opportunity they aimed at. I went to the Half King and pressed him in the strongest terms to go; he told me that the commandant would not discharge him until the morning. I then went to the commandant, and desired him to do their

business, and complained of ill treatment; for keeping them, as they were part of my company, was detaining me. This he promised not to do, but to forward my journey as much as he could. He protested he did not keep them, but was ignorant of the cause of their stay; though I soon found out. He had promised them a present of guns, &c. if they would wait until the morning. As I was very much pressed by the Indians to wait this day for them, I consented, on a promise that nothing should hinder them in the morning.[28]

Previously, while Washington had waited for Legardeur's response, he had ordered that the party's horses be sent back to Fort Machault to allow them adequate rest and recuperation so they would be fit for the return trip to Logstown and on to Virginia. It was planned that Washington's party would return to Fort Machault on foot and by canoe, where they would collect their rested horses for the remainder of their journey.

On Sunday, December 16, 1753, in spite of Tanacharison's promise to be ready to travel, and Legardeur's assurance that he would facilitate a timely departure, Washington was forced to confront increased efforts by the French to delay the departure of Tanacharison and his Indians in an attempt to entice them away from the Virginians. The French efforts were centered around the speech belt that Tanacharison was determined to return. Legardeur initially declined to accept the speech belt from Tanacharison. Instead he promised lasting friendship and peace between the French and the Ohio Indians. Even after he grudgingly accepted the belt,[29] Legardeur assured the half-king that he wanted to live in peace and continue to trade amicably with the Indians. As proof the French commander said he would immediately send trade goods to Logstown. In addition, Legardeur gave the Indians quantities of liquor and promised them additional presents if they would remain at Fort Le Bœuf so that they could hold further councils. Washington was hard pressed to convince the Indians to leave with him. It was only after Tanacharison was reminded that he had given his word to accompany Washington that the half-king agreed to leave. Somewhat reluctantly, the Indians turned their backs on further French hospitality and gifts to set off with Washington in the direction of Fort Machault where they would reclaim their rested horses. The snow and ice made the journey extremely difficult, often forcing the party into the water to pull their canoes over shoals, ice jams, and other debris that made the water route over French Creek almost impassable. In several instances, they were forced to portage their canoes and equipage for considerable distances around obstructions. They finally reached Fort Machault at Venango on Saturday, December 22, 1753, and once again availed themselves of Captain Joncaire's hospitality while they rested and prepared for the next leg of their journey.

Washington was well aware that as Legardeur had tried to seduce Tanacharison and his Indians to the French, Joncaire would certainly continue that effort. Adding to Washington's concern was the half-king's intent to remain behind at Fort Machault for a few additional days, because Kaghswaghtaniunt was unable to walk due to sickness and injuries. Tanacharison said he would remain at the French fort until the ailing Indian was able to travel, and even then they would take the longer route down river by canoe. However, Tanacharison said he would send Guyasuta with Washington's party to hunt for them. The half-king said he hoped to meet Washington at the Forks where he would give Washington a speech for Dinwiddie that Washington would write down and deliver to the lieutenant governor. Before he left Fort Machault, Washington warned Tanacharison to guard against Joncaire's flattery, and admonished him not to allow any fine speeches to influence the Indians toward the French. Tanacharison told Washington that he should not be concerned, "for he knew the French too well, for anything to engage him in their behalf."[30] However, Tanacharison delayed at Fort Machault longer than he anticipated and did not meet Washington on the Virginian's return journey. Washington had returned to Virginia by the time the half-king passed the Forks. Tanacharison arrived at Logstown on Tuesday, January 15, 1754, in the company of a party of French soldiers that Joncaire sent along as an escort.[31]

To Washington's dismay, the horses he had sent ahead to Fort Machault to be rested for the return journey had not sufficiently recovered their strength. Washington and his group started out on the horses anyway, but soon realized that their mounts and packhorses were in such bad shape that their progress was drastically slowed. Washington and Gist dismounted to spread the baggage among all the horses in order to lighten the loads of each, but it didn't help much. The men soon found it impossible to remain mounted and were forced to travel on foot leading their exhausted animals. Washington said he put himself into "Indian walking dress,"[32] which was most likely moccasins and a hunting shirt instead of boots and a regimental coat. He wrote that he trudged along with the slow moving group for three frustrating days, "til I found there was no Probability of their getting home in a Reasonable Time. The Horses grew less able to travel every Day; the Cold increased very fast; and the Roads were becoming much worse by a deep Snow, continually freezing: Therefore I was uneasy to get back, to make Report of my Proceedings to his Honour the Governor, I determined to prosecute my Journey the nearest Way through the Woods, on Foot."[33] They had been retracing their route along the Logstown–Venango Trail, but Washington decided that he and Gist would leave the rest of the group in order to make better time. On Wednesday, December 26, 1753, Washington and Gist separated from the party and set off by themselves overland leaving Van Braam in charge of the horses, baggage, and the other members of the group. Washington described readying himself for the trek. "I took my necessary Papers; pulled off my Cloaths; and tied myself up in a Match Coat [a heavy overcoat of wool or skins]. Then with Gun in Hand and Pack at my Back, in which were my Papers and Provisions. I set-out with Mr. Gist, fitted in the same manner."[34] Gist apparently was not convinced that Washington would be able to undertake the grueling winter trek through the wilderness. The young major, though strong, was more used to covering distances on horseback than on foot. Gist wrote in his journal: "I was unwilling he should undertake such travel, who had never been used to walking before this time. But as he insisted on it, I set out with our packs, like Indians, and travelled eighteen miles. That night we lodged at an Indian Cabin, and the Major was much fatigued."[35]

On December 27, Washington and Gist had just passed Murdering Town, where they encountered an Indian who apparently had been waiting for them and who greeted Gist personally.[36] The Indian offered to lead them to the Forks via a shorter route and both men, pleased at the prospect of a shortcut, accepted the Indian's offer to guide them. Although the Indian had greeted Gist by name, the frontiersman didn't know the Indian, but believed he had seen him "at Joncaire's at Venango"[37] when they had stopped at Fort Machault. Since the Indian appeared friendly and offered to guide them, he did not initially arouse any suspicion. In fact, the Indian was very helpful, and when it was apparent that Washington was fatiguing, he offered to carry Washington's pack. Gist however, began to get suspicious when he noticed that the Indian was leading them in a more northeasterly direction, but the frontiersman refrained from alerting Washington so as not to unduly concern him. The Indian next offered to carry Washington's gun, but for some reason Washington also began to mistrust the Indian, and when he refused to give up his gun, the Indian's demeanor became surly. The Indian next tried to convince the white men to change course. He told them there were many Ottawa Indians around who would kill them if they were discovered and he suggested that they go to his cabin that was located a little farther to the north, and remain there until the danger from hostile Indians had passed. Washington refused and insisted that they head directly to the Forks. Then, before Gist and Washington had time to take notice, the Indian accelerated his pace until he was about 15 yards ahead of the two men. The Indian then turned abruptly and fired his musket in the direction of Washington and Gist. Fortunately the shot missed them both and the bullet smacked into a tree. Before the echo of the gunshot had died away, Gist was after the Indian, who bolted away and was hurriedly trying to reload his musket. Washington and Gist were soon on the

Indian and Gist would have killed him on the spot, had not Washington prevented the frontiersman from slaying the Indian. Gist was certainly not happy with Washington's order not to harm the Indian, but he grudgingly obeyed. However, they didn't know what to do with the Indian. Not willing to remain constantly on guard against further treachery on the part of the Indian and not wanting to kill him, they decided on a plan of subterfuge. Washington and Gist built a fire and acted as if they were going to camp there for the night, and then they released the Indian who immediately disappeared into the darkness. A short time after the Indian departed, Gist and Washington abandoned the campsite and walked until morning to put as much distance as possible between them and any pursuers.

Two days later, on Saturday, December 29, 1753, Washington and Gist reached the west bank of the Allegheny River about two miles above Shannopin's Town and approximately five miles from the Forks. They had hoped to be able to walk across the frozen river to the east bank, but the solid ice only extended to about 50 yards from either shore, with swift open water and treacherous ice floes in the middle. Washington recorded in his journal, "There was no Way for getting over but on a Raft: Which we-set about, with but one poor Hatchet, and finished just after Sun-setting. This was a whole Day's Work: we next got it launched, and went on Board of it: Then set-off. But before we were Half Way over, we were jammed in the Ice, in such a Manner that we expected our Raft to sink, and ourselves to perish. I put out my setting Pole to try to stop the Raft, that the Ice might pass by; when the Rapidity of the Stream threw it with so much Violence against the Pole, that it jirked me out into ten Feet Water: But I fortunately saved myself by catching hold of one of the Raft Logs. Notwithstanding all our Efforts we could not get the Raft to either Shore; but were obliged, as we were near an island, to quit our Raft and make to it."[38] Coming ashore on the little island in the Allegheny River,[39] the two soaked and freezing men were saved only by Gist's frontier savvy and his ability to quickly start a fire and construct a crude shelter. The night was bitterly cold, and Gist, who primarily tended the fire and worked to dry their garments, bore the brunt of the elements. Washington wrote that "the Cold was so extremely severe, that Mr. Gist had all his fingers, and some of his Toes frozen."[40] Gist was more upbeat when he wrote that "...the cold did us some service for in the morning it was frozen hard enough for us to pass over on the ice."

Washington and Gist travelled the ten miles to John Fraser's cabin at the mouth of Turtle Creek on the Monongahela the same day that they left the little island in the Allegheny, which was Sunday, December 30, 1753. They rested at Frazer's cabin until Tuesday, January 1, 1754, but took time to visit the staunchly pro–English Queen Aliquippa, who had recently moved her village to the mouth of the Youghiogheny on the Monongahela (present McKeesport, Pennsylvania). The old queen told the two men that the reason she moved from her village at McKee's Rocks was to distance herself from the French, and she would never go back to the Ohio River area until the English built a fort there.[41] Leaving Fraser's cabin on January 1, Washington and Gist stopped for two days at Gist's new settlement, where Washington bought a horse and tack before continuing on to Wills Creek, where the two men arrived on Sunday, January 6, 1754. Washington wrote in his journal that at Wills Creek he "met 17 Horses loaded with Materials and Stores for a Fort at the Forks of Ohio."[42] The party was under the command of William Trent (1715–1787), en route to build an Ohio Company of Virginia storehouse at the mouth of Red Stone Creek on the Monongahela. Washington apparently wrote his journal entry a considerable time after the fact, because at the time Washington and Trent met at Wills Creek, Trent had only received orders to build a storehouse at Red Stone, but had not yet been told to proceed to the Forks. However, Trent's men and tools used for the construction of the Red Stone storehouse would certainly be later used in the construction of the fort at the Forks.

Gist took leave of Washington at Wills Creek, and Washington continued on to Williamsburg. He stopped at Belvoir Plantation on Friday, January 11, for a short rest before continuing on to Williamsburg. Belvoir was the home of George William Fairfax (1729–1787) and his wife Sally Cary Fairfax (ca. 1730–1811), who were very close friends and neighbors of Washington. George Fairfax's sister Anne was the widow of Washington's brother Lawrence, who died the previous July of 1752.

Washington departed Belvoir Plantation and arrived at Williamsburg on Wednesday, January 16, 1754, where he presented Dinwiddie with a detailed report of his mission along with Lagardeur's letter of reply.

6

The Race to the Forks

> *I summon you in the Name of the King my Master, by Vertue of Orders which I got from my General, to retreat peaceably with your Troops from off the Lands of the King and not to return, or else I find myself obliged to fulfill my Duty and compel You to it.*—Captain Claude-Pierre Peċaudy de Contrecœur to Ensign Edward Ward at Fort Prince George

Lieutenant Governor Dinwiddie's protest letter to the French was a somewhat tepid response to the French army's invasion of the Ohio territory, but it wasn't long before Dinwiddie followed up with more forceful actions. The previous summer, the French had built a chain of forts as far as the Allegheny, but their dash to the Forks had stalled out at Venango. However, the Virginia lieutenant governor knew full well that come spring, the rested and reinvigorated French army would once again be on the move toward the Forks. During the winter of 1753–54, while Washington was still engaged on his mission to forts Machault and Le Bœuf, Dinwiddie took measures to assert Virginia's claim to the Ohio by initiating construction of the long-promised "strong house" at the Forks of the Ohio. For the task, he selected William Trent. Trent was a seasoned frontier veteran and a very good choice for the mission. He was born in Lancaster County, Pennsylvania, around 1715. In 1746, during King George's War, he was appointed captain of Pennsylvania troops and spent most of 1746 and 1747 fighting the French along the Canadian frontier north of Albany. He was honorably discharged in late 1747 and subsequently formed a partnership with George Croghan to engage in trade with the Ohio Indians. Around 1752, he was hired by Virginia as the colony's Indian agent and was also employed by the Ohio Company of Virginia as their factor or agent authorized to transact business in their behalf. In those capacities, Trent represented both the Colony of Virginia and the Ohio Company of Virginia at the Logstown Council in May 1752, which was also attended by Tanacharison and Christopher Gist. As noted earlier, it was at this council that the English were invited to build a strong house at the Forks. While still at the Logstown Council of 1752, Trent was directed by the Virginia commissioners to proceed on to Pickawillany to take gifts to the Ohio Indians and reaffirm their chain of friendship with Virginia. Andrew Montour (ca. 1720–1772),[1] an Indian of mixed blood and an accomplished linguist in French, English and several Indian dialects, was hired to accompany Trent as his interpreter. Trent and Montour departed Logstown on Saturday, June 21, 1752, for the 326-mile trek to Pickawillany.[2] Coincidentally, the very day Trent left Logstown, Pickawillany was attacked and destroyed by French Indians and French militia under the leadership of Charles Langlade and the Ottawa Chief Pontiac. Trent and Montour reached Pickawillany on Sunday, July 20, 1752, but found the town virtually abandoned, except for a few survivors of the disastrous raid a month earlier. As an expression of sympathy, Trent gave a scarlet cloak to Old Briton's son, a full set of clothes to the widow of the slain chief and distributed other trade goods to the few Indians who were still at Pickawillany.[3] On the return trip, they stopped at several other Indian villages along the way and distributed the remainder of the gifts that were originally meant for the Pickawillany Indians.

In July 1753, Trent was sent by Lieutenant Governor Dinwiddie to build a fortified storehouse for the Ohio Company of Virginia at the mouth of Red Stone Creek on the Monongahela River. Trent was on this mission when he met Washington at Wills Creek upon Washington's return from forts Le Bœuf and Machault. Being considerably closer to the Ohio territory, the Red Stone storehouse was meant to serve as a more advanced depot for trade goods, which would facilitate the Indian trade by shortening the traders' supply lines. The storehouse on Red Stone Creek was occasionally referred to as a "fort," however the structure was never used as a fort nor was it ever intended to be one.[4] As mentioned previously, this misconception likely resulted from the ancient Indian earthworks in the vicinity that were called "Red Stone Old Fort."

In January 1754, while Trent was still at Red Stone Creek working on the storehouse, a messenger, which some sources indicate was the frontiersman Thomas Cresap, brought word that Dinwiddie had commissioned Trent a captain in the Virginia militia. Trent's new orders were to raise a company of 100 frontiersmen to construct and garrison a fort in the area of the Forks of the Ohio "with the least practicable delay, suitable in strength to resist any ordinary attack." His orders also stated that he should "capture or destroy any hostile or resisting force."[5] Being ordered to raise a company of 100 men was one thing and actually raising a company on the frontier was another. Recruiting men to serve in the wilderness was particularly difficult under the best of circumstances, but Trent tried his best. He sent recruiters and messengers to his friends, acquaintances and officials throughout the neighboring colonies asking for volunteers, but he could only enlist about 40 men[6] with which to seize the Forks of the Ohio, construct a fort there, and hold it against the French.

Trent and his small company, armed only with muskets, some rifles, and the necessary tools for fort building, arrived at the Forks on Sunday, February 17, 1754. They immediately set to work, felling trees and clearing ground for the construction of the fort they would name Fort Prince George, in honor of King George II's son, the future George III. Tanacharison was there to greet Trent and his party, pledging Indian support. The half-king promised to supply food for Trent's men and also to provide warriors if the French should attempt to interfere. Tanacharison, however, was not overly impressed with Trent's tiny command or for that matter the English response to the French incursion in general. On one hand, the English were finally willing to commit troops to challenge the French army that was moving down the Allegheny, but the size of Trent's minuscule force didn't give Tanacharison any measure of confidence when compared to Legardeur's massive, veteran, artillery-equipped army. However, the half-king was philosophical, believing that once the British were in for a penny, they would be in for a pound, and since this small force of Virginians was all he had for the present, it would have to make do until he could somehow draw the regular British army into a war against the French. As the first logs of the fort were laid, Trent's men and Tanacharison's Indians drank toasts in celebration of winning the race to the Forks, but no one really believed that the contest was over. They knew the French would arrive in the spring.

Other colonial governors, particularly those whose colonies were nearer to the Ohio frontier, became increasingly concerned about the French invasion, and felt obliged to take some sort of action. None of them wanted to rush to support Dinwiddie and the Ohio Company of Virginia's business venture, but a formidable French army fortifying the western frontier of the English colonies was a worrisome situation. Memories of French and Indian depredations in recent wars were still too vivid for them to not view a nearby powerful French presence with trepidation. Pennsylvania Royal Governor James Hamilton felt it was in the interest of Pennsylvanians to assess the potential French threat. In January of 1754, Hamilton sent George Croghan and Andrew Montour to Logstown to confer with Tanacharison and Scarouady regarding the French invasion, and to attempt to evaluate the severity of the threat to Pennsylvania. John Patten, a trader who was familiar with the Indians of the area, accompanied Croghan and Montour. The Pennsylvania delegation arrived at Logstown after Washington and Gist had already left the area of the Forks on their return to Virginia, and also very soon after Tanacharison had arrived at

Logstown from Fort Machault. Croghan's party were met at Logstown by several French soldiers led by Lieutenant Michel Maray de La Chauvignerie (ca. 1710–?), a tough and experienced officer who had accompanied Tanacharison from Fort Machault to Logstown, where he was instructed to set up an outpost.[7] The French soldiers apparently brought ample quantities of liquor, because most of the Indians at Logstown were completely drunk when Croghan, Montour, and Patten arrived. Worse yet, La Chauvignerie recognized John Patten as the English trader the French had arrested near the Miami village of Quiskakon in 1750. At that time they had confiscated Patten's goods and sent him to Fort Detroit, then on to Québec, and from there he was sent to Paris, France. Patten was eventually released through the intervention of Lord Albemarle and returned to Pennsylvania by way of England.[8] Now once again recognized as "trespassing" on French territory, Patten was arrested on the spot. Surprisingly, the French did not detain Croghan as they did Patten. If anything, Croghan, the "king of the Pennsylvania traders" was more notorious than perhaps any of the English traders operating in the Ohio territory, and in addition, the French had previously put a price on his head. Either La Chauvignerie did not recognize Croghan, or more likely, he considered him a diplomatic emissary of the Pennsylvania governor. Patten was fortunately rescued when Croghan and Montour were able to sober up Tanacharison in time to intervene and secure Patten's freedom before La Chauvignerie sent him to Fort Machault. Since they had been chosen by Captain Joncaire to escort the half-king to Logstown and to set up an outpost there, La Chauvignerie was reluctant to inflame the Indians by creating an incident, so Patten was grudgingly released.

In private council with Croghan and Montour, Tanacharison and Scarouady reaffirmed their determination to resist the French. Even the Delaware chief Shingas, who later sided with the French, proclaimed his support for the English. The chiefs restated their request that the Virginians build a fort at the Forks that would also house Indian warriors who were allied with the English. In addition, the half-kings also invited the Pennsylvanians to build a fort in the area. The Indians requested whatever assistance the Virginians and Pennsylvanians could provide them. Tanacharison made a plea to the governors of Virginia and Pennsylvania for "whatever assistance he will think proper to send us, may be kept safe for us as our enemies are just at hand and we do not know what day they may come upon us."[9] The Pennsylvania delegation left Logstown on Saturday, February 2, 1754, 15 days before William Trent and his small company arrived at the Forks to begin work on Fort Prince George, or "Trent's Fort," as it was popularly called during its construction.

The French were aware that English colonists were moving toward the

Forks, and French and Indian scouting parties were continually gathering information regarding the Virginians' intentions and progress. In February 1754, Captain Joncaire at Fort Machault sent the local Delaware chief Custaloga to ascertain the level of English activities in the area. Custaloga, with a large party of warriors, combed the area in the vicinity of the Monongahela and Ohio Rivers. When he returned to Fort Machault on Monday, February 18, 1754, Custaloga reported to Joncaire that "when he arrived at Teyaondeshongen [Monongahela], he had delegated a chief of his tribe to go to a fork in that river [the mouth of Red Stone Creek]. The courier says he saw a thousand men building a fort there, that as soon as this fort is finished, they are to come and build another at the mouth of that same river [the Forks]."[10] Although the report greatly inflated the number of men at work at Red Stone, Custaloga's scouts had either obtained accurate intelligence or merely deduced that Trent's next construction project was to be a fort at the Forks of the Ohio.

La Chauvignerie at Logstown was also aware of the Virginians' intentions to fortify the Forks. He was also concerned that the arrival of the English would turn the Indians in the area of the Forks against the French. Gathering every scrap of information available, he sent a letter dated February 26, 1754, to Legardeur at Fort Le Bœuf conveying a sense of urgency. "The Indians here have not been well disposed toward us for several days.... I have just learned from old Dejiquequé[11] that the English, numbering One Thousand men, were to arrive in three days at the fork firstly to take possession of the aforesaid Théaoudaôgoin [Monongahela] River and that they were to call the Nations from here to go meet this party no doubt in order to conclude the preparation they have to make for their Settlement or our Destruction."[12] On Wednesday, March 6, 1754, La Chauvignerie sent scouts from Logstown to reconnoiter the English construction at the Forks. In the vicinity of the Forks, the scouts encountered a deserter who gave them information regarding the storehouse at Red Stone Creek and also told them that six cannon consisting of six and eight-pounders were being sent to arm Trent's fort.[13] The fort was certainly planned to accommodate cannons, and the deserter must have assumed that artillery was on the way, but in fact no guns larger than swivel guns were en route to the Forks at that time.

At the Forks, Trent and his men were making a great effort to complete the fort in anticipation of the imminent arrival of the French army. Rumors were rife that the French were preparing to move down the Allegheny. George Croghan reported after a visit to the Forks that the men there were working very hard, which "seemed to give the Indians great pleasure and put them in high spirits."[14] At the Forks, Tanacharison urged that a palisaded stockade be built first to facilitate defense, but Trent's initial effort was to construct a stoutly built stronghouse of squared logs, pierced with loopholes for muskets. Both Trent and Tanacharison were correct to hurry the preparation of defenses at the Forks, because the French were in fact on the move.

Reports of English activities reached Duquesne in Québec, and the Governor-General took the extraordinary measure of launching a mid-winter expedition to secure the Forks before the English could effectively fortify it. But first he had to appoint a new commander. The previous fall, shortly after arriving as Marin's replacement, Legardeur requested to be relieved, citing ill health as the reason.[15] On Christmas Day in 1753, Captain Claude-Pierre Pećaudy de Contrecœur (1705–1755) was appointed to replace Legardeur as commander of French troops along the Ohio. Contrecœur was a colonial officer of regular troops who had been in the king's service since age 16. He had been second-in-command during Céloron's 1749 expedition and had commanded at Fort Niagara during Marin's march down the Allegheny in 1753. Contrecœur's journal and family letters indicate that neither he nor his wife were enthusiastic about the new assignment. Now that he was the commander of Fort Niagara, he and his family were finally living together and enjoying comfortable quarters after spending the previous years apart or in rugged service on the frontier. However, orders were orders, especially when issued by the governor-general, and Contrecœur duly reported to Québec to take command of the expedition. Duquesne's orders were "to take possession of the Belle Rivière, where you will have Fort de Chiningué built."[16] Logstown was sometimes referred to by the names Chiningué or Chenango. That implied that in addition to building a fort at the Forks, Contrecœur was ordered to extend the chain of French strongpoints at least as far as Logstown. Duquesne realized that the English might arrive at the Forks first, so the governor-general added that Contrecœur should "hasten to interrupt and even destroy their work from the start."[17] In a subsequent letter to Contrecœur dated Sunday, January 27, 1754, the governor-general specified that he expected the fort at the Forks to be named Fort Duquesne.

Contrecœur's force of 500 French regulars and militia left Québec on Tuesday, January 15, 1754, and were joined by 300 troops in Montréal. They marched out of Montréal on Saturday, February 2, 1754, dragging sledges laden with ammunition, food and equipment sufficient for two months. The first stages of the more than 600-mile winter journey were extremely arduous, requiring exhausting snowshoe travel most of the way while pulling their heavily laden provision sleds. Often their daily progress was so trifling that they scarcely moved beyond sight of their previous night's bivouac. After they crossed the Niagara portage, however, the ice on Lake Erie had thawed sufficiently to allow the troops to travel via batteaux as far as Fort Presque Isle, which they reached on Friday, March 8, 1754. The trek south over Presque Isle Portage and down French Creek continued to be exhausting. Although the air temperature was rising with approaching spring, the road that had been previously so laboriously constructed was now in terrible condition and needed to be repaired. Water travel was restricted by tangles of fallen trees and other debris that choked French Creek after a severe winter storm had earlier battered the area. The French force stopped at Fort Le Bœuf, where Contrecœur formally relieved Legardeur of command, then Contrecœur continued on to Fort Machault, where he and his men arrived toward the end of March 1754.

Shortly after Contrecœur marched into Fort Machault, the military engineer and artillerist Captain François-Marc-Antoine Le Mercier and an additional 350 reinforcements arrived. They had been recuperating in Québec from the previous summer's grueling expedition to the Allegheny with Marin. Le Mercier brought further orders from Duquesne specifying that Contrecœur leave only a handful of troops at Forts Presque Isle, Le Bœuf and Machault, and take the rest of the army to the Forks with all possible speed. Apparently, Duquesne had received La Chauvignerie's intelligence report with its inflated 1,000-man estimate of Trent's force. Duquesne correctly reasoned that by now they had already begun construction of a fort there. Concerned that an alarming number of English troops had arrived at the strategic location ahead of the French, the governor-general believed that it would require a maximum effort to dislodge them. Duquesne was so disquieted by the reports of a potent English army at the Forks that he considered it necessary to further reinforce Contrecœur. In May 1754, Duquesne dispatched additional troops under Captain Michel-Jean-Hughes Péan (1723–1782) to support Contrecœur's operation. Péan's orders specified that if in Contrecœur's opinion, Péan's services were not needed or if the increased troop strength was insufficient to dislodge the British, Péan should abort the rendezvous with Contrecœur and resume his journey to Fort Detroit. By the time Péan reached the Fort Presque Isle Portage in June 1754, he learned that Contrecœur no longer needed his assistance. He tarried at Fort Preque Isle until the end of July, then continued on to Fort Detroit.

With Trent at work on Fort Prince George, Lieutenant Governor Dinwiddie needed to find troops to garrison and defend the fort. Since Washington had recently returned from his mission to the Ohio and was knowledgeable about the area, as well as experienced in dealing with the Indians and the French, Dinwiddie tasked Washington to raise the initial contingent of troops to defend the Forks. Once again, the fact that members of the Washington family were stockholders in the Ohio Company of Virginia likely influenced Dinwiddie to select him, as much as for Washington's frontier experience.

Dinwiddie undoubtedly considered that the young Virginian's financial interest in the Ohio Company would enhance his diligence regarding the success of the enterprise.

But first Dinwiddie had to make it possible for Washington to raise troops for the venture. The daily pay for Virginia militia volunteers was 15 pounds of tobacco, and if that didn't entice sufficient volunteers, the lieutenant governor was prepared to conscript the rest. Dinwiddie also turned to his neighboring colonial governors for troops, but they were not eager to send their citizens to support Dinwiddie's Ohio Company business venture. Even the Virginia colonial legislators in Williamsburg balked at Dinwiddie's request for funds for additional troops. Some members argued that reports of the French advance were blatant attempts to sway the burgesses to support the interests of the Ohio Company, and at least one member even expressed the opinion that the Forks of the Ohio in actuality belonged to France. To Dinwiddie's dismay, the burgesses also stated that the Virginia militia could not be used outside the colony, and the Forks of the Ohio likely fell into that category. The best concession that Dinwiddie was able to wrest from the burgesses was an appropriation of £10,000 for protection of the frontier.[18] Thwarted by his own colony's legislature, Dinwiddie looked at other means of raising troops. There were several units of British regulars in the colonies, including independent companies that were not attached to any regiment. After sending messages to their respective governors, two companies based in New York and one in South Carolina were placed at Dinwiddie's disposal. The more immediate problem was still the number of troops that could be mustered and how quickly they could reach the Forks. Even if the independent companies of regulars from New York and South Carolina could reach the Forks in time, their combined numbers were still too small a force to defend against a sizable French army. It would require an additional several hundred militia troops to augment the regular companies in order to stand any chance against the veteran French army that was presently moving down the Allegheny River.

Dinwiddie had originally planned for a force of 600 militia, but recruiting became unexpectedly difficult. Volunteers were few and far between and the quality of those enlisted was generally disappointing. Washington complained to Dinwiddie that "you may, with almost equal success, attempt to raise the dead to life again as to raise the force of this country."[19] To spur enlistments, Dinwiddie offered as an inducement a bonus of 200,000 acres of land to divide among those who enlisted, but even so, volunteers only trickled in, and those were usually of very poor quality. On Saturday, March 9, 1754, Washington again wrote that those who enlisted were generally "loose, Idle persons, that are quite destitute of House, and Home; and I may truly say many of them of

Cloaths; which last render's them very incapable of the necessary Service as they must uavoidably be expos'd to inclement weather in Marches etc.; and can expect no other, than to encounter almost every difficulty that's incident to a Soldiers Life. There is many of them without Shoes, other's want Stockings, some are without Shirts, and not a few that have Scarce a Coat, or Waistcoat, to their Backs; in short, they are as illy provided as can well be conceived."[20]

While Washington continued to recruit troops, Dinwiddie commissioned Joshua Fry (1700–1754), as colonel in overall command of the force that would defend the Forks. Washington would be Fry's second-in-command with the rank of lieutenant colonel. Fry had been a professor of mathematics at the College of William and Mary, and around 1744 he and his family moved to Goochland County between present Charlottesville and Scottsville, Virginia. In 1749, he and Peter Jefferson (1708–1757), were commissioned to determine a section of the Virginia–North Carolina boundary, and in 1751, he collaborated with Peter Jefferson in compiling the "Map of the Inhabited Parts of Virginia." Peter Jefferson was the father of Thomas Jefferson. In 1750, Fry was commissioned a colonel of Virginia militia and a member of the Governor's Council, and in 1752, he was delegated to represent Virginia at the Logstown Council that included the Six Nations of the Iroquois and the tribes of the Ohio territory. It's likely that Dinwiddie selected Fry to command the mission on the basis of his rank as colonel of militia, but mostly because of his previous experience in dealing with the Indians of the Ohio area.

Frustrated by the slow pace of recruitments, Dinwiddie decided he would send a smaller force, because he believed it was imperative to have troops on the Ohio as soon as possible. He opted to make do with a regiment of 300 men instead of waiting until he recruited the full 600, which was his original plan. A full-strength eighteenth century regiment numbered between 600 and 1,000 men. Dinwiddie's smaller Virginia Regiment would be less than half the size of a full-strength regiment and would be comprised of six companies of 50 men each. To increase the manpower that could be used against the French, Dinwiddie tried to augment his force with Indians. He hoped to entice a thousand Cherokee and Catawba warriors from the Carolinas, but two issues frustrated that endeavor. The Catawbas were allies of the British, but at the same time they were bitter enemies of the Iroquois and were reluctant to join them as allies. In addition, Royal Governor James Glen (1701–1777) of South Carolina suspected that Dinwiddie was trying to take over the lucrative trade with the southern Indians, so Glen successfully campaigned to convince the southern Indians to stay at home.

During March of 1754, messages arrived continually at Williamsburg from Trent and Gist warning that the French were on the move and that reinforcements were urgently needed at the Forks. Trent reported that Monsieur René-Hippolyte LaForce had warned the Ohio Indians that if they sided with the English, "neither they nor the English there would see the Sun above 20 Days longer; 13 of the Days being then to come."[21] Dinwiddie felt he couldn't wait any longer. On Sunday, March 31, 1754, Washington received his orders to march at once for the Forks with whatever men he had. Colonel Fry would follow as soon as possible with the rest of the men. Washington wrote:

> The last of March 1754.
> March 31. I received a commission from the Governor, dated the 15th instant,[22] for the lieutenant-colonelcy of the Virginia regiment under the commanding officer Joseph [Joshua] Fry, Esquire, with orders to take under my command the troops which were then in quarters at Alexandria, and to march with it towards Oyo and aid Captain Trente in constructing fortresses and in defending the possessions of His Majesty against the enterprises and hostilities of the French.[23]

Two days later on Tuesday, April 2, 1754, Washington wrote:

> Everything being ready in execution of our orders, we began our march on April 2, with two companies of infantry, commanded by Captain Peter Hog[24] and Captain-lieutenant Vambraan, five subaltern officers, two sergeants, six corporals, a drummer, and one hundred and twenty soldiers, a surgeon-major, a Swedish gentleman volunteer [Carolus Gustavus de Splitdorph],[25] two wagons guarded by a lieutenant, sergeant, corporal, and twenty-five soldiers."[26]

Work progressed on the fort at the Forks, and even though Trent was doing the best that he could with his tiny band of laborers, the pace of construction did not give much comfort to Tanacharison. The Indians themselves were unaccustomed to heavy construction and for the most part were unwilling to take part in the strenuous labor required to build the fort. They did, however, consume a fairly large portion of Trent's meager food supply. Soon there was nothing to eat other than some Indian corn and whatever scant game the Indians brought in. Trent continued to send urgent appeals for reinforcements, provisions, and equipment, but he only received vague assurances that Virginia troops and companies of British regulars would be dispatched. In desperation, Trent decided to travel to Wills Creek to personally plead for whatever assistance he could get. Trent's second-in-command was the trader John Fraser, who had been commissioned a lieutenant in Trent's small force. However, Fraser was at his cabin at the mouth of Turtle Creek, where he was desperately working to save his furs, equipment, and trade goods. Fraser was certain that when the French arrived they would not only evict the British from the Forks, but would likely pillage and destroy any English trading posts in the area.

With Fraser adamant about taking care of his personal business, Trent felt he had no choice but to leave his brother-in-law, Ensign Edward Ward[27] in command of the small force at the Forks. Before he left, however, Trent acted on Tanacharison's advice and ordered the construction of a palisaded stockade around the English stronghouse.

After Trent departed for Wills Creek, Ward felt overwhelmed by the pressures of supervising the completion of the fort and preparing an effective defense against the advancing French army. Work was nearing completion when on Saturday, April 13, 1754, scouts brought word that a large French force equipped with artillery was nearby and descending the Allegheny. Ward rushed the eight miles to Fraser's house on Turtle Creek and asked the trader to return with him to the Forks to assume command of the garrison and direct the defense of the fort. Fraser, who in Trent's absence was technically in command at the Forks, unabashedly refused. He asked the astonished Ward, "What can we do?"[28] He added that "he had a shilling to loose for a penny he should gain by his Commission at that time. And that he had Business which he could not settle in under Six Days."[29] Ward was disgusted with Fraser's attitude, and he returned to the Forks alone declaring that he would not only complete the fort, but would defend it against the entire French army, and that he would "hold out to the last extremity before it should be said that the English retreated like cowards before the French forces appeared."[30]

In the meantime, Washington's two rather small companies were struggling to reach the Forks in time to help defend Fort Prince George, but it was rough going. Washington, dressed in a fine regimental uniform, rode at the head of the column, but his men for the most part were dressed in homespun linen, linsey-woolsey,[31] or buckskin, and while some had shoes, most wore moccasins. Their baggage train consisted of a line of lumbering wagons that carried food, supplies, and ammunition. They had no artillery except for a few small-caliber swivel-guns, which were very small cannons that, depending on their size, could fire up to a one-pound ball or one pound of shot. They were short-range antipersonnel weapons that were generally mounted on a swiveling fork or rotating stand that provided them with a very wide range of movement.

After departing Alexandria on Tuesday, April 2, 1754, Washington and his men only traveled six miles before they were forced to camp for the night. The following days, they were able to increase their rate of march to about 11 miles a day, but even at that rate, it would take them several weeks to travel the roughly 220 miles to the Forks. From the time Washington's force departed their first campsite on Wednesday, April 3, 1754, there is minimal information recording their daily progress or even the exact route of their march to Wills Creek. It is known that they crossed the Blue Ridge Mountains at Vestal's

Gap[32] during the first week, and ferried across the Shenandoah River toward Winchester on Wednesday, April 10, 1754. At Winchester, Washington was met by Captain Adam Stephen (1718–1791)[33] and the militia company that Stephen had recruited from the area. These reinforcements brought Washington's regiment up to approximately 160 men, but it was still only about half the force Washington and Fry hoped to have at the Forks. Even the youthfully optimistic Washington realized that they would need a considerably larger number of troops to stand a chance against the French army. Two of the officers, Captains Andrew Lewis and Robert Stobo, remained in Alexandria where they attempted to recruit additional men, and Colonel Fry was working his way through Virginia to join Washington while also trying to attract volunteers to augment his force. Washington spent almost a week in Winchester attempting to secure wagons and teams for the arduous trek to the Forks, but no sooner would Washington find a wagon and mark it for impressment into government service than the wagon and team would disappear, hidden away by its owner. Only a small fraction of the wagons were obtained for the march, and an exasperated Washington wrote to Dinwiddie, "we got but ten after waiting a week.... some of those so badly provided with teams that the soldiers were obliged to assist them up the hills.... It was known [the people] had better teams at home."[34]

Figure 8. Half-pounder swivel-gun. The brass barrel is approximately 20 inches long, with a 22-inch wooden handle attached. It was a close range antipersonnel weapon that fired a half-pound projectile or the equivalent weight in grape-shot (photograph by author at Fort Ligonier, Pennsylvania).

As near as can be calculated, Washington departed Winchester on about Tuesday, April 16, 1754. On Wednesday, April 17, they encountered Christopher Gist, who had been sent to Virginia at the urging of Tanacharison to find out when English reinforcements could be expected at the Forks. Gist reported that the fort was begun, but its construction was not very advanced. He also related that the half-king was so concerned by the French advance, and angry at the English delay, that he and his Indians threatened to abandon the area around the Forks rather than face the French juggernaut with only Trent's minuscule force for support. On Friday, April 19, 1754, still some 30 miles from Wills Creek, they met a messenger from Trent who brought the alarming news that a French army numbering more than 800 and supported by artillery was coming down the Allegheny in a flotilla of canoes and batteaux. Washington relayed the message on to Williamsburg, adding his own urgent request for immediate reinforcements. They were too late. Two days previous, on Wednesday, April 17, 1754, the French army had arrived at the Forks.

On Saturday, April 13, 1754, Ensign Ward at the Forks received word that a massive French force of more than 1,000 men would arrive on or about April 17. The small detachment worked at a frenzied pace to complete the defenses before the French arrived, and somehow they were just able to get it done. The gates to the palisaded stockade were hung on Tuesday, April 16, 1754, the day before the French arrived.

From his spies who had been constantly observing the construction of Fort Prince George, Contrecœur had a good grasp of what to expect as far as the fortification was concerned, but he was not as confident of the intelligence he received regarding the size of the English garrison that would defend it. Most recently, his spies reported that the English personnel at the Forks numbered only about 50 men, but that number drastically conflicted with the earlier reports of upwards of 1,000 English troops in the area of the Forks. Unwilling to meet a potentially large, hostile force before his men were in battle formation, Contrecœur landed his troops at Shannopin's Town on the Allegheny, about three miles above the Forks. He bivouacked there for the night of Tuesday, April 16, 1754. The next day, Wednesday, April 17, with updated intelligence, Contrecœur and his army proceeded the remaining three miles downriver and disembarked a short distance from Fort Prince George. Ward and his small garrison were huddled in the fort as Contrecœur's professional soldiers quickly swarmed ashore and established a perimeter. Four of the French cannon were unloaded and assembled on carriages.

Ensign Ward and his small command watched with increasing trepidation from behind their palisaded walls as the French troops smartly formed-up on shore while their artillery deployed to cover them. Then, with flags flying and

6. The Race to the Forks

Six-pounder cannon similar to the type of field artillery that accompanied Contrecœur's force at the Forks. It would fire a six-pound projectile or the equivalent weight in grape-shot or canister (photograph by author at Fort Ligonier, Pennsylvania).

drums beating, the French ceremoniously marched to a point just beyond musket range—about 150 yards from the fort—while Captain Le Mercier continued forward with a small guard and called for a parley.[35] Ward was unsure of what to do, and as far as he was concerned there did not seem to be any good options. Undoubtedly cursing both Trent and Fraser for being absent, Ward quickly assembled a small guard and nervously marched out of the fort to meet with the French representatives. Tanacharison accompanied Ward to the meeting with Le Mercier. Thankfully, Ward found Le Mercier gracious to a fault and though he treated Ward with sympathetic kindness, he left no doubt whatsoever that he was there to evict the English from the Forks. He handed Ward a letter that Contrecœur had written the previous day that was filled with polite Gallic obliqueness and sanctimoniousness, but minced no words in demanding the immediate abandonment of the fort and English withdrawal from the area.

> A Summon by order of Contrecœur, Captain of one of the Companies of the Detachment of the French marine, Commander-in-Chief of his Most Christian

Majestie's Troops now on the beautiful River, to the Commander of Those of the King of Great Britain at the Mouth of the River Mohongialo.

Sir:

Nothing can surprise me more than to see you attempt a Settlement upon the Lands of the King my Master, which obliges me, now, Sir, to send You this Gentleman, Chevalier Le Mercier, Captain of the Bombardiers, Commander of the Artillery of Canada, to know of you, Sir, by Vertue of what Authority You are come to fortify Yourself within the Dominions of the King my Master. This action seems so contrary to the last Treaty of Peace concluded at Aix-la-Chapelle between his Most Christian Majesty and the King of Great Britain, that I do not know to whom to impute such an Usurpation, as it is incontestable that the lands situated along the beautiful River belong to his Most Christian Majesty.

I am informed, Sir, that your Undertaking has been concerted by none else than by a Company who have more in View the advantage of a Trade than to endeavor to keep the Union of Harmony which subsists between the Crowns of France and Great Britain, altho' it is as much the Interest, Sir, of your Nation as Our's to preserve it.

Let it be as will, Sir, if you come into this Place charged with Orders, I summon you in the Name of the King my Master, by Vertue of Orders which I got from my General, to retreat peaceably with your Troops from off the Lands of the King (and not to return, or else I find myself obliged to fulfill my Duty and compel You to it. I hope, Sir, You will not defer an Instant, and that You will not force me to the last Extremity); in that case, Sir, You may be persuaded that I will give Orders that there shall be no Damage done by my Detachment.

I prevent You, Sir, from the trouble of asking me one Hour of Delay, nor to wait for my consent to receive Orders from your Governor; He can give you none within the Dominions of the King my Master. Those I have received of my General are my laws, so that I cannot depart from them.

If, on the contrary, Sir, You have not got Orders, and only come to trade, I am sorry to tell you that I cannot avoid seizing You and to confiscate your Effects to the Use of the Indians our Children, Allies, and Friends, as You are not allowed to carry on a contraband Trade. It is for this Reason, Sir, that we stopped two Englishmen last year who were trading upon our Lands; moreover, the King my Master asks nothing but his Right, he has not the least Intention to trouble the good Harmony and Friendship which reigns between his Majesty and the King of Great Britain.

The Governor of Canada can give Proof of having done his utmost Endeavors to maintain the perfect Union which reigns between Two Friendly Princes, as he has learned that the Iroquois and the Nepissingues of the Lake of the Two Mountains had struck and destroyed an English Family towards Carolina, he has barred up the Road and forced them to give him a little Boy belonging to that family, which was the only one alive, and which Mr. Wlerich, a Merchant of Montréal, has carried to Boston; and what is more, he has forbid the Savages from exercising their accustomed Cruelty upon the English our Friends.

I could complain bitterly, Sir, of the Means taken all last Winter to instigate the Indians to accept the hatchet and to strike Us while We were striving to maintain the Peace.

I am well persuaded, Sir, of the polite Manner in which You will received Monsieur Le Mercier, as well out of Regard to his business as his Distinction and personal Merit. I expect You will send him back with one of your Officers, who will bring me a precise answer. As You have got some Indians with You, Sir, I join with Monsieur Le Mercier an Interpreter, that he may inform them of my Intentions upon the subject.

I am, with great Regard, Sir,
Your most humble and most obedient Servant,
Contrecœur
Done at our Camp, April 16, 1754[36]

Ward was in a quandary. The young ensign was charged with defending the Forks, and did not want to surrender his post without a fight, but being outnumbered twenty-to-one by a veteran army supported with artillery could only end in the slaughter of his small command. Tanacharison advised Ward to try to delay by stating that he was not authorized to make such a decision. Ward explained to Mercier that as a mere ensign, he did not have sufficient authority to surrender the fort. That could only be done by Captain Trent who had gone to Wills Creek or Lieutenant Fraser at Turtle Creek. Ward asked for time to at least summon Lieutenant Fraser from his home eight miles away, since Fraser was technically in command during Trent's absence and was the more appropriate person to carry on negotiations with the French commander. Le Mercier politely but firmly refused Ward's request and told Ward that he had exactly one hour to accept the terms and "retreat peaceably with your troops"[37] or the French army would remove them by force. Ward realized that resistance would be futile and agreed to abandon the Forks, much to the frustration of the enraged Tanacharison, who angrily watched as the English surrendered their fort to the French without so much as a shot being fired.

Contrecœur's terms allowed the English to spend the night camped near the fort, but specified they must leave the Forks by noon the following day. They were allowed to take their weapons and all of their possessions with them. In an outward gesture of politeness, but more likely to obtain intelligence, the English and their Indian allies were invited to dinner in the French camp. The French commander asked many questions concerning the British government, to which Ward professed ignorance. Wine flowed freely and one of the topics discussed was the disposition of the Virginians' construction tools; axes, saws, mattocks, etc. Contrecœur knew that Ward's garrison was desperately short of provisions, and he offered rations and money in exchange for the tools.[38] Some sources indicate that Ward took advantage of Contrecœur's offer and sold him the construction equipment,[39] but Trent steadfastly claimed that he refused Contrecœur's offer. Ward's deposition letter of Tuesday, July 2, 1754, to Dinwiddie states that "the French Commander desired some of the Carpenter's Tools, offering money for them, to which he [Ward] answer'd he loved his King and Country too well to part with any of them."[40]

On the morning of Tuesday, April 18, 1754, Ward and his small command began their march east as the French raised the fleur-de-lis flag over the fort. One of the French soldiers wrote, "We took possession of the fort in which there were only fifty men and four cannons, but no provisions at all."[41] The "four cannons" mentioned were most likely swivel guns. Other than swivel guns, the Virginians did not have any proper, large-caliber artillery at the Forks at that time.

When Contrecœur learned that the Virginians had absolutely no provisions, he graciously provided three-days' rations to help sustain Ward's troops. Tanacharison watched as the English and the French waged their strangely genteel form of warfare, and the half-king was beside himself with anger and frustration. Tanacharison realized that he had grossly overestimated the strength and resolve of the English to stop the French advance, and now with the French in undisputed control of the Ohio territory, he was concerned that the Ohio Indians would be more than inclined to accept French supremacy. Worse, he realized that French influence over the Ohio Indians would negatively impact his leadership and stature. His only chance to reverse this state of affairs would be to force the situation and somehow strike a spark that would ignite a war between England and France.

7

The Spark is Struck

Tu n'es pas encore mort, mon pére! (Thou are not yet dead, my father)—Tanacharison to Jumonville

On Thursday morning, April 18, 1754, as the Virginians marched away from the Forks, they saw that the French soldiers were in the process of tearing down the fort's palisades that they had so laboriously constructed. Contrecœur realized that the puny fort built by the Virginians would not suffice as the premier French fortification guarding the Ohio territory, much less one bearing the name of Governor-General Duquesne. One French soldier wrote that they "destroyed the fort, which was no more than an enclosure of upright stakes,"[1] however, the timbers prepared by the Virginians for Fort Prince George were put to good use in the construction of the new French fortification there. In a letter to Contrecœur dated Saturday, May 11, 1754, Duquesne wrote, "I am glad that you have found a good supply of posts and squared timber; for the English are good judges of wood and excel in workmanship."[2] To the Indians, the destruction of Fort Prince George was tangible confirmation of the British capitulation of the Forks, and it caused the already distraught Tanacharison to lose his composure. Ward reported that the half-king "stormed greatly at the French at the time they were obliged to march out of the Fort and told them it was he Order'd that fort and laid the first log of it himself."[3] Even more insulting to Tanacharison was that "the French paid no regard to what he said."[4] To the half-king this was a humiliating loss of stature and an indication that neither the French nor the Ohio Indians any longer regarded him as a force to be reckoned with.

Washington, in the meantime, was on the way with his small force, vainly hoping to reach the Forks in time to reinforce Trent. However, when he arrived at Cresap's trading post at Old Town (present Oldtown, Maryland),[5] about 15 miles from Wills Creek, Washington received word that the French had indeed captured Fort Prince George, occupied the Forks, and evicted the Virginia garrison there. Washington wrote in his journal: "April 20th Came down to Colonel Cresap's to order the detachment, and on my Route, had notice that the Fort was taken by the French."[6]

Washington arrived at Wills Creek about Sunday, April 21 or Monday, April 22, 1754. On the 22nd, Ensign Ward and his small detachment from the Forks straggled into Wills Creek and reported to Washington. Washington wrote in his journal that the news of the Fort being taken by the French "was confirmed by Mr. Ward, the Ensign of Captain Trent, who had been obliged to surrender to a Body of one thousand French and upwards, under the Command of Captain Contrecœur, who was come from Venango Presque Isle with sixty batteaux, and three hundred canoes, and who having planted eighteen pieces of Cannon against the Fort, afterwards had sent him a Summons to withdraw."[7] Ward added that Tanacharison and his Indians remained steadfastly loyal to the English, and the half-king had sent a wampum belt with Ward, along with two young Mingo warriors who were to see with their own eyes and confirm that the English troops were indeed marching to the Indians' assistance.

In light of Ward's news that the French had captured the Forks, Washington's original orders to garrison and defend Fort Prince George were no longer applicable. To determine the best course of action, the young commander held a council of war at Wills Creek on Tuesday, April 23, 1754. According to Ensign Ward, the French at the Forks consisted of more than 1,000 troops supported by 18 pieces of artillery, some of which were 9-pounders. Washington's force, on the other hand, numbered about 160 men plus the 33 or so effective troops that returned with Ward from the Forks. The heaviest ordinance they had were a few small-bore swivel guns. This force was much too small and too lightly armed to try to reclaim the Forks, but with the anticipated reinforcements, including those recruited by Colonel Fry and Captain Stobo, the Virginians might soon be able to challenge the French on somewhat equal terms, at least with respect to manpower. In the meantime, Washington decided that he would take his force as far as the storehouse at Red Stone from where he could observe the French and gather intelligence regarding their strength and disposition. At Red Stone, he would await reinforcements, and also Colonel Fry, who would take over command of the expedition. The decision to lead his troops to Red Stone Creek was unusual in that Washington, on his own initiative, decided to cross the Alleghenies and penetrate disputed territory, where his small force would be exposed to a possible attack by a veteran French army that was at least six times larger than his and was supported with a battery of field artillery.

However, Washington believed that he needed to respond to Tanacharison's urgent request for help in a timely manner. Though the young lieutenant colonel did not have sufficient strength to confront the French, he decided that by moving his force to Red Stone Creek, he would tangibly demonstrate to the half-king that help was on the way. Washington was convinced that Tanacharison was loyal to him and firmly under his control, but he also felt it was necessary to respond to the chief's pleas for assistance in order to maintain that loyalty or risk permanently losing the support of the half-king and his Indians. Interestingly, Tanacharison, who was very savvy and intelligent, regarded Washington as someone he could influence. The half-king needed the British to help him maintain his stewardship over the Ohio Indians, and he viewed the young and fairly naïve Washington as his best hope of achieving British intervention against the French. Tanacharison believed that he could manipulate the young Virginian and cause him to be the agent by which a large British force would come to evict the French from the Ohio territory.

Washington reported his intentions to Dinwiddie and added, "I thought it proper also to acquaint the Governors of Maryland and Pennsylvania of the news."[8] In a letter to Governor Sharpe of Maryland dated Wednesday, April 24, 1754, Washington described his intentions.

> Sir,
>
> I have arrived here with a detachment of One hundred and Fifty men. We daily expect Colonel Fry with the remaining part of the regiment and the artillery; however, we shall march quietly across the Mountains, clearing the roads as we go, that our cannon may, with the greater ease, be sent after us; we proposed to go as far as Red-Stone Creek, which falls into the Monongahela, about thirty-seven miles this side of the Fort which the French have taken, as far as the Ohio. A store is built there by "the Ohio Company," wherein may be placed our ammunition and provisions.[9]

To emphasize the urgency for reinforcements and support from all the neighboring colonies, Washington added: "Besides the French forces above mentioned we have reason to believe, according to accounts we have heard, that another Party is coming to the Ohio; we have also learnt that six hundred of the Chippeways and Ollowais [Ottawa] Indians, are coming down the River Scioto in order to join them."[10] If French regulars at the Forks were not enough to cause concern among the English colonies, the threat of an army of savage northern Indians let loose on the Virginia, Maryland, and Pennsylvania frontiers should certainly do the trick.

Washington sent one of the Mingo warriors back to Tanacharison with a message that the British army was indeed on the way and that Washington's force was building the road to accommodate the large numbers of English troops, cannons, and provisions that would follow. He requested that

Tanacharison join his force on the march to assist in council, and signed the message with the name "Conotocarious" (Taker of Towns), the name Tanacharison had given Washington the previous winter. Washington's message read:

> To the Half-King, and the Chiefs and Warriors of the Shawanese and Loups our Friends and Bretheren. I received your speech by brother Bucks who came to us with the two young men six days after their departure from you. We return you our greatest thanks and our hearts burn with love and affection towards you, in gratitude for your constant attachment to us, as also your gracious speech, and your wise counsels.
>
> This young man will inform you, where he found a small part of our army, making towards you, clearing the roads for a great number of our warriors, who are ready to follow us, with our great guns, our ammunition and provisions. I cannot delay letting you know the thoughts of our hearts, I send you back this young man, with this speech, to acquaint you therewith, and the other young man I have sent to the Governor of Virginia, to deliver him your speech and your wampum, and to be an eye-witness of the preparations we are making, to come in all haste to the assistance of those whose interest is as dear to us as our lives. We know the character of the treacherous French, and our conduct shall plainly show you how much we have it at heart. I shall not be satisfied if I do not see you before all our forces are met together at the Fort which is in the way, wherefore, I desire with the greatest earnestness, that you, or at least one of you, Scruneyattha [Scarouady] and send a necklace of wampum, should come as soon as possible and meet us on the road, and to assist us in council. I present you with these bunches of wampum, to assure you of the sincerity of my speech, and that you may remember how much I am your Friend and Brother.
>
> Signed
> G° Washington or
> Conotocarious[11]

The first work parties left Wills Creek on Thursday, April 25, 1754, ahead of Washington's main body of troops, to begin clearing the road along the route of the old Nemacolin Trail. The work was arduous as they hacked a narrow trail through the dense forest and thick underbrush, but they knew that it would get even more difficult when they reached the high ridges of the Alleghenies. Washington led the rest of his troops out of Wills Creek a few days later and it wasn't long before every man was employed in constructing the narrow road. The spring rains made fording and bridging the numerous streams especially difficult. At one point they were barely able to progress 20 miles in 15 days.[12] To make matters worse, the troops encountered Indians and traders fleeing east with wild rumors of hostile Indians and a large advancing French army under the command of Monsieur LaForce, whom Washington had encountered the previous winter. It's not exactly known what LaForce's status and role was in the French army, but he seems to have been an important cog in the French war machine on the Ohio. French records indicate he was merely "commander of stores" or commissary, but he was very active in leading French troops, and he appears to have been an influential emissary to the Indians. The traders also reported that French reinforcements numbering upwards of 800 troops had arrived at the Forks.

On Thursday, May 9, 1754, Washington met the trader Robert Callender (1726–1776), who said that he observed a number of French soldiers led by LaForce in the vicinity of Gist's plantation. These reports were worrisome to Washington, who was becoming increasingly edgy about French troops between him and Red Stone Creek. On Saturday, May 11, 1754, Washington detached 25 men under Captain Adam Stephen and Ensign William Chevalier La Peyronie (?–1755) to proceed as far as Gist's plantation. Gist's plantation was part trading post and part company town; it contained a fortified storehouse and the homes of about a dozen settler families. The site of Gist's plantation is on present U.S. Route 119 between Uniontown and Connellsville, Pennsylvania, approximately 4.5 miles southwest of Connellsville.

Stephens and Peyronie were to ascertain "where LaForce and his party were; and in case they were in the neighborhood, to cease pursuing and to retire to a safe place." Washington ordered that they should "closely examine the woods round about, and if they should find any Frenchman apart from the rest, to seize him and bring him to us, that we might learn what we could from him." He added, "we were also desirous to enquire what were the views of the French, what they had done, and what they intended to do and to collect everything, which could give us the least intelligence."[13] Washington's orders must have had some ambiguity as far as Adam Stephen was concerned, because while Washington recalled that he ordered Stephen to cease pursuing and retire to a safe place if they should encounter LaForce, Stephen recorded in his diary that Washington ordered him to "apprehend" LaForce. The aggressive Stephen may have interpreted Washington's order to seize any Frenchman to include LaForce, and to bring him in for interrogation.

On Sunday, May 12, 1754, an express rider caught up with Washington, bringing news that "Colonel Fry, with a detachment of one hundred men and upwards was at Winchester and was to set out in a few days to join us." The message also stated that "Col. Innes[14] was marching with three hundred and fifty men, raised in [North] Carolina, that it was expected that Maryland would raise two hundred men, and that Pennsylvania had raised ten thousand pounds to pay the soldiers raised in other Colonies, as that Province furnished no recruits."[15] As heartening as this message was, the Maryland troops were not raised, and the troops with Innes would not join Washington in western Pennsylvania. Innes was a crony of Dinwiddie's, and though he had some prior military experience, his march to meet Washington was marked by ineptitude and bad management. After a plodding two-month march across Virginia, Innes finally reached Winchester on Tuesday, July 9, 1754; too late to be of any use to Washington. During Innes's march, desertions depleted his command from about three hundred and fifty men to about one hundred and fifty. Worse yet, most of those who remained with Innes were without weapons of any kind, and when they later learned of Washington's defeat at Great Meadows, most of the remainder of Innes's troops dispersed without orders and returned home.

On Friday, May 17, 1754, Ensign Ward, on his return from briefing Dinwiddie in Williamsburg, caught up with Washington near the great crossing of the Youghiogheny River (present location between Addison, Pennsylvania, and Markleysburg, Pennsylvania, approximately where U.S. 40 crosses the Youghiogheny River), and informed him that Dinwiddie approved Washington's course of action in taking his small force toward Red Stone Creek. This was gratifying news to the young commander, especially since he had embarked on a risky venture on his own initiative. Dinwiddie also sent word that two companies of regulars were marching to join Washington. Captain James Mackay (ca. 1718–1785)[16] was leading the Independent Company of Regulars from South Carolina to join Washington, and they might be expected at any day, and the Independent Company of Regulars from New York could be expected in about ten days. In fact, the Independent Company from New York did not arrive at Wills Creek until after the Battle of Great Meadows. When the New York Independent Company finally reached Wills Creek, they remained there. Each of the regular companies was composed of about 100 troops in addition to the officers. As a side note, Dinwiddie informed Washington that both Captain Trent and Lieutenant Fraser were to be tried for leaving the Forks and thereby abandoning their men to fend for themselves against the French army. Fraser and Trent were in fact tried by court-martial for the offense of absenting themselves from the fort before it was besieged, however, both were exonerated and afterward promoted.

Ward also related some information that Dinwiddie did not include in his message. The Virginia legislature set the maximum pay for Washington at 12 shillings, 6 pence, which was less than the 15 shillings originally promised by Dinwiddie. Washington calculated that at the prevailing exchange rate between colonial and British currencies, Washington would receive about 10 shillings a day less than his counterparts in the regular companies. This affected all of Washington's troops, who would be paid considerably less than their regular army counterparts. Worse, it was decided that officers would not be given an extra allowance to supplement their rations. In effect, the Virginia legislature decreed that Washington and his officers would not be fed any differently than the lowest ranking Virginia soldier. Washington undoubtedly kept this demeaning news to himself, but word leaked out, and in a protest letter to Dinwiddie, Washington's outraged officers threatened to quit work and resign when the higher-paid and better-fed officers of the regular independent companies arrived. Washington supported his officers with a letter of his own to Dinwiddie, but rather than threaten to quit, he offered to serve as a volunteer instead of accepting a degrading "shadow pay." Writing their protest letters seemed to assuage much of the frustrations of the officers, and they continued on as before. However, Washington was concerned that the matter would again resurface once the independent companies arrived.

That same evening, two Indians came into Washington's camp claiming they had been at the Forks of the Ohio five days previous. They told Washington that the construction of Fort Duquesne was progressing rapidly and that most of the troops were employed in construction duties. They said that when they left, the fort was "already breast-high, and of the thickness of twelve feet, and filled up with Earth. Stone, &c."[17] The Indians estimated the number of French troops to be about 600, but they said that the French claimed they had 800 and expected their numbers to double to about 1,600 within the next few days.

On Sunday, May 19, 1754, Washington sent a message to Tanacharison via one of the half-king's Indians. In the message, Washington told Tanacharison to be of good courage, because his brethren the English under Washington's command were on the way. He added that Lieutenant Governor Dinwiddie was very sorry for the treatment Tanacharison had received from the treacherous French, and was sending additional forces to join Washington so that they could assist the Indians and protect them.

During his grueling trek through the densely forested mountain wilderness, Washington received disconcerting information from various sources that a route over Chestnut Ridge was almost impossible for wagons and artillery. As a result, he considered that the army might conceivably travel by batteaux or canoe via the Youghiogheny River to the Monongahela and thence to Red Stone Creek. However, before committing to the river route, Washington wanted to see for himself whether the Youghiogheny was navigable. On Monday, May 20, 1754, he, along with four soldiers and one Indian, embarked by canoe down the river. They travelled only a short distance when they met a trader named Peter Suver, who discouraged Washington from attempting to move his troops down the Youghiogheny. Suver said the river was choked with shallow water and unnavigable rapids. He also added that portaging around those places would be impossible, because the dense mountains came down so close to the river. However, Washington wanted to see for himself. He travelled about ten miles before he realized that the route down the Youghiogheny was not practical and he abandoned the idea. The Ohiopyle Falls area (var. Ohio Pile), which Washington undoubtedly encountered, is beautiful but almost impassable. The rapids fall about 60 feet in the course of one mile, and one cascade has a perpendicular drop of 46 feet.

As Washington slogged his way westward, Contrecœur at Fort Duquesne was keeping track of the approaching English troops. His earlier scouting parties, including those under LaForce, gave him a fairly accurate estimation of the size and strength of Washington's force, but Contrecœur was at a loss regarding the Virginians' intentions. Surely, they did not mean to try to reclaim the Forks with such a small number of men. Whatever their intentions, it appeared that the English were planning to invade French-claimed territory, and Contrecœur would have to do something about it. On Thursday, May 23, 1754, the French commander sent Ensign Joseph Coulon de Villiers de Jumonville (1718–1754) and a small detachment of some 30 troops to discover the whereabouts of the English force, and to find out if they had in fact entered French territory. Jumonville was ordered to first report the location of the English troops to Contrecœur, and then present the intruders with a peaceful summons that demanded their immediate withdrawal from French territory. Ensign Jumonville was 35 years old and had an undistinguished military career. His military service was unlike those of his three brothers, who had all distinguished themselves in the regular army. It is supposed that Jumonville was given the mission by Contrecœur to help him with his advancement. However, while Jumonville was technically in command, the party included two officers, Monsieur LaForce, who likely was there to look after the untested ensign, and Ensign Pierre Jacques Drouillon de Macé (1727–1780), who reportedly was sent along as an interpreter.

Jumonville's detachment proceeded southwest from the Forks on a collision course with Washington, who was approaching his last major obstacle, Chestnut Ridge. By Friday, May 24, 1754, after a month of backbreaking advance through the forest, Washington's troops had only covered about two-thirds of the distance to Red Stone Creek. During the trek from Wills Creek, about a dozen men had deserted and the rest were exhausted to the point of collapse. The young commander received rumors of advancing French troops almost daily, and frustratingly, there was still no sign of the promised reinforcements. Washington's force had hacked and dug their way over a series of increasingly higher ridges and had just crossed the formidable Laurel Ridge, but the massive 2,500-foot Chestnut Ridge still loomed ahead and blocked their way to Red Stone Creek. In the valley lay an open alpine grassland called

7. The Spark is Struck

Great Meadows (present Farmington Township, Pennsylvania), which was watered by a stream called Great Meadow Run and intersected by a tributary brook called Indian Run. The grassy field was a few hundred yards wide and stretched about two miles long.

By that time, his men desperately needed a period of rest and recuperation, so Washington decided to establish a camp at Great Meadows before tackling Chestnut Ridge, which loomed above them to the west. Great Meadows was not a bad choice for rest. It was fairly level, there was adequate pasturage and it provided a plentiful supply of water. In addition, the location of Great Meadows was strategic. It lay 51 miles from Wills Creek and 18 miles from the Great Crossing of the Youghiogheny, 12 miles from Christopher Gist's plantation, 26 miles from Red Stone Creek, and about 55 miles from the French garrison at the Forks of the Ohio. It was a good place to set up a camp to rest the men and plan how best to proceed toward Red Stone Creek.

As they neared the last of the natural boundaries separating the English colonies from the disputed territory, Washington became increasingly aware of the vulnerability of his relatively small force. He decided that they should proceed with caution, lest they have a chance encounter with a large number of French regulars. Tanacharison, on the other hand, was doing his part to provoke the war he needed between the French and the English. In a blatant embellishment of facts, the half-king sent a message to Washington warning him of an imminent French attack. The translator John Davidson wrote the message for Tanacharison and it reached Washington on Friday, May 24, the same day the Virginians arrived at Great Meadows. While Davidson was a good translator, he was a barely literate writer. The message read:

> To the forist his Magesties Commander Offeverses to hom this meay concern.
> An acct. Of a French armey to meat Miger Georg Wassiontton therfor my Brotheres I deisir you to be awar of them for deisind to strike the forist English they see tow deays since they marchd I cannot tell what number the hif King and the rest of the Chiefes will be with you in five dayes to Consel- no more at present but give my serves to my Brother's the English.
> The Half King
> John Davidson[18]

The poorly written message was filled with ambiguities that undoubtedly perplexed Washington. It mentioned a French army that was on the march, but it gave no hint of its size or location. Since there was no punctuation, Washington couldn't tell whether the phrase "I cannot tell what number" referred to the French troops or the number of Indians with Tanacharison. At any rate, Washington was very concerned, since he had been hearing from other sources about French parties scouting the area. However, this was the first warning he received of an army of French regulars marching out specifically to engage his force. The young commander questioned the Indians who had brought in the message, but admitted that he was unable to learn much if anything more from them. The Indians said that they were aware of parties of Frenchmen roaming the area, but they did not know of any large force of French troops that were heading for Great Meadows. However, Washington was able to learn a little of the French situation at the Forks. The Indians reported that the French were erecting Fort Duquesne and that the sides facing the land were well enclosed, but the sides facing the rivers were almost defenseless. They reported that the French artillery was not yet mounted at the fort and that many of the French were sick. They also said that the French were having some difficulty convincing the Indians to guide them toward the English.

Even though the Indian messengers seemed to contradict some of what was in Tanacharison's message, Washington was loath to disregard it. Coincidentally, about two o'clock that afternoon, an English trader came into camp and reported that he had seen two Frenchmen at Gist's plantation the previous night and had learned that a strong detachment of French troops were on the march. To Washington's mind, this was confirmation of Tanacharison's warning, and he immediately put his weary troops to work preparing defensive positions. Washington centered his defenses at the natural entrenchments provided by the streams in the meadow so that his troops would be prepared for an imminent attack by the French in the least possible time. He put men to work clearing brush, and he positioned his wagons to serve as makeshift fortifications. Washington wrote to Dinwiddie, "We have with Natures assistance made a good Intrenchment, and by clearing ye[19] Bushes out of these Meadows, prepar'd a charming field for an Encounter."[20] After ensuring that all the weapons were serviceable and ammunition was adequate, the Virginians spent an uneasy night. Sentries were on the alert for any sign of the French, and the remainder of the troops nervously tried to sleep in their clothes with their weapons handy.

Saturday, May 25, 1754, dawned with no sign of the enemy. While most of the men were ordered to improve the defenses, Washington sent out scouting parties to try to learn the proximity of the French. Washington wrote in his journal, "Detached a scouting party at Chavert [no explanation for Chavert has been determined] to go along the roads, and sent other small parties to scour the woods. I gave the Horse-men orders to examine the country well, and endeavor to get some views of the French, of their forces, of their movements, etc."[21] The scouting parties returned in the evening without having located the French, even though they had ranged far in the direction of the

7. The Spark is Struck

Forks. Their inability to discover any French troops was even more disquieting to Washington. Reports consistently indicated that the French were coming, and the fact that he had no idea of their strength or proximity was even more worrisome. Washington hoped that with each hour, Colonel Fry and the long awaited reinforcements would arrive.

The following day, Washington received a message from Colonel Fry stating that Lieutenant Governor Dinwiddie had arrived in Winchester where he wanted to meet with Tanacharison. Though the message indicated that Fry was on the march, it was also evident that he had not yet reached Wills Creek. It would likely be several days or even weeks before Fry and the much needed reinforcements would arrive at Great Meadows. Washington realized that he most likely would have to deal with the French threat on his own, and he nervously continued to plan for a French attack that he believed was imminent.

On Monday, May 27, 1754, Washington's anxiety level escalated rapidly when his friend Christopher Gist arrived in camp with a report that French troops were very nearby and that he had seen their tracks not more than five miles from Great Meadows. It was one thing to receive reports of French sightings from fearful English traders who were fleeing the area, but a report of nearby French regulars from a frontiersman of Gist's stature was truly alarming. Washington's journal states, "Mr. Gist arrived early in the morning, who told us that Mr. LaForce, with fifty men whose tracks he had seen five miles from here, had been at his plantation the day before, towards noon, and would have killed a cow, and broken every thing in the house, if two Indians, whom he had left in charge of the house, had not prevented them from carrying out their design."[22] To put Gist's report in perspective, he did not actually see the French soldiers, but was relaying information from the Indians at his plantation. To them an armed party of 30 or so uniformed soldiers was an impressive force and most likely one that was on the warpath. Undoubtedly, the troops were Ensign Jumonville's detachment that had passed Gist's plantation on the way to locate Washington's force. Gist's Indians erred slightly in their estimation of the number of French troops, but their recognition of LaForce, who was with Jumonville, certainly identifies it as Jumonville's detachment. While at Gist's, the French had asked the Indians about Tanacharison and his whereabouts, because they believed that he was with the English. They reasoned that by learning the location of the half-king, it would lead them to Washington's position.

While Gist's Indians had overestimated the number in Jumonville's detachment, Washington, on the other hand, believed that they might have grossly underestimated the size of the French force. In an attempt to get better intelligence, he sent out a scouting party of 65 troops under the command of

Captain Hog. Next he capitalized on the French officer's query regarding Tanacharison's whereabouts by issuing some propaganda of his own. Washington told the half-king's Indians who were still in camp that the reason the French wanted to know the chief's location was "that the French wanted to kill the Half-King."[23] It apparently had the desired effect, because the Indians said that if it were true that Tanacharison were killed or even insulted, they would incite the Mingoes to take up the hatchet against the French.

Throughout the day, Washington's men frantically worked to improve their defenses while scouting parties combed the area looking for the French force that was reported in the vicinity. Washington and his troops were fatigued from stress, physical exertion and very little sleep. They were on their third day of round-the-clock high alert, expecting the French regulars and their Indians to attack at any time. There was no hope of reinforcements in the short term, and every report indicated that the French were very nearby indeed. Washington's men prepared for another miserable, restless night with sentries posted all around as the troops tried to sleep with their weapons handy. To make matters worse, a steady rain began to fall, which turned the camp into a quagmire.

About eight o'clock in the evening of Monday, May 27, 1754, an Indian named Silverheels[24] came into Washington's camp with a message from Tanacharison informing the Virginians that the half-king, who had been on his way to rendezvous with them at Great Meadows, came across the tracks of two men, which he followed. The tracks led to a very secluded area where Tanacharison believed a large force of French soldiers were hidden. Silverheels said that the half-king and his Indians were camped near the French bivouac, which was about six miles from Great Meadows. This information was consistent with Gist's earlier report about a French war party in the vicinity. It also reinforced in Washington's mind the thought that a hostile enemy force with intentions to attack was near at hand. Night had fallen and the steady rain turned the darkness into an inky blackness, but rather than wait for the enemy to launch their attack, Washington decided to reconnoiter the French force so that he would have a better idea of what he might be up against. He left his camp at Big Meadows on high alert with sentries and pickets posted, and then with Silverheels guiding, he set off with about 40 men to find Tanacharison's camp.

The trek of Washington and his detachment up the forested slope of Chestnut Ridge in the blackness of the night and in heavy rain was very challenging. Washington wrote:

> I sent out forty men and ordered my ammunition to be put in a place of safety, fearing it to be a stratagem of the French to attack our camp; I left a guard to defend it, and with the rest of my men, set out in a heavy rain, and in a night as

dark as pitch, along a path scarce broad enough for one man; we were sometimes fifteen or twenty minutes out of the path before we could come on it again, and we would often strike against each other in the darkness: All night long we continued our route, and on the 28th about sun-rise we arrived at the Indian camp.[25]

A rested Tanacharison greeted an anxious Washington and his wet, tired and haggard force. In addition to their grueling night trek through the soggy mountainous forest, none of the Virginians had a decent rest since arriving at Great Meadows more than three days previous. The half-king could see that Washington and his men were stressed by fatigue, and their anxiety was exacerbated by the proximity of what they believed was a potent enemy force. Tanacharison and Washington held a hurried council during which the half-king easily convinced the young commander that the French were obviously planning to attack, and it would be more prudent for Washington to attack them first. Washington stated in his journal that "after having held a council with the Half-King, we concluded to attack them together; so we sent out two men to discover where they were, as also their posture and what sort of ground was thereabout."[26] Tanacharison had about a dozen warriors and Washington had about 40 men. Scarouady had accompanied Tanacharison, and the two half-kings and Washington agreed that the element of surprise would give them a good chance against the French regulars. The two scouts quickly returned with the news that the French were camped in a hidden glen about a mile away, and it appeared that they were completely unaware that Washington's force and Tanacharison's Indians were in the vicinity. It was agreed that an early morning attack on the French troops before they had broken camp offered the best chance of success. The combined force left the Indian camp with Tanacharison and his warriors leading the way and Washington and his troops cautiously following Indian-fashion through the early dawn greyness of the forest.

Although they moved stealthily through the wet forest, it did not take long to reach the French bivouac. Jumonville's detachment of about 30 men was camped in a hollow at the foot of a stone cliff that rose sharply from the glen floor. The bivouac was fairly well hidden and protected. The location was most likely selected in an attempt to find protection from the incessant rain rather than as a place of stealth and concealment. There were no sentries posted, and the French soldiers had stacked their arms off to one side in a protected area under an overhang where they would be less susceptible to the constant rainfall. It's difficult to explain why Jumonville did not exercise basic military discipline in posting armed sentries, or why the more experienced Monsieur LaForce did not intervene in that matter. One likely explanation is that they believed their role was diplomatic rather than military and did not require a defensive perimeter. Jumonville's orders were to discover the English party and after reporting its location to Fort Duquesne, he was ordered to merely deliver a peaceful summons from Contrecœur to "the first English officer that he could find,"[27] which was a message that invited the English to withdraw from French territory. Contrecœur's summons read:

> Word has reached me by way of the savages, that you have come with an armed force upon the lands of the King, my master; but I am hardly able to believe it. Since I ought to neglect nothing to be informed correctly about it, I am sending Sieur Dejumonville to find out, and in case he finds you there, he is to summon you in the name of the king, in virtue of the orders I have received from my general, to retire peaceably with your troops. Otherwise, Monsieur, I shall be obliged to compel you in all the ways that I believe most efficacious for the honor of the arms of France. The sale of the Belle River territory by the savages gives you such poor title that I could not be prevented from meeting force with force.
> I warn you that if any act of hostility occurs after this summons, which is the last I shall send you, you will have to answer for it, since our intention is to maintain the concord which now reigns between the two friendly princes. Whatever your intention may be, I am convinced you will show M. Dejumonville all the consideration that he deserves and send him back at once to inform me of your intentions.[28]

While the French considered themselves to be on a diplomatic mission, Washington, who surveyed the French encampment from the concealment of the surrounding forest, and with Tanacharison's prompting, immediately came to a different conclusion. Since the French had chosen such an obscure and secretive bivouac, they obviously were up to no good. He reasoned, likely with the half-king's help, that the French force had been skulking in the vicinity of Washington's encampment for several days. Since they had not revealed themselves or sought a parlay, it could only be assumed that they were there to cause harm to the Virginians. The fact that the French had not posted pickets or sentries and were likely in the ravine seeking refuge from the rain did not apparently register with Washington. Nor did he consider that Jumonville's party had conceivably not yet learned where Washington and his men were camped. Washington only saw a substantial number of armed French troops who were attempting to remain concealed, and he concluded, with Tanacharison's encouragement, that at a minimum the French were there to secretly spy and gather intelligence on the Virginians at Great Meadows.[29]

Washington planned to deploy his men to encircle the French encampment, but he saw that his right flank would be the most difficult to conceal as they advanced and would be visible to the French from some distance away. However, there was no way around it. He sent the Indians under Tanacharison around to the north side of the glen, to advance south once the attack started,

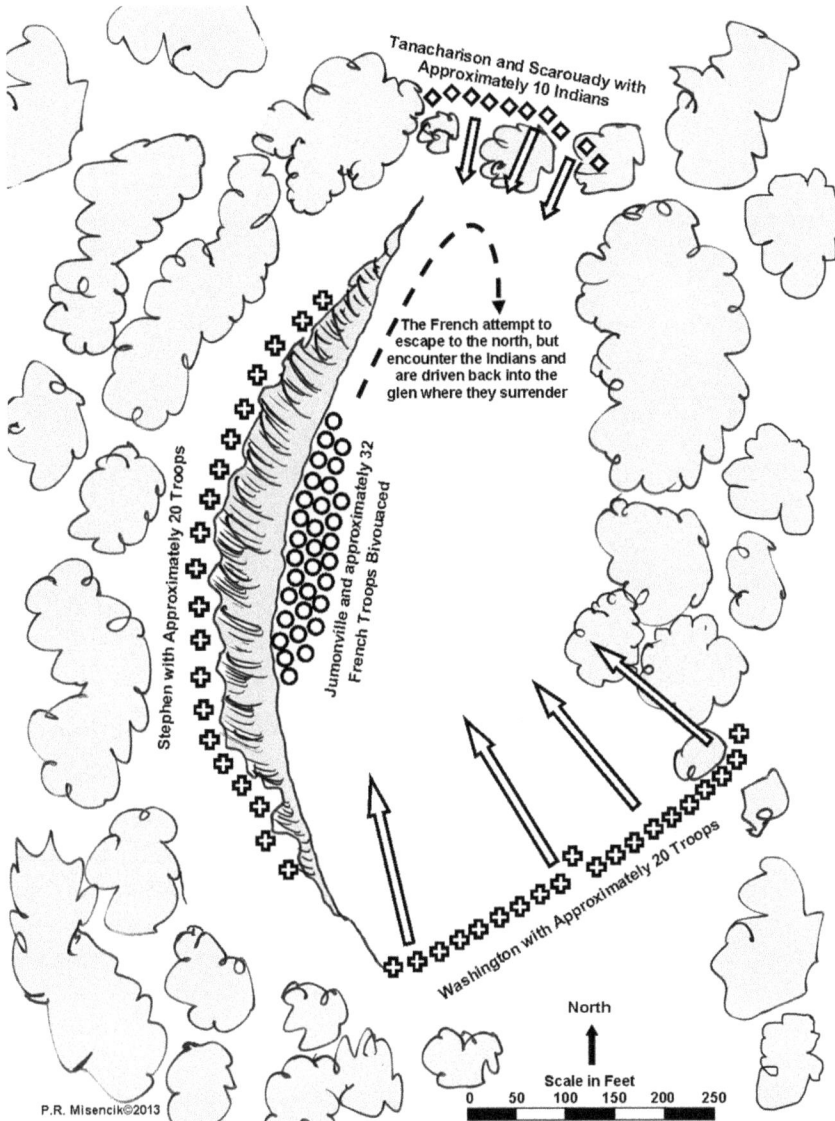

Figure 10. The skirmish at Jumonville Glen.

to cut off a French retreat or redeployment to the north. He then positioned Captain Adam Stephen with about 20 men on his left flank to the west in a commanding position at the top of the cliffs. A portion of Stephen's line extended down the hill southwest to the floor of the ravine. Washington, with the remaining 20 or so men, led the more exposed right flank, which stretched

View of Jumonville Glen from approximate position of Washington's wing. Stephen's men were deployed along the top of the rock wall (photograph by author).

from the south to the southeast of the glen. Sometime around seven o'clock in the morning, when he was certain the men under Stephen and Tanacharison were in position, Washington signaled his men to stealthily advance toward the French encampment. At about 100 yards from the French camp, Washington's line of men emerged from the covering of the woods and continued to advance in the clear. The distance was still too far for accurate musket fire, and since he was up against French regulars, the young commander wanted to make every shot count.

When the advancing Virginians stepped into the open, French soldiers who were preparing for breakfast spotted them almost immediately. The sight of an armed force marching toward them in line of battle startled them, and they quickly raised the alarm and rushed for their stacked muskets to defend themselves. Now that he was discovered, Washington swiftly advanced his line to less than 50 yards, well within killing range of his muskets. Then a shot rang out. Nobody recalled who fired first, but within seconds a full-scale engagement erupted. Stephen's troops poured fire from the tops of the rock face down into the milling French troops, and Washington's men fired

7. The Spark is Struck 113

View of French bivouac area from Stephen's position atop rock outcropping. (photograph by author).

volley after volley from the floor of the glen. In the first exchanges several French and a few Virginians were bowled over by the heavy musket balls. It was obvious to both sides that the French were getting the worst of it. The French troops began a fighting withdrawal to the north, but soon ran into Tanacharison and his Indians, who forced them back into the ravine. The fight lasted no more than 15 minutes and it ended when Jumonville cried out for a cease-fire. The firing slackened off and eventually stopped, but before the shocked Washington could intervene, the Indians rushed forward and tomahawked all but one of the wounded Frenchmen, and then they began to scalp the dead. Some accounts maintain that Washington allowed the Indians to murder the wounded, because he understood that it was their way of fighting and also because he did not want to be burdened by tending to the enemy casualties. It was when Tanacharison demanded that the unwounded French be turned over to the Indians to be killed and scalped that Washington firmly took charge and denied the half-king's demand in no uncertain terms. The Indian chief was clearly unhappy with Washington's refusal, but rather than risk a fight with the Virginians, the half-king gathered his Indians and stood sullenly by as the French were herded together at the center of the ravine.

What happened next has been the subject of discussion among historians, in that there are differing versions of the event. What is common among the various accounts is that Jumonville was alive when the firing ceased and was killed after he and the survivors of his command were taken prisoner. The most persistent and perhaps believable account comes from John Shaw, a private in Washington's regiment who admittedly was not present, but related in a sworn statement what others who were in the ravine at the time had told him. According to Shaw, Jumonville called out through his interpreter that he had something to tell the commander of the English force, after which Washington and his Virginians closed in around Jumonville to hear what he had to say.[30] Jumonville began to read his summons aloud in French, which ironically Tanacharison understood, but Washington did not. The French commander apparently intended to read the document through and then allow his interpreter to translate it into English. Tanacharison listened for a few moments and realized that the summons was indeed a peaceful directive to the English to withdraw, but it also contained an unmistakable threat of strong retaliation for any act of hostility to Jumonville. Unwilling to allow the war that he had worked so diligently to foment be avoided through diplomatic negotiations, Tanacharison, in a calculated move, forced the issue. He approached Jumonville and interrupted the French commander, asking if he was English, to which Jumonville replied that he was indeed French. Tanacharison, then softly said, "Tu n'es pas encore mort, mon père" (you are not yet dead, my father),[31] and before Washington or any of the Virginians could act, the half-king swung his tomahawk and split Jumonville's skull, which killed him instantly. Then, as the horrified Virginians and their French prisoners watched, Tanacharison scooped out a handful of Jumonville's brains and washed his hands with them.

Washington, Tanacharison and their men thought they had captured or killed the entire French force, however, one Frenchman did escape to carry the word back to Contrecœur at Fort Duquesne. A Canadian soldier named Mouceau[32] was fortunate to be in the woods answering a call of nature when the Virginians attacked. He observed some of the engagement from his place of concealment, but admittedly fled the scene immediately after the cease-fire and just as Jumonville was trying to read Contrecœur's summons to Washington. He traveled barefoot all the way back to Fort Duquesne, where he reported the attack on Jumonville, but at the time he had no idea that Jumonville had been killed. However, shortly after Mouceau arrived at Fort Duquesne with news of the attack, Contrecœur learned of the death of Jumonville from a messenger sent by none other than Tanacharison. The half-king recalled Contrecœur's admonition in the message Jumonville carried: "I warn you that if any act of hostility occurs after this summons, which is the last I shall send you, you will have to answer for it,"[33] and the wily chief wanted to make certain that Contrecœur was fully aware of the English attack on his emissaries. To further inflame the situation, the half-king's message described Washington's sneak attack on Jumonville's detachment, and he also self-servingly reported that Contrecœur's emissary had been cold-bloodedly murdered during the cease-fire. Now Contrecœur would have no option but to regard Washington's actions as an act of war and would be obliged to retaliate. That would certainly ensure the war between the French and English that the Indian chief desired. Tanacharison's version to the French commander omitted his role in Jumonville's death by claiming that after the cease-fire and while Jumonville was trying to read Contrecœur's message, the ensign was shot down where he stood. The half-king also added that the Virginians were determined to murder the rest of the French party, but Tanacharison and his warriors formed a wall of protection around the captives and were able to save them from being barbarously slaughtered by Washington's troops.

After the fight, Washington was undoubtedly torn with emotions. On one hand he experienced the euphoria of leading men in his first battle, and not only had he survived, but he had emerged victorious against veteran French troops. On the other hand, he was concerned about how his actions would be judged by his superiors and indeed by the king himself. Most worrisome was the realization that Jumonville may have in fact been an emissary, and Washington, without any real provocation, had launched a surprise attacked on the French delegation that killed the envoy and several of his men. The fact that Jumonville was cold-bloodedly slaughtered after the cease-fire was particularly disconcerting in that it could cast dishonorable aspersions on Washington. That and the fact that this small engagement would likely result in war between France and England made Washington realize that some sort of damage control had to be initiated immediately.

8

Rationalization and Justification

> *These officers pretend they were coming on an embassy; but the absurdity of this pretext is too glaring ... they were sent as spies, rather than anything else.* —Washington to Dinwiddie

Even as the smoke was clearing from the engagement in the ravine, the surviving French soldiers began to protest their being treated as prisoners of war. They insisted that as escorts of the slain Jumonville, who was indeed an emissary of the French crown, they should be treated with diplomatic consideration and immediately returned to Contrecœur at Fort Duquesne. Washington, of course, could not accede to their demands for the simple reason that to do so would be to admit that Jumonville and his party were, in fact, emissaries on a diplomatic mission. Accepting responsibility for killing a French envoy along with a third of his command in an unprovoked ambush was something Washington was not willing to do. Another difficulty for Washington was that two of his captives were the redoubtable René-Hippolyte LaForce and Pierre-Jacques Druillon de Macé. Both were influential in the French command structure, and Washington was reluctant to allow them to present their version of the Jumonville affair before he was able to. Washington examined all of the documents that the French possessed in hopes of finding something that would refute the French officers' diplomatic claims, but those hopes were soon ended in frustration. Contrecœur's official summons seemed to confirm rather than refute the claim that the French party was diplomatic, and a close study of the rest of the documents also indicated that the French were on a peaceful mission. Included in the documents were orders from Contrecœur, listing all of the members of Jumonville's command and instructions to discover the road that the English were constructing into the area, and to ascertain whether the Indian claims were true that the English were preparing to attack the French at the Forks. A review of Contrecœur's orders to Jumonville was no help to Washington at all.

8. Rationalization and Justification

The orders only stipulated that if Jumonville's party should discover any hostile activities on the part of the English, Jumonville was merely to serve the English commander with Contrecœur's summons, wait for a reply, and return to inform Contrecœur of the English commander's response and intentions.

Almost immediately, Washington began to justify his actions and malign the claims of the French. Interestingly, he devoted very few written lines in his personal journal or in his letters to Dinwiddie regarding the engagement itself, but he did expound in great detail on the perfidiousness of the French detachment's intentions and on the righteousness of his own actions. His details of the fight in the glen were very sketchy and inferred that Jumonville was killed in the fight itself rather than after the cease-fire. He wrote in his journal: "We had thus advanced pretty near to them when they discovered us; I then ordered my company to fire; my fire was supported by that of Mr. [Thomas] Waggoner and my company and his received the whole fire of the French, during the greater part of the action, which lasted a quarter of an hour before the enemy was routed. We killed Mr. de Jumonville, the Commander of that party, as also nine others, we wounded one and made twenty-one prisoners, among whom were M. LaForce, M. Drouillon and two cadets. The Indians scalped the dead and took away the greater part of their arms, after which we marched on with the prisoners under guard."[1] On Wednesday, May 29, 1754, Washington wrote two letters regarding the action in the glen that had occurred the previous day. The first was sent by express to Lieutenant Governor Dinwiddie with Washington's version of the event, and the second was dispatched to Colonel Joshua Fry, who was on his way to take command of Washington's force. The letter to Fry simply stated that "yesterday, I engaged a party of French, whereof ten were killed, one wounded, and twenty-one taken, with the loss of only one of mine killed and two or three wounded, among whom was Lieutenant Waggener."[2] His letter to Dinwiddie was equally lacking in details about the battle and the death of the French Commander: "I thereupon in conjunction with the Half-King and Monacawacha [Scarouady] formed a disposition to attack them on all sides, which we accordingly did, and after an engagement of about fifteen minutes, we killed ten, wounded one, and took twenty-one prisoners. Amongst those killed was M. de Jumonville, the commander."[3]

While his descriptions of the engagement and particularly the death of Jumonville was noticeably lacking in detail, Washington was very meticulous and exhaustive in detailing every aspect of the actions taken by Jumonville's detachment. He elaborated on anything that could possibly be construed as deceitfulness on the part of the French to refute their claim of being emissaries. He went to great lengths to particularly assure Dinwiddie that had he not taken action, the devious French would certainly have launched a surprise attack against the Virginians. He wrote in his journal,

> They had informed me that they had been sent with a summons to order me to retire. A plausible pretense to discover our camp and to obtain knowledge of our forces and our situation! It was so clear that they were come to reconnoiter what we were, that I admired their assurance when they told me they were come as an Embassy; their instructions were to get what knowledge they could of the roads, rivers, and all the country as far as the Potomac; and instead of coming as an Embassador, publicly and in an open manner, they came secretly, and sought the most hidden retreats more suitable for deserters than for Embassadors; they encamped there and remained hidden for whole days together, at a distance of not more than five miles from us; they sent spies to reconnoiter our camp; the whole body turned back 2 miles; they sent two messengers mentioned in the instruction, to inform M. de Contrecœur of the place where we were, and of our disposition, that he might send his detachments to enforce the summons as soon as it should be given.
>
> Besides, an Embassador has princely attendants, whereas this was only a simple petty French officer. An Embassador has no need of spies, his person being always sacred: and seeing their intention was so good, why did they tarry two days within five miles distance from us without acquainting me with the summons, or at least, with something that related to the Embassy? That alone would be sufficient to excite the strongest suspicions, and we must do them the justice to say, that, if they wanted to hide themselves, they could not have picked out better places than they had done. The summons was so insolent, and savoured of so much Gasconade [extravagant boasting], that if it had been brought openly by two men it would have been an excessive Indulgence to have suffered them to return.[4]

Returning to the Indian camp after the fight in the ravine, Washington delivered Dinwiddie's invitation to Tanacharison, telling him that Dinwiddie desired to meet the half-king at Winchester in order to hold a council. Washington was hopeful that the half-king would be able to refute possible accusations that Jumonville was a peaceful emissary whose party had been attacked without provocation, and more importantly explain how Jumonville had been slain after the cease-fire if that should become an issue. However, Tanacharison refused, saying that he would not go, because his people were in too great a danger "from the French whom they had attacked."[5] He told Washington that he would send runners to all of the allied Indian tribes, summoning them to take up the hatchet in support of the English, and that he would personally bring the Indians to Washington's camp at Great Meadows. Disappointed in Tanacharison's refusal to meet with Dinwiddie, Washington and his men marched back to their camp at Great Meadows with the captive Frenchmen in tow.

8. Rationalization and Justification

In his May 29 letter to Dinwiddie, Washington expounded on the perfidy of Jumonville and his detachment:

> These officers pretend they were coming on an embassy; but the absurdity of this pretext is too glaring, as you will see by the instructions and Summons enclosed. Their instructions were to reconnoiter the country, roads, creeks, and the like, as far as the Potomac, which they were about to do. These enterprising men were purposely chosen out to procure intelligence, which they were to send back by some brisk dispatches, with the mention of the day that they were to serve the summons; which could be with no other view, than to get a sufficient reinforcement to fall upon us immediately after. This, with several other reasons, induced all the officers to believe firmly, that they were sent as spies rather than anything else, and has occasioned my detaining them as prisoners, though they expected, or at least had some faint hope, that they should be continued as ambassadors.
>
> They, finding where we were encamped, instead of coming up in a public manner, sought out one of the most secret retirements, fitter for a deserter than an ambassador to encamp in, and stayed there two or three days, sending spies to reconnoiter our camp, as we are told, though they deny it. Their whole body moved back near two miles, and they sent off two runners to acquaint Contrecœur with our strength, and where we were encamped. Now thirty-six men would almost have been a retinue for a princely ambassador, instead of a petit. Why did they, if their designs were open, stay so long within five miles of us, without delivering their message, or acquainting me with it? Their waiting could be with no other design, than to get detachments to enforce the summons, as soon as it was given. They had no occasion to send out spies, for the name of an ambassador is sacred among all nations; but it was by the track of those spies, that they were discovered, and that we got intelligence of them. They would not have retired two miles back without delivering the summons, and sought a skulking-place (which, to do them justice, was done with great judgment), but for some special reason. Besides, the summons is so insolent, and savors so much of gasconade, that if two men only had come to deliver it openly, it would have been too great an indulgence to send them back.[6]

Washington sent the captive Frenchmen under guard to Dinwiddie, warning the lieutenant governor that "the principal officers taken are M. Drouillon and M. LaForce, of whom your honor has often heard me speak, as a bold enterprising man, and a person of great subtlety and cunning."[7] However, Washington must have been concerned that when LaForce and Drouillon related their version of the fight in the glen and the death of Jumonville it would conflict with his own. He hurriedly dashed off another letter to Dinwiddie to caution him not to be swayed by the French captives. The undated letter stated, "Since writing my last I have still stronger presumption, indeed almost confirmation, that they were sent as spies, and were ordered to wait near us, til they were truly informed of our intentions, situation, and strength, and were to have acquainted their commander therewith, and to have lain lurking here for reinforcements before they served the summons, if served at all."[8] Writing about the French captives that were en route to Williamsburg, Washington reiterated, "I doubt not but they will endeavor to amuse you with many smooth stories, as they did me; but they were confuted in them all, and, by circumstances too plain to be denied, almost made ashamed of their assertions. I dare say you will treat them with respect, which is due to all unfortunate persons in their condition. But I hope you will give no ear to what they will have an opportunity for displaying to the best advantage, having none present to contradict their reports. I have heard, since they went away, that they should say they called to us not to fire; but that I know to be false, for I was the first man that approached them, and the first whom they saw, and immediately upon it they ran to their arms, and fired briskly till they were defeated."[9] Washington's letter then took on a more deadly demeanor. From initially stating that they should be treated with respect and unfortunate prisoners of war, Washington now wrote, "I thought it expedient to acquaint your Honor with the above, as I fancy they will have the assurance of asking the privileges due to an embassy, when in strict justice they ought to be hanged as spies of the worse sort."[10]

In his correspondence to Dinwiddie, Washington also referred to Tanacharison's appraisal of Jumonville's force as further justification of his attacking the French party. Washington added a warning to the lieutenant governor of the consequences of releasing LaForce. "The sense of the Half-King on this subject is, that they [the French] have bad hearts, and that this is a mere pretense; that they never designed to come to us but in a hostile manner, and if we were so foolish as to let them go again, he never would assist us in taking another of them. Besides, LaForce would, if released, I really think, do more to our disservice, than fifty other men, as he is a person whose active spirit leads him into all parties, and has brought him acquainted with all parts of the country. Add to this a perfect use of the Indian tongue, and a great influence with the Indians. He ingenuously enough confessed, that, as soon as he saw the commission and instructions, he believed, and then said he expected some such tendency, though he pretends to say he does not believe the commander [Jumonville] had any other than a good design."[11] Of course, unknown to Washington, Tanacharison, in his message to Contrecœur, attempted to fan the flames of the developing war by describing Washington's actions concerning the death of Jumonville in the worst possible way.

9

The Half-King Gets His War

We have with Natures assistance made a good intrenchment and by clearing the Bushes out of these Meadows prepar'd a charming field for an encounter. —Washington to Dinwiddie

On Thursday, May 30, 1754, after having returned to Great Meadows, Washington sent the French prisoners under a guard of 20 men commanded by Lieutenant John West (?–1777) to Lieutenant Governor Dinwiddie, who was on his way to Winchester. At the same time he immediately began to prepare for French retaliation with the construction of a more substantial fortification at Great Meadows. His journal entry for May 30 read, "Detached Lieutenant West, and Mr. Spiltdorph, to take the prisoners to Winchester with a guard of twenty men. Began to erect a fort with small palisades, fearing that when the French should hear the news of that defeat we may be attacked by considerable forces."[1]

Work on the Great Meadows fortification was initially carried out at a furious pace. On Friday, May 31, 1754, Washington wrote to his brother John Augustine Washington (1736–1787), relating the engagement in the ravine, and Washington's expectation of a French attack.

To John Augustine Washington
Camp at Great Meadow
May 31, 1754

Since my last we arrived at this place, where three days ago we had an engagement with the French, that is, a party of our men with one of theirs. Most of our men were out upon other detachments, so that I had scarcely 40 men remaining under my command, and about 10 or 12 Indians; nevertheless we obtained a most signal victory. The battle lasted about 10 or 15 minutes, with sharp firing on both sides, till the French gave ground and ran, but for no purpose. There were 12 killed of the French, among whom was Mons. De Jumonville, their commander, and 21 taken prisoners, among whom are Mess. La Force and Drouillon, together with two cadets. I have sent them to his honour the Governor, at Winchester, under a guard of 20 men, conducted by Lieutenant West. We had but one man killed, and two or three wounded. Among the wounded on our side was Lieutenant Waggener, but no danger, it is hoped, will ensue. We expect every hour to be attacked by a superior force, but if they forebear one day longer, we shall be prepared for them. We have already got entrenchments, are about a pallisado which I hope will be finished to-day. The Mingoes have struck the French and I hope will give a good blow before they have done. I expect 40 odd of them here tonight, which, with our fort and some reinforcements from Col. Fry, will enable us to exert our noble courage with spirit.

P.S. I fortunately escaped without any wound, for the right wing, where I stood, was exposed to and received all the enemy's fire, and it was the part where the man was killed, and the rest wounded. I heard the bullets whistle, and believe me, there is something charming in the sound.[2]

On Saturday, June 1, 1754, Tanacharison, Queen Aliquippa and about 85 Indian men, women and children arrived at the Great Meadows encampment. Now that the war he worked so hard to provoke appeared to have begun, the half-king wanted to make certain it continued. Washington was glad to have Tanacharison's warriors to augment his small force, but the addition of women and children only threatened to deplete the Virginians' meager rations. Washington suggested that Tanacharison send the women and children away to the east, but the half-king refused and Washington was forced to feed them, since it would have been an intolerable breach of protocol to refuse them food. To keep Washington in a warlike frame of mind, Tanacharison said that a French party from Fort Duquesne had been sent out to "take and kill all the English they should meet."[3] As a result, the half-king said that he sent Scarouady to Logstown with wampum belts and four French scalps to convince the Indians there to join in the war against the French. The result was that soon after, a few additional Indian families arrived at Great Meadows, also wanting to be fed.

By Sunday, June 2, 1754, a rough palisade had been erected, and Washington held a prayer service inside the walls. Washington named the stockade Fort Necessity. The fortification was a circular palisade of upright split logs assumed to have been approximately seven feet high[4] and about 50 feet in diameter. The palisade wall was constructed of split white oak logs with the flat side facing outward. Smaller unsplit logs were used to fill the gaps along the inside of the palisade wall. The use of split logs for the palisade was not common in fort construction and indicates the hurried nature in erecting Fort Necessity. Washington certainly wanted to erect defenses quickly in anticipation of an imminent French attack, but he was hampered by a lack of manpower as well as a shortage of time. Split oak logs meant that only half the number of trees had to be felled, and a split log could be carried by two men. He originally had only about 160 men, and 20 of them had been

9. The Half-King Gets His War

sent to escort the prisoners to Winchester. A good number of the rest were on patrols, picket duty, on scouting missions, or too sick to work. Using split logs was an innovative answer. They would provide fairly effective protection against musket fire, and if the French arrived with artillery, even whole logs would not withstand cannon fire. The fort was almost a perfect circle with a three-foot wide gateway at the west side of the palisade. The palisade wall was pierced in several places to allow muskets to be fired from within, but there was no fire step or platform to allow troops to fire over the top of the palisade wall. Tanacharison, who arrived the day before, was certainly not impressed with Washington's defenses. The chief could see that the forest to the south and southeast was well within effective musket range of the fort, and worse, the higher ground there would allow hidden attackers to rain enfilading fire down on the defenders from the cover of the forest. The amateurish placement and dubious construction of the tiny fort caused Tanacharison to reflect that only someone very inexperienced, foolish or mad would attempt to defend it against veteran regulars. The half-king expressed his opinion to Washington in the strongest terms that the fort would be a death-trap once the French arrived, and was very chagrined that Washington paid no attention to his advice. Instead, Washington insisted that the fort could withstand an attack by 500 men. The half-king had staked his authority and indeed his reputation on backing Washington, and was disgusted that the young Virginian was going to risk it all by trying to defend "that little thing upon the meadow" as Tanacharison disdainfully referred to Washington's fort.

On Wednesday, June 5, an Indian arrived who had been at Fort Duquesne, and from him Washington first learned of Mouceau's escape from the attack in the ravine. The young commander now knew that Contrecœur was aware of the English attack on Jumonville's party, and therefore the French commander could be expected to retaliate at any time. The Indian said that Mouceau could scarcely walk after having spent six days barefoot and starving during his return to Fort Duquesne. Washington was not aware that Tanacharison's messenger had already informed Contrecœur of the death of Jumonville and a third of his men, and the captivity of the survivors of the fight in the ravine.

Realizing that Contrecœur was now aware that hostilities had taken place between French and English troops, Washington was impatient for the arrival of Colonel Fry and especially the reinforcements Fry was bringing with him. Washington was concerned about the ability of his small force of raw militia to mount any sort of effective defense against Contrecœur's regulars. In addition, he was anticipating Colonel Fry's arrival so that Fry would take over command of the defense of Great Meadows and bear the brunt of the decision-making now that a full-scale battle was certain to erupt at any time.

However, on Thursday, June 6, 1754, Christopher Gist arrived at Great Meadows with the grave announcement that Colonel Joshua Fry had been severely injured by a fall from his horse, and after lingering for a few days, Fry died at Wills Creek on Friday, May 31, 1754. Gist's message added that because of the death of Fry, Dinwiddie had elevated the 22-year-old Washington to the rank of colonel. Washington was to remain in command of the English troops until such time as Colonel James Innes arrived with his contingent of reinforcements. Innes would then take over as commander-in-chief of the expedition, and Washington would be his second-in-command. In the meantime, Innes and his troops were dawdling ineffectually across Virginia and would not reach Winchester for more than another month, much too late to be of any use to Washington at Great Meadows. When they finally reached Winchester, where they received word of Washington's defeat at Great Meadows, most of Innes's force simply dispersed and returned home.

Washington realized that he was now principally responsible for mounting an effective defense against the French troops, should they attack before Innes arrived. Gist told Washington that Major George Muse was bringing in the three companies that had been recruited by Fry, and because of the death of Fry, Muse was promoted to lieutenant colonel and was now Washington's second-in-command. Adam Stephen was promoted to major and Jacob Van Braam was promoted to captain. Gist also told Washington that the French prisoners under Lieutenant West had arrived at Winchester and their capture appeared to have caused "great satisfaction to the Governor."[5]

The news of Colonel Fry's death spurred Washington to complete the defenses at Great Meadows. Construction on the fort had begun as soon as Washington returned from his encounter with Jumonville, but now that he did not expect anyone to take over command in the short term, he wanted to make the fort as strong as possible to withstand the expected French attack. The rough palisade had been hurriedly erected by Sunday, June 2, 1754, but now the troops worked to improve the total defenses. Washington's available manpower presented a problem. With 20 men escorting the prisoners to Winchester, his available force at Great Meadows consisted of approximately 140 raw troops plus about 40 or 50 Indian warriors. Contrecœur, on the other hand, reportedly had 2,000 or so veteran French regulars that he could send against the Virginians. The situation improved somewhat when on Sunday, June 9, the first of Washington's long anticipated reinforcements arrived. Lieutenant Colonel George Muse (1720–1790), Captain Robert Stobo (1726–1770), and Captain Andrew Lewis (1720–1781) commanded the three companies of reinforcements that marched into the Great Meadows encampment.

While he was thankful for the additional manpower, Washington was somewhat chagrined to see that the total of all three companies comprised only about 140 men or about the normal compliment of one full-strength company.[6] With their arrival, Washington now had about 280 troops with which to face the French, but he still did not have any artillery. Muse brought in nine swivel-guns, which were the only weaponry larger than a musket available to Washington at Great Meadows. The new arrivals also reported that the independent company of regulars from South Carolina had reached Wills Creek, and would soon arrive at Great Meadows.

Captain Stobo, who was recognized as a military engineer, took on the task of improving the Great Meadows defenses. Realizing that the 50-foot, circular Fort Necessity was far too small to be effectively defended from within

Reconstructed Fort Necessity (photograph by author).

Reconstructed Fort Necessity showing the wooded high ground near the fort. The white sign designates the forest edge at the time of the battle (photograph by author).

the walls alone, Stobo laid out protective earthworks to expand the defensive perimeter. There were now about 300 troops and Indian warriors at Great Meadows, with 100 or so South Carolina regulars expected at any time. How best to deploy defenses for about 400 troops was Stobo's main question. The interior circumference of the fort was about 155 feet, and could at best accommodate 50 defenders along the inside walls. Since time was believed to be critical, the quickest way to expand the defensive position was to construct earthworks around the perimeter of the fort. The most critical area was to the south of the fort where the forest was within musket range, and that was where Stobo concentrated his efforts. A number of men were detailed to construct a log storehouse in the center of the fort to be used as a powder magazine and to store supplies. At the same time another group labored at digging entrenchments outside the fort. The two V-shaped entrenchments were laid out with the respective points aiming southeast and northwest of the fort. The trenches

Reconstructed Fort Necessity showing earthworks and mounted swivel-gun (photograph by author).

could only be dug to a depth of about two feet before reaching the water table. Dirt taken from the ditch was piled outside the trench to form a parapet for additional protection, and most likely additional dirt was added in an attempt to raise the parapet to a height of at least four and one-half feet above the floor of the trench. However, even with the earthworks, the defenses were not very suitable for 400 men. Washington's troops would be compacted to a point where enemy fire into the mass of men would likely hit someone.

Work continued at a frantic pace at Great Meadows. It seemed every time a patrol returned or a visitor arrived, they brought more rumors of advancing French troops. Indians that came into the encampment claimed that a large party of 90 or more French regulars were in the area. On Tuesday, June 11, 1754, Washington sent out a scouting party, and the next day, two of his scouts returned with news that a small party of French soldiers had been spotted in the forest. The next day, Wednesday, June 12, Washington led a detachment of about 130 troops and 30 Indians to reconnoiter the French. He gave Muse orders to continue work on the defenses, place all ammunition and supplies in the fort, and establish a strong perimeter guard.

Washington had not travelled far before he encountered a group of Indians who had nine French deserters with them. The deserters said that about 400 French reinforcements were expected at Fort Duquesne, but they also claimed that as many as 100 troops at Fort Duquesne were eager to desert. They added that a number of the Ohio Indians, including Delaware and Shawnee, had taken up the hatchet and joined with the French against the English. Washington took the deserters back to Great Meadows and had them clothed and fed, after which he somehow convinced them to write letters to their colleagues at Fort Duquesne who might be inclined to desert.

On about Friday, June 14, 1754,[7] the independent company of South Carolina regulars under command of Captain James Mackay marched smartly into Great Meadows. Washington viewed their arrival with mixed emotions. He was grateful for the additional troops, and being regulars, they were better trained and better equipped than his raw militia. On the other hand, Wash-

Inside palisade and gate of Fort Necessity, with author's wife, Sally Misencik (photograph by author).

9. The Half-King Gets His War

ington realized that maintaining an effective command structure at Great Meadows would be a challenge. He was well aware of the prejudice regular officers had for provincials. Regulars officers believed that no matter how low their rank, they still held a superior position to any provincial officer. Mackay was no different. As a regular officer, Mackay insisted that since his commission

Figure 17. Reconstructed log building inside Fort Necessity, with author (photograph by Sally Misencik).

came from the king himself, he certainly did not think it fitting or proper to take orders from a colonial officer regardless of the colonial's rank. The fact that Washington was 22 years old and completely unschooled in military science did not help matters any. Mackay, born in Scotland, came from a military family, and had come to North America with James Oglethorpe. In addition, he was a veteran of 15 years spent mostly fighting Indians in the south. While Mackay refused to place himself and his men under Washington's command, he wisely did not insist on commanding the Virginia troops. Washington also prudently did not press the issue of overall command, which resulted in a de facto split in the command structure. MacKay and Washington remained coolly cordial to each other. However, the South Carolinians established their own separate camp at Great Meadows, and Mackay refused to share a common password or countersign with the Virginians. In some cases Mackay's men even declined to return salutes.[8] Worse yet, Mackay would not put his men to work to improve the defenses, construct roads, or engage in any other manual labor. Washington wrote to Dinwiddie, complaining that "Captain Mackay says, that it is not in his power to oblige his Men to work upon the Road, unless he will engage them a Shilling Sterling a Day, which I would not choose to do; and to suffer them to March at their ease, whilst our faithful Soldiers are laboriously employed, carry's an air of such distinction that it is not to be wondered at if the poor fellows were to declare the hardship of it. He also declares to me that this is not particular to his Company only, but that no Soldiers subject to Martial law can be obliged to do it for less. I therefore shall continue to compleat the work we have begun with my poor fellows; we shall have the whole credit, as none others have assisted."[9] Washington added, "I can very confidentially say that his [Mackay's] absence would tend to the public advantage."[10]

Tanacharison observed this turmoil in the British command with a growing amount of consternation. He had worked hard to force a fight between England and France, but it appeared that the English troops were more interested in fighting among themselves. Washington sensed the Indians' unease and attempted to assuage it. Altogether about 25 Indian families comprising roughly 85 individuals were at Great Meadows. Washington realized that the Indians were becoming increasingly nervous about the Virginians' abilities to defend themselves against the French, much less protect the Indians who had sided with the English. Tanacharison, who had hoped to bring all of the Ohio Indians over to the side of the English, was beginning to realize that goal was hopeless. The powerful, veteran French army exuded professionalism, efficiency and competence, while the British appeared incapable of building adequate defenses or even of maintaining effective interaction among themselves.

9. The Half-King Gets His War

The Ohio Indians by and large believed it was in their interest to side with the French, and now they considered it suicidal to even consider going over to the English. The few Ohio Indians who may have been inclined toward the British would now rather wait and see how the situation developed before declaring themselves. However, those Indians at Great Meadows who had taken the overt action of joining the English felt very vulnerable indeed. Washington was aware of Tanacharison's trepidation, which infected the other Indians at Great Meadows, and he attempted to bind them more firmly to the British cause before they melted away into the forest, or worse yet, joined with the French. In a ceremonial gesture, Washington distributed wampum, medals, and other gifts to the Indians and bestowed on Tanacharison the name "Dinwiddie," which he told the half-king meant "the Head of All." Returning the compliment, Tanacharison reaffirmed the name "Connotaucarious,"[11] or "Town Destroyer," for Washington. The ceremonial council seemed to be going very well in strengthening the bond with the Indians, until Washington committed a faux pas that the half-king interpreted as an insult. During the council, Queen Aliquippa let it be known that she felt that she was getting too old to conduct business for her people, so she was delegating her son Canachquasy to take over for her in council. Without considering the consequences, Washington publicly bestowed the name "Colonel Fairfax" upon Canachquasy, telling him that the name meant "The First in Council."[12] While this pleased Queen Aliqippa and Canachquasy, it greatly irked Tanacharison, who felt that naming the young warrior "The First in Council" diminished his own stature among the Indians.

Mackay's intransigence in refusing to allow his men to do manual labor, either in preparing the defenses of Great Meadows or in road building, forced Washington and his Virginians to go it alone. While the South Carolina regulars lolled about their camp, the Virginia troops sweltered in the hot sun, putting the finishing touches on the small, palisaded fort, and the construction of entrenchments and earthworks. He also employed his men in clearing brush for a considerable distance around the fort, so that the fort's defenders would have visually unimpeded fields of fire. By the 16th of June, there was still no sign of the French, and Washington decided to leave MacKay's troops to guard Great Meadows, while he took most of the remainder of his Virginia troops over the ridge to Gist's plantation with the thought of constructing defenses there. The journey over Chestnut Ridge was a nightmare. Even when traversing the mountain by the narrow Nemacolin Trail, the route was arduous, but now that Washington was dragging wagons over the forbidding ridge, a road had to be hacked, dug and graded through the virgin forest with trees often five feet in diameter blocking the way. Wagons broke down and had to be either

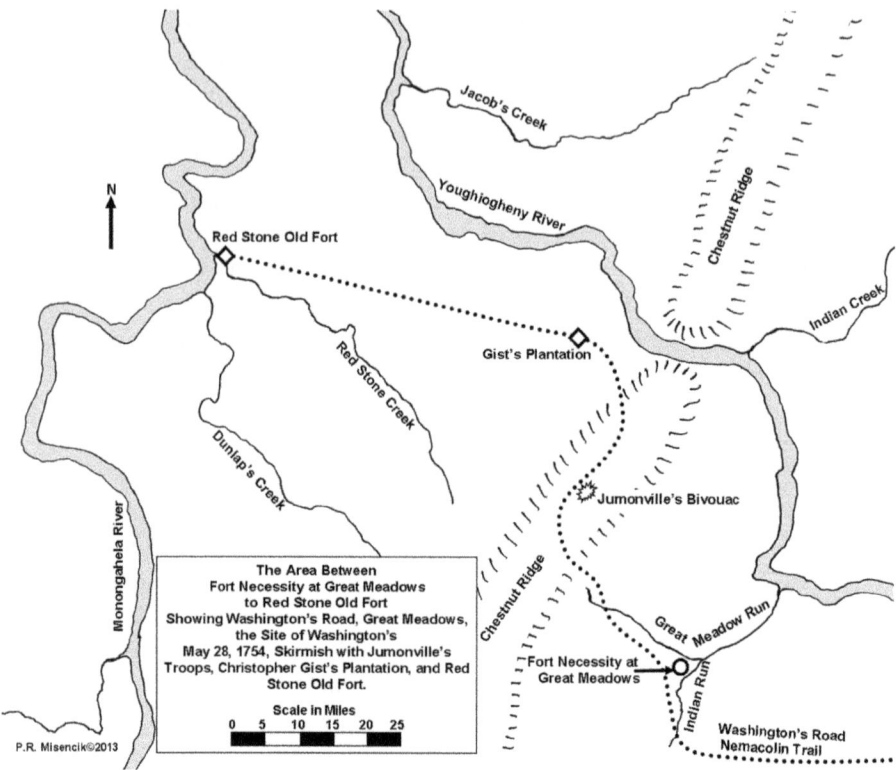

Figure 18. The area between Great Meadows and Red Stone Old Fort.

painstakingly repaired or cannibalized for parts, and many of the horses dropped dead from the exertion of struggling up the steep grade. Most of the Indians accompanying the Virginians became exasperated at the slow pace and returned to Great Meadows. Even Tanacharison did not accompany Washington to Gist's, but promised to join him later there. It took almost two weeks to cover the roughly 13 miles to Gist's plantation, but even before they arrived Washington sent out runners inviting the Ohio Indians to come to the plantation for a council. Washington sent a messenger back to Great Meadows asking Tanacharison and his Indians to come to Gist's plantation, and he also asked Mackay to join him there.

Washington arrived at Gist's plantation on about Thursday, June 27, 1754, and immediately began to fortify the place as best as he could. The Virginians tore down Gist's fences and used the timbers to start construction of a small palisade, while at the same time Gist's house was being fortified as much as possible. Washington still hoped to move his base to Red Stone, but he needed

Trace of Washington's road atop Chestnut Ridge. The road was improved by Braddock's army the following year (photograph by author).

to have ready defenses to fall back on in case the French arrived. So while most of the men toiled to fortify Gist's, Washington detached Captain Lewis with 60 men to continue building the road toward Red Stone. At the same time, he sent another small detachment under Captain William Polson[13] to scout out the whereabouts of any approaching French force.

Several Ohio Indians were already at Gist's plantation when Washington arrived, and more of the Delaware, Shawnee, Wyandot, and Mingo were steadily coming into the plantation. Washington held a council with the Indians to attempt to gain their loyalty and their assurance that they would support the British in a war against the French. In that respect the council was a failure; the majority of the Ohio Indians would have nothing to do with Washington's plan to battle the French. In fact a number of the Indians at the council had been sent there by the French to act as spies. They were to report on the strength and intentions of the British force, and also to gauge the loyalties of the Indians attending the council. True to their custom, most of the Indians at the council criticized the French and avowed their loyalty and friendship to the English, but in the short time he had been on the frontier, Washington had learned enough of Indian diplomacy not to be deceived. When the council ended, the Indians melted away. Even Tanacharison, who had arrived in time for the council, departed with his Mingos. Washington was left with only a few Delaware Indians who agreed to stay and act as scouts.

Mackay and his independent company arrived at Gist's on the evening of Friday, June 28, 1754, and Washington called the officers together for a series of councils of war to consider a prudent strategy. At first, they decided to continue to fortify Gist's plantation, but it wasn't long before the impracticality of that plan was realized. With the French reportedly approaching in large numbers, it would simply take too long to construct adequate fortifications at Gist's. Washington and his officers unanimously decided to return to Great Meadows where better defenses had already been prepared and where the long-awaited supplies and reinforcements would more quickly be received. Some officers even suggested that it might be more sensible to retreat as far as Wills Creek until sufficient troops and artillery could be amassed to successfully challenge the French. In any case, remaining at Gist's was out of the question. Washington received a series of reports that as many as 1,600 French and Indians were on the march and were heading for Gist's plantation, and it was imperative that they begin their withdrawal as soon as possible. In the minutes of the council of war, Washington wrote that he had learned from deserters that the French were expecting additional reinforcements, but worse, two English deserters had informed the French of the number, situation, and present deployment of the English troops. With an attack by a superior force imminent, there wasn't time to tarry. The defensive works around Fort Necessity were fairly complete and the bulk of Washington's meager food supplies, with about 25 head of cattle, was located there.[14] Washington concluded that in the short term, Great Meadows would be the better location to face the French army.

Washington's force began the trek back to Great Meadows almost immediately, departing Gist's on Sunday, June 30, 1754. Since many of the wagons and horses had been destroyed on the journey to Gist's, the troops had to abandon much of their baggage and equipment on the return march to Great Meadows. Some of the few remaining wagons were pulled by Virginia troops for want of horses. It became necessary for the officers to give up their saddle mounts so they could be pressed into service as pack animals. Even Washington gave up his mount to be used as a packhorse, which was used to carry military equipment. Rather than abandon his personal effects, Washington paid the generous sum of four pistoles[15] to soldiers whom he engaged to carry part of his personal baggage back to Great Meadows.[16]

While the Virginians suffered from hauling their supplies and equipment back over the mountain, the independent company under Mackay refused to help, claiming it was not an appropriate occupation for a regular soldier of the king.[17] Instead, Mackay's company marched out as they had marched in, carrying only their own personal arms and baggage. This, of course, further eroded the morale of the Virginia troops, who suffered terribly in dragging their equipment on the road they had so arduously carved over Chestnut Ridge. What irked them more was the idea that on their road, the better paid and better fed independent company leisurely marched without lending a hand, even in the most difficult situations.

Washington's troops reached Great Meadows in the evening of Monday, July 1, 1754, and as soon as they arrived, Washington conducted a thorough inspection of the troops. The Virginians in particular were totally exhausted from transporting themselves and their equipment and supplies back from Gist's plantation. In addition, many of the troops sustained injuries, while others were sick from fatigue and meager rations. None of the troops had eaten any bread for the previous eight days, and, in fact, had scarcely eaten any food at all. Washington realized that the troops desperately needed nourishment, rest and recuperation before they could either fight or retreat farther. Any thought of continuing on to Wills Creek was completely out of the question. When the French arrived, as they were expected at any time, Washington would have to fight them at Great Meadows.

The only good news that awaited Washington upon his return to Great Meadows was word that about 20 days earlier, two independent companies of regulars from New York had arrived at Alexandria, Virginia, and it was assumed that by now, they should have at least reached Wills Creek en route to Great Meadows. Washington immediately sent a dispatch rider to meet them and hurry them on as quickly as possible. Unfortunately, the New York independent companies had not yet departed Alexandria, because of a lack of appropriation from the Virginia Burgesses to fund their expedition. Lieutenant Governor Dinwiddie had solicited the New York companies without advising the Virginia House of Burgesses. The Virginia Assembly then balked at paying for New York troops that were engaged in the king's business. In fact the Yorkers, as they were called, would not reach Wills Creek until September 1754, much too late to be of any assistance to Washington at Great Meadows.

By Tuesday, July 2, 1754, some of the troops were fit enough to work on improving Fort Necessity and the earthworks surrounding the small fort. Indian scouts were regularly arriving with news of a large number of French troops that was advancing in their direction. This information spurred the healthier men to work harder and also inspired many of the sick to do the best they could to help improve the defenses. While the troops in camp worked feverishly on the defensive positions, Washington ordered most of the remaining men into the forest to form a double ring of pickets around the camp to provide as much warning as possible of the enemy's arrival. Tanacharison observed these efforts with increasing frustration, and he stridently advised Washington that any attempt to fight the French under the existing circumstances was not only foolish, but also suicidal. He argued that the flimsy palisade that Washington called a fort was not large enough to protect the majority of the men, and would not even provide suitable protection for those who were inside the walls. Worse yet, those troops who were huddled in the ditches outside the palisade would be well within musket range of the surrounding forest. Not only would the nearby forest provide cover to the enemy, but they would also be on higher ground with the ability to fire down into the entrenchments and even the fort itself. Tanacharison insisted that the only sensible course of action was to abandon the foolish idea of engaging the French at Great Meadows and retreat to Wills Creek until a larger, more potent army could be assembled. Washington not only ignored the half-king's advice, but also angered the chief by ordering him and his Indians on scouting missions and to assist in the work on the defenses, as if they were subject to British military command.

Early the next morning, the camp was alerted when a soldier who had been wounded by the enemy while on picket duty was brought into camp. A short time later, at about nine o'clock, other picket workers rushed into camp with the alarming news that a large body of French troops and their Indian allies were only a few miles away. To make matters worse, it started to rain, and as the morning wore on, the rain increased in intensity. Washington ordered the troops to take up their battle formation, and as the men maneuvered they could hear the sound of distant firing as the English pickets were driven in by the advancing French and Indians. Twenty-two-year-old Washington hurriedly deployed his troops, and likely assessed his odds for the coming fight. The reports he received indicated that as many as a 1,500 French and Indians were coming against him, but his Virginia militia only numbered about 250 effectives, due to sickness, injuries, and desertions. Of course, Mackay's regulars were there and would increase Washington's force by another hundred men, but Washington was not sure how or even if Mackay would use them against the French. Regardless, even with Mackay's troops, Washington faced daunting odds of better than three to one. In addition to his manpower concerns, the incessant rain was causing other difficulties. Ironically, when Washington first arrived at Great Meadows, he praised it as a "charming field for an encounter," but now he must have been having second thoughts; the place was rapidly turning into a muddy swamp. Having earlier touted the streams crossing the meadow as a source of ample fresh water, it was becoming apparent that the water that nurtured the lush meadow was a disadvantage in rainy weather. The ground was essentially a saturated bog, and during the rain, the hundreds of plodding feet quickly turned the area surrounding the fort into a thick, viscous quagmire. To add to his consternation, Washington discovered that the Indians, whom he had relied on for scouting and as additional manpower in the coming fight, had all disappeared.

To Tanacharison, Washington's plan to fight the French at Great Meadows was madness. The half-king's scouts were consistently bringing in information about the whereabouts and size of the French and Indian force. At the very least, the approaching enemy was considerably larger than Washington's small command. Tanacharison was frustrated by the young commander's unwillingness to heed sound advice and retreat at least to Wills Creek in order to gather sufficient troops that could stand a chance against a veteran French force. Only a fool would fight against the present odds or even attempt to defend "that little thing on the meadow," and the wily Tanacharison was certainly no fool. Disheartened and disgusted that the first battle of the war that he had worked to bring about would undoubtedly end in a defeat for the British forces, Tanacharison and his Indians slipped away into the forest leaving Washington to fight the French without him.

The sounds of sporadic gunfire grew nearer, and shortly before eleven o'clock in the morning, the pickets who had manned the perimeter in the surrounding forest came rushing headlong into camp, shouting that the French were close behind them. Washington had previously ordered his troops to form up under arms, and now they stood in the meadow just outside the trenches, nervously peering into the heavy rainfall for any sign of the enemy. They didn't have to wait very long. At about eleven o'clock in the morning, out of the pouring rain and mist, a long line of French infantrymen materialized at the western edge of the forest about 600 yards away.

10

Battle at Great Meadows

> *As our intention has never been to trouble the peace and good harmony which reigns between the two friendly princes, but only to revenge the assassination which has been done one of our officers....* —Captain Sieur Louis Coulon de Villiers in Articles of Capitulation

Washington's troops, including the independent company of regulars, were aligned in battle order on the meadow in the customary European manner of engagement. The rain by this time was a steady downpour and the main focus of the troops was to try to keep their powder dry, which was a challenge with eighteenth-century firelocks. Washington had assumed that the French would also deploy on the meadow, and the two forces, arrayed in line abreast formations, would fire volleys at each other from ever decreasing distances until a climactic bayonet charge would decide the winner. The maximum effective range of a musket was around 100 yards and generally the opposing forces closed to less than that distance before engaging in musketry. The English troops, however, were surprised when the French soldiers loosed an ineffective volley from almost 600 yards away. That prompted Washington's men to respond with a volley from their swivel guns that were mounted on posts near the fort, but despite the fact that they had a longer effective range, 600 yards was far too distant to cause much, if any, damage.

The French commander was Captain Sieur Louis Coulon de Villiers (1710–1757), the half-brother of Ensign Joseph Coulon de Jumonville, who was killed by Washington's force in the fight in the glen on Tuesday, May 28, 1754. Coulon de Villiers had a notable career in the French colonial regular army. In 1733, he had been severely wounded in a fight against the Sauk Indians, a battle in which his father and one brother were killed. He was perhaps the most distinguished warrior of a family of military men, and was commonly referred to as "Le Grand Villiers."[1] In 1748, he was given command of Fort des Miamis, and in 1753 he was promoted to Captain. In 1754, Governor-General

Duquesne sent Villiers in command of 600 Canadian troops and 100 Indians to the Forks in support of Contrecœur's efforts to secure the Ohio territory for France. Villiers arrived at Fort Duquesne on Wednesday, June 26, 1754, where he learned of the ambush and death of his half-brother Jumonville 29 days previous. Villiers immediately requested and was granted command of the force that would avenge the death of his half-brother, and also drive the British out of territory claimed by France. On June 28, 1754, Villiers led his force of about 600 French and Canadian troops and about 150 Indians[2] out of Fort Duquesne. The veteran force moved rapidly. They passed Red Stone Creek on June 30, and arrived at Gist's plantation in the morning of July 1. As Villiers surveyed the abandoned and unfinished defenses at Gist's plantation, Indian scouts brought in a Virginian who had deserted from Washington's force. The man told Villiers that Washington's troops had left Gist's only two days previous. He said that when Washington learned of the French advance, he led his troops back to Great Meadows where they had previously begun building fortifications. After spending the night at Gist's, Villiers hurried his force over the road Washington had so painstakingly constructed in hopes that he could catch the English force before they had time to prepare formidable defenses. He wrote in his journal, "The weather was inkling to rain, but I saw the necessity of anticipating the enemy in the works he might construct. I even flattered myself that he would be less on his guard in such bad weather."[3]

Villiers reached the site of the fight in the glen at about noon of Tuesday, July 2, 1754, where he found the body of his half-brother Jumonville and the other scalped and mutilated bodies of the ill-fated party. After burying the dead, Villiers and his men set off again through the steadily increasing rain. The French and Indian force descended Chestnut Ridge and camped for the night a few miles from Great Meadows. Early in the morning of Wednesday, July 3, 1754, the French cautiously continued their advance and almost immediately began to encounter Washington's pickets that were screening Great Meadows. The veteran French and their Indian allies steadily drove the English pickets before them until about eleven o'clock in the morning, when Villiers caught sight of the palisades of Fort Necessity through the rain and mist. After forming up his men at the edge of the forest, Villiers, for some reason, ordered a volley fired in the direction of the English troops at the impossible range of about 600 yards, to which Washington's troops responded with a fusillade from their swivel-guns.

The exchange of gunfire certainly announced the opening of hostilities, and Washington anticipated that the French infantry would march toward them in line of battle while regularly loosing volleys of musketry. Expecting a conventional battle, the Virginia commander ordered his troops to stand firm

10. Battle at Great Meadows   141

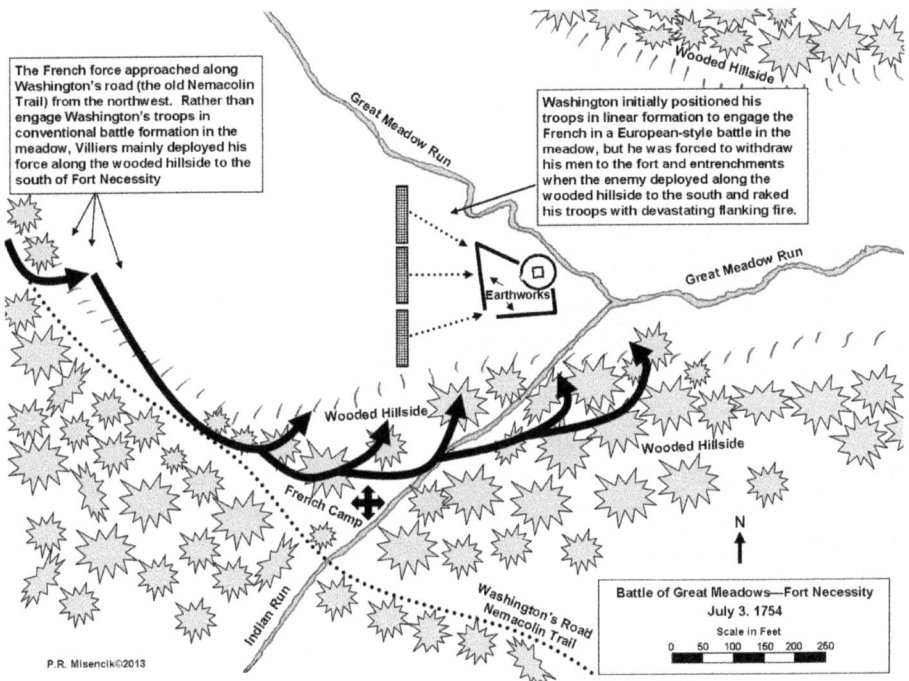

Figure 20. Battle of Great Meadows—July 3, 1754.

and to hold their fire until the French closed within musket range. However, despite their superior numbers, the French were not inclined to leave the forest and march forward onto the field in straight lines to trade murderous volleys with the English. Villiers instead had his men rapidly deploy along the forest edge, but in doing so, he uncharacteristically committed a tactical blunder by presenting his flank to Washington's troops. Washington, however, did not take advantage of the French error by advancing his troops to smash the French flank. Instead, he ordered his swivel-guns to fire at the French at a range that was far too great to do any effective execution. Villiers described this first meeting in his journal: "I sent scouts who were to go close to the camp; and twenty more to support them; and I advanced myself in order; when some of my people returned to tell me that we were discovered; and that the English approached in order of battle to attack us: as it was said that they were close to me, I put my troops in order of battle, and in a manner suited to woods fighting. It was not long before I perceived that my scouts had led me wrong; and I gave order to my troops to advance toward that side from which I apprehended an attack. As we were not acquainted with the ground, we presented our flank to the fort from whence they began to cannonade us."[4]

While Villiers's troops deployed along the forest edge, Washington's troops continued to maintain their formation just ahead of the trenches surrounding Fort Necessity. Villiers, a veteran of the previous war (King George's War, 1740–1748), did not consider the option of engaging in a brutal face-to-face exchange of musketry at point-blank range. Instead he opted to deploy his men in whatever manner would give him the greatest tactical advantage. He sent the majority of his French and Indians into the tree-covered hills to the south of the small English fort, and from a distance of about 60 yards, they began to fire from the cover of the tree line into Washington's troops that were lined up in the meadow below. The raking fire from the woods was devastating as the heavy musket balls tore into the ranks of Washington's men. Stunned by the ferocious fire from the forest edge, Lieutenant Colonel George Muse, Washington's second-in-command, pulled his Second Division from the line without orders and took refuge in the trenches. This action would cause Muse to be tainted as a coward. The unexpected withdrawal of Muse's division exposed the Carolina independent company to the galling French fire, and Washington had no choice but to order all of the troops to fall back to the fort and the trenches for protection. There they tried to defend themselves as best they could while they awaited the expected French assault. The rain was falling in torrents and the ground was a quagmire. Worse yet, the trenches were completely filled with water, making it almost impossible to keep cartridges dry or prevent muskets from fouling. Fortunately for Washington's troops, Villiers had no intention of launching an assault against the Fort Necessity positions. Instead the French and Indians sniped at anything that moved, killing horses, cattle and dogs along with the troops huddled in and around the tiny fort. Within a short time, every cow, horse and dog had been killed. Early in the engagement, Washington's men were somehow able to fire several volleys "with great Alacrity and Undauntedness,"[5] but the pouring rain began to render muskets unserviceable until only a desultory and sporadic English gunfire answered the steady French and Indian musketry from the woods. Being sheltered under the canopy of trees, the French and Indians found it somewhat easier to keeps their weapons serviceable.

As the afternoon wore on, it was becoming ever more desperate for the English troops. The numbers of Washington's men killed and wounded were steadily rising, while the French did not appear to have suffered many losses at all. The uneven contest continued for over nine hours, and as dusk approached, Washington surveyed his troops and found that about a third of his men were casualties: either dead or wounded. To add to Washington's woes, soldiers broached the rum supply, thinking it was only a matter of time before they were slaughtered, and within a short time most of the remaining militia troops were roaring drunk. Major Adam Stephen wrote that "by the continued Rains, and Water in the Trenches, the most of our Arms were out of Order, and we had only a Couple of Screws[6] in the whole Regiment to clean them. But what was still worse, it was no sooner dark, that one-half of our Men got drunk."[7] Washington now realized that most of his remaining men would be unable or unfit to defend themselves against an attack by a combined force of French and Indians. From his experience in the fight against Jumonville, he recalled how difficult it was to control the Indians once their bloodlust was up, so the prospect of the Virginians being massacred was very real indeed. Since they were trapped by a superior force, the only apparent option left to Washington and his troops was to try to sell their lives as dearly as possible.

It was totally unexpected when, at about eight o'clock in the evening, the French fire ceased, and a voice called out from the tree line that the French were willing to parley. Washington immediately suspected a deceit of some kind, but in actuality Villiers had concerns of his own. His men were wet and tired from the long march over Chestnut Ridge, and his Indians, who had no interest in siege-type warfare, were threatening to leave the next morning. Fortunately his casualties were very light, with two French and one Indian killed, and 15 French and two Indians wounded. However, of immediate concern was his dwindling supply of ammunition. Villiers had made the choice to travel as lightly and rapidly as possible in his pursuit of Washington, and had anticipated a quick, decisive fight when he caught up with the Virginians. As a result, he did not have the staying power for a drawn-out siege. Villiers wrote in his journal that because of the prolonged firing, "I saw that we would in a little while be without ammunition."[8] Another factor that influenced Villiers was his belief that English reinforcements were nearby and on their way to Great Meadows. His journal states, "Rumor said that the beat of drums and the firing of cannon had been heard in the distance."[9] In fact, there were no English reinforcements nearer than Wills Creek.

When the offer to parley came from the French lines, Washington called back, refusing to allow any member of the French force to enter his lines. In answer, Le Mercier, who was speaking for Villiers, offered safe parole to any of Washington's officers who would come into the French camp to negotiate. Washington didn't believe he had an alternative, so he decided to see what the French would offer in the way of terms. He had only two officers who could speak French, Captain Van Braam and Ensign William La Peyronie. While La Peyronie was from France and very fluent in the French language, Van Braam's first language was Dutch, and as a result, he was not as adept at translating between French and English. To complicate matters, La Peyronie had been seriously wounded during the fight and had to be assisted into the French camp. Even so, they were the only officers among Washington's men who could read, write, and converse in French, so the two were dispatched through the darkness and rain to meet with the French commander.

After the customary exchange of pleasantries, the negotiators got down to business. Van Braam and La Peyronie expected the worst, because everyone realized that the small English force was totally beaten. They were surprised, however, when Villiers stated that since France and England were not at war, he was inclined to offer very generous terms. Washington and his troops would surrender their positions with full honors of war, and with flags flying and drums beating, they would be allowed to return home with all their personal effects. They would also be permitted to take their weapons and one swivel-gun with them. Taking the swivel-gun was in accordance with "the honors of war," where a defeated force was generally allowed to haul away at least one piece of artillery. Villiers added that Washington must accept the terms quickly, because 500 more Indians were expected, and the French commander was concerned that once they arrived, he would not be able to control them and prevent a massacre if Washington delayed in accepting the terms of capitulation.

Van Braam and La Peyronie returned to Fort Necessity and related what transpired. Washington was surprised by the generosity of Villiers's terms, and he also realized that he had no choice; they were at the mercy of the French. Washington only insisted that the terms be put in writing, so he sent Van Braam back to the French camp to secure the document. La Peyronie remained at Fort Necessity because was too weak from his wounds to take further part in the negotiations.

After what seemed like a very lengthy absence, Van Braam finally returned with two copies of the articles of capitulation, which were both written in French. Translated, the terms read:

> Capitulation granted by Mons. De Villiers, Captain of infantry and commander of troops of his most Christian majesty, to those English troops actually in the fort of Necessity which was built on the lands of the King's dominions July the 3rd, at eight o'clock at night, 1754.
>
> As our intention had never been to trouble the peace and good harmony which reigns between the two friendly princes, but only to revenge the assassination which has been done on one of our officers, bearer of a summons, upon his party, as also to hinder any establishment on the lands of the dominions of the King, my master. Upon these considerations, we are willing to grant protection of favor, to all the English that are in the said fort, upon conditions hereafter mentioned

Article 1

We grant the English commander to retire with all garrisons, to return peaceably into his own country, and we promise to hinder his receiving any insult from us French, and to restrain as much as shall be in our power the Savages that are with us

Article 2

He shall be permitted to withdraw and to take with him whatever belongs to them except the artillery, which we reserve for ourselves

Article 3

We grant them the honors of war; they shall come out with drums beating, and with a small piece of cannon, wishing to show by this means that we treat them as friends

Article 4

As soon as these Articles are signed by both parties they shall take down the English flag

Article 5

Tomorrow at daybreak a detachment of French shall receive the surrender of the garrison and take possession of the aforesaid fort

Article 6

Since the English have scarcely any horses or oxen left, they shall be allowed to hide their property, in order that they may return to seek for it after they shall have recovered their horses; for this purpose they shall be permitted to leave such number of troops as guards as they may think proper, under this condition that they give their word of honor that they will work on no establishment either in the surrounding country or beyond the Highlands during one year beginning from this day

Article 7

Since the English have in their power an officer and two cadets, and, in general all the prisoners whom they took when assassinated Sieur de Jumonville they now promise to send them with an escort to Fort Duquesne, situated on Belle River, and to secure the safe performance of this treaty article, as was as of the treaty, Messrs. Jacob Van Braam and Robert Stobo, both Captains shall be delivered to us as hostages until the arrival of our French and Canadians herein before mentioned. We on our part declare that we shall give them an escort to send back in safety the two officers who promise us our French in two months and a half at the latest.

Made out in duplicate on one of the posts of our blockhouse the same day and year as before.[10]

As soon as Van Braam returned, Washington and his officers studied the document throughout the night. According to Villiers's verbal instructions to Van Braam, Washington was to signal his acceptance of the terms by not raising his flag the following morning. The rain was pouring down, and the only available lights were a few flickering candles. As a result, Washington and his officers relied on Van Braam's translation, which likely was based in large part on his recollections of his conversation with Villiers. Eventually, Washington and Mackay both signed the document. The terms in themselves were as negotiated, and generous indeed for the circumstances, however, what they missed and would later became an issue were the phrases that read "only to revenge the assassination which has been done on one of our officers, bearer of a summons, upon his party" and "the prisoners whom they took when assassinated Sieur de Jumonville." In essence, by signing the document, Washington had admitted to the assassination of a diplomatic emissary.

Later, when he realized the full import of that admission, Washington and his officers placed the blame squarely on Van Braam for his faulty translation. In fact, the Dutch officer was vilified for knowingly presenting the terms *l'assasin* and *l'assasinat* as "killed," "loss of" or "the death of" rather than the correct translation, "assassination." Adam Stephen wrote, "When Mr. Van Braam returned with the French Proposals, we were obliged to take the Sense of them by word of Mouth: It rained so heavily that he could not give us a written Translation of them; they were wrote in a bad Hand, on wet and blotted Paper so that no Person could read them but Van Braam who had heard them from the mouth of the French Officer. Every Officer then present, is willing to declare, that there was no such word as Assassination mentioned; the Terms expressed to us were 'the Death of Jumonville.' If it had been mentioned, we could have got it altered, as the French seemed very condescending, and willing to bring Things to a Conclusion."[11] Washington also blamed Van Braam for knowingly or unknowingly influencing him to admit to being an assassin. He wrote, "That we were willfully or ignorantly deceived by our interpreter in regard to the word 'assassination,' I do aver and will to my dying moment; so will every officer who was present. The interpreter was a Dutchman little acquainted with the English tongue, and therefore might not advert to the tone and meaning of the word in English, but whatever his motives were for so doing, certainly it is he called it the 'death' or the 'loss' of the Sieur Jumonville. So we received and so we understood it until, to our great surprise and mortification, we found it otherwise in a literal translation."[12]

Van Braam never was able to escape the disgrace of having been responsible for sullying Washington's honor. In fact, when the house of Burgesses of Virginia subsequently voted to express their thanks to Washington and his officers for their gallant defense at Great Meadows, they specifically and pointedly excluded two officers: Lieutenant Colonel George Muse for cowardice and Captain Jacob Van Braam for treachery in purposely misrepresenting the articles of capitulation. Notwithstanding the fact that the French words *l'assasin* and *l'assasinat* should have caught the attention of Washington at the time, it's easy to understand the 22-year-old commander or his friend Adam Stephen's after-the-fact assertion that they were not aware of the document's true translation. Historians have generally supported the claim that Van Braam purposely misrepresented the translation. This is most likely a result of Washington's later heroic stature as "father of his country," and Parson Mason Locke Weems's (1759–1825) promotion of the legend of Washington, particularly the great man's inability to tell a lie. However, it is reasonable to question whether in fact Van Braam did intentionally mistranslate the words or why he might do so.

One explanation is that Van Braam may have accepted that Jumonville's death was, in fact, a cold-blooded murder that occurred after the French force surrendered in the glen, and after the firing had ceased. After all, Van Braam was present at the time and was undoubtedly as startled as Washington when Tanacharison split the French commander's skull with his tomahawk while Jumonville attempted to read his summons. To Van Braam, the articles of capitulation only mentioned the "assassination" of Jumonville in general and did not refer to Washington as the assassin. Van Braam was fully aware that Tanacharison had murdered the French commander, and the Dutchman likely accepted the term "assassination" in that context. If he glossed over the word in his translation on the night of July 3, 1754, it might have been to present the document in slightly more politically palatable language, in order to have the matter over and done with, especially since the half-king was no longer at Great Meadows. Washington himself was certainly eager to extricate the remainder of his force from an extremely critical situation, and may not have devoted the attention to the document that it deserved.

It was only after the fact that Washington and Stephen attempted to lessen their responsibility of endorsing a document that proved to be not only embarrassing, but would also lead to later questions about their honoring their parole. In addition to the assassination issue, Washington technically violated the terms of the capitulation when he accompanied Braddock into the area less than a year later. In signing the document, he specifically agreed that he and his men were giving their "word of honor that they will work on no establishment either in the surrounding country or beyond the Highlands during one year beginning from this day." Washington offered no explanation why he disregarded that specific article, but Adam Stephen justified it in a bit of convoluted legalese. He wrote, "We obliged ourselves not to attempt an Establishment beyond the Mountains: This was translated to us, 'Not to attempt Buildings or Improvements on the Lands of his Most Christian Majesty.' This we never intended; but denied that he had any Lands there, and therefore thought it needless to dispute that point."[13] In essence, by claiming they only agreed not to trespass on the French king's land, they felt no compunction in marching toward Fort Duquesne during the time of their parole, because they simply denied that the area west of the mountains belonged to the French king.

The British flag was not raised over Fort Necessity the following morning of Thursday, July 4, 1754. That signaled Washington's acceptance of the articles of capitulation. Soon after, Villiers marched his troops down to take possession of the fort. The Indians also came down, and although the French soldiers were able to control them to a degree, the Indians began to pillage the weapons and belongings of Washington's troops. To make matters worse, another large number of Indians had arrived during the night, and though the fight was over, they too wanted to share in the spoils of war. The Indians were not only numerous but also aggressive, and they caused deep concern to Washington's troops by their intimidating behavior. As a result many soldiers did not offer much resistance when the Indians grabbed whatever they wished. The only thing Washington's men wanted at that time was to leave as quickly as possible. Villiers wrote that "the Indians, who had in every respect, complied with my desires, had laid claim to the pillage. I opposed it, but the consternation of the English was so great that they ran away and left behind them even their flag and a pair of the colors."[14] When the French officially took possession of the fort, they found several casks of liquor, and Villiers immediately ordered that it be destroyed, rather than allow it to cause the Indians to become even more unruly, unpredictable, and belligerent. Villiers wrote in his journal that he wanted to prevent any further problems with the Indians, which liquor consumption would have inevitably caused.

Washington and his men prepared as best they could to evacuate Great Meadows, but since they did not have a single horse remaining, everything would have to be carried by the men themselves, even the wounded. Their first task was to bury their dead, and then prepare the wounded for transport. It soon became obvious that several of the badly wounded men could not be moved at all and would have to remain at Great Meadows until wagons from Wills Creek could recover them. With Villiers's approval, Washington left an ensign, a sergeant, and eleven soldiers to care for those left behind and also to guard any personal effects that could not be carried out.

Two others that would remain behind as hostages of the French were Captain Robert Stobo and Captain Jacob Van Braam. In accordance with the terms of the capitulation they would be held hostage until such time as the English released the 21 French prisoners who were captured in the fight with Jumonville and who were now in Williamsburg. It's not certain how Stobo and Van Braam were selected or whether they volunteered. Some credit the fact that they were not married and had no other families in Virginia as the reason they were chosen. Some anecdotal evidence suggests that Stobo volunteered, but Van Braam was assigned. Those troops who were leaving were making the difficult choices of what to carry and what to leave behind. Fearing attacks by the Indians along the way, Washington instructed his troops to take as much ammunition as they could carry; whatever gunpowder they had left over was surreptitiously emptied onto the soggy meadow so neither the French nor the Indians could use it against them. Regardless of the small guard remaining behind, no one doubted that as soon as they departed, the personal effects of Washington's men would be looted. Washington, who was loathe to leave his finery to be pillaged by the French and Indians, offered to sell some to Van Braam, who was staying behind. The Dutchman agreed to buy Washington's silver-fringed broadcloth coat for £6 and his scarlet waistcoat for £7. Other articles of Washington's increased Van Braam's debt to £17, and to settle, the Dutchman assigned two months pay to Washington. Since the hostages were not permitted to have weapons, Captain Stobo gave his sword to an officer in his company.

The French were courteous for the most part and observed the English preparations with very few signs of disrespect. However, one incident was noteworthy. Apparently, a French soldier looking for war souvenirs found an untended portmanteau, so he threw it over his shoulder and carried it off. Major Adam Stephen's servant happened to notice the act and cried out that a Frenchman had run off with Stephen's luggage. Stephen recognized his portmanteau on the shoulder of the Frenchman and immediately took off in pursuit. Upon hearing the commotion he caused, the culprit broke into a run, hoping to disappear among a group of his comrades. Undaunted, Stephen plunged into the mass of men and grabbed the thief, snatched his possession, and sent the offending Frenchman reeling with a sharp kick. Stephen at the time was mud-covered, stockingless, and dressed only in a dirty body shirt and breeches. Two French officers stopped Stephen, admonished him for striking a French soldier, and threatened that his actions were contrary to the terms of the capitulation and could jeopardize the truce. The hot-headed Stephen angrily damned the capitulation and told the French officers that by their actions they themselves had broken its terms already. Shocked at such a saucy and belligerent response from the man they originally supposed was a lowly enlisted man, one of the officers asked Stephen if he was an officer. In answer, Stephen opened his portmanteau and pulled out his crimson, lace trimmed regimental coat and put it on, showing that indeed he was an officer. That diffused the situation. While the French would not tolerate an enlisted man striking one of their own, an officer, regardless of his allegiance, was another matter.

The French officers immediately began chatting with Stephen in a friendly and comradely manner. One mentioned that since the French had demanded hostages for the return of those who were with Jumonville, the English should also demand hostages against the safe return of Stobo and Van Braam. In fact, they would gladly volunteer to be the hostages, because they desired to go to Virginia where, they heard, there were a great many Belles and Mademoiselles.[15]

Finally, at about ten o'clock in the morning, Washington's men were ready to depart. As the English troops formed up for the march, the French with flags flying and drums beating formed up in two long parallel lines through which the defeated English troops would pass. Washington ordered his drums to beat, and with their flags flying high, he and his 293 remaining officers and men, including the wounded, marched as smartly as they were able out of Great Meadows. It was the fourth of July.

Epilogue

The paths of glory lead but to the grave—Thomas Gray—"Elegy Written in a Country Churchyard"

Thus ended 22-year-old George Washington's first major command, and also his association with Tanacharison, the half-king. His campaign was conducted amateurishly, which resulted in a crushing defeat and a humiliating capitulation. A month after the fight at Great Meadows, Tanacharison summed up his dissatisfaction with Washington's leadership:

> The Colonel was a good-natured man, but had no experience; that he took upon him to command the Indians as his slaves, and would have them every day upon the Out Scout, and attack the Enemy by themselves, and that he would by no means take the advice of the Indians; that he lay at one place from one full moon to another, and make no fortifications at all but that little thing upon the meadow, where he thought the French would come up to him in the open field; that had he taken the Half King's advice and make such fortifications as the Half King advised him to make, he certainly would have beat the French off; that the French had acted as great cowards and the English as fools in that engagement; that he [the half-king] had carried off his wife and children; so did the other Indians before the battle begun, because Colonel Washington would never listen to them, but was always driving them on to fight by his direction.[1]

In addition to Washington's inexperience, it was his bad fortune that Captain Sieur Louis Coulon de Villiers was his adversary; he was a hardy, able and wily veteran with more than 20 years of frontier warfare experience. While Villiers was tough, his troops were for the most part tougher. Most were recruited from the hardy coureurs des bois or "woods runners," Canadian frontiersmen who were more at home in the forest with the Indians than in the towns and villages of New France. They knew how to live and fight in the woods, and they generally disdained the European methods of warfare, preferring to fight from cover rather than in the open. Villiers and his troops gave Washington his first lesson on frontier warfare, and to his credit, Washington learned from the experience. He realized that a successful campaign required more than a hodgepodge of troops in the field. It required a well-trained and equipped force, adequate military intelligence, a reliable system for supplies and reinforcements, and a well-developed strategy—none of which Washington had when he embarked on his campaign. Though the capitulation at Great Meadows was a bitter pill for Washington to swallow, he learned from it. It was the last time in his military career that he would suffer the indignity of surrendering.

When Washington marched out of Great Meadows, his force was comprised of 293 officers and men that included a great many wounded. The going was slow and they were only able to cover about three miles before they bivouacked for the night. It took them five days to cover the 51 miles to Wills Creek. During the trek they buried those that had died along the way and they also had to leave some of the more seriously wounded in the care of able-bodied soldiers. When they reached Wills Creek on Tuesday, July 9, 1754, Washington's force numbered only 165 officers and men. Thirty-nine men had been left along the road, and some of the troops simply deserted. In addition, several of the stragglers and some of the wounded left behind were captured or killed by pursuing Indians, who disregarded Villiers's guarantee of safe conduct. Captain Stobo and the French soldier J.C.B. reported that the Indians brought prisoners into Fort Duquesne. J.C.B. recorded that those who were unable to make the trek back to the fort were killed and scalped outright, and the rest who were brought in were forced to run the gauntlet. The Indians tortured some of the English prisoners to death outside the walls of the fort.

Assessing the actual casualties is somewhat difficult since both sides reported different numbers. Washington claimed that as a result of the battle, his force suffered 30 killed, 70 wounded, and 19 missing. Captain Mackay reported that the independent company of regulars sustained 17 casualties, one of which was an officer. It's not certain whether Washington included Mackay's casualties along with the Virginians in his listing. Washington made the extravagant claim that the French lost over 300 killed in the battle, including an unidentified high-ranking officer. Villiers, on the other hand, claimed his force only lost two French and one Indian killed, and 15 French and two Indians wounded. He added that some others of his force received such slight injuries that they did not require medical aid. The French commander reported that they counted 70 or 80 of Washington's force killed or mortally wounded, about twice the number Washington reported. Apparently, both commanders were eager to inflate the damage they caused on their opponent. In addition to his victory, Villiers was also able to boast that "we made the English agree to give us in their own hands, that they had committed an assassination on us, in the camp of my brother," and "we compelled them to evacuate the country as belonging to the most Christian King."[2]

After Washington departed, Villiers methodically destroyed Fort Necessity and burned as much of the timbers as he was able before he began his march back to Fort Duquesne. Before they left, a French soldier, who apparently was pillaging luggage that was left behind, found Washington's portmanteau and discovered his papers and journal, which Villiers took with him. On Friday the fifth of July they arrived at Gist's plantation, where Villiers ordered the buildings burnt to the ground and Washington's incomplete entrenchments demolished. En route to Fort Duquesne they also destroyed the storehouse at Red Stone Creek. Villiers recorded in his journal, "I burned as I went along all the settlements I met with."[3] The French force arrived at Fort Duquesne on Sunday, July 7, 1754, where Villiers turned his command back over to Contrecœur. When Governor-General Duquesne received news of the engagement at Great Meadows, he commended Villiers's victory and also praised his humanity and restraint in sparing so many English lives, despite the fact that the English had killed his half-brother only a short time before.

The war was, in fact, started, but it would take another 20 months before England and France went through the formality of officially declaring it on Saturday, May 15, 1756. Despite not being officially at war, England responded to the French capture of the Forks and the defeat of Washington's little army at Great Meadows with a massive expedition that was intended to send the French reeling back into Canada and reclaim the Ohio territory for England in the process. To accomplish this, Major General Edward V. Braddock (1695–1755) arrived in Virginia in February 1755 with two regiments of regular soldiers. Braddock's grand strategy was a three-pronged assault against New France and the disputed Ohio territory. One part of the plan was to send General William Johnson north against the French stronghold of Fort St. Frédéric, at Crown Point on Lake Champlain. Johnson, the British agent to the Iroquois, was commissioned a major general even though he did not have any credible military experience. The second prong of the plan was to send Massachusetts regiments to reinforce Fort Oswego,[4] where they would interdict French reinforcements from Montréal and would later support Braddock's eventual assault on Fort Niagara. Fort Oswego was constructed on the west side of the mouth of the Oswego River and was strategically located on Lake Ontario between the French forts Frontenac to the north at the source of the Saint Lawrence River and Niagara to the west.

The main part of the campaign's thrust would be led by Braddock himself, who would take his artillery-supported regiments against Fort Duquesne.

After capturing the French stronghold at the Forks, they would proceed up the Allegheny River, capturing the French forts of Machault, Le Bœuf, Presque Isle, and ultimately Fort Niagara. However, it didn't work out the way Braddock planned.

On Wednesday, July 9, 1755, less than ten miles from their goal, Braddock's force was disastrously routed and Braddock was mortally wounded when his force was attacked by an inferior number of French and Indians. In the north, William Johnson's expedition was slightly more successful when his force of 1,500 colonial troops and 200 Indians narrowly won a victory against 1,500 French, Canadians and Indians at the Battle of Lake George. Even though the French suffered heavier casualties, including the capture of their commander Baron de Dieskau, Johnson was unable to follow up with his attack against Fort Saint Frédéric. Instead, Johnson built Fort William Henry at the southern end of Lac Saint Sacrement, which Johnson renamed Lake George to signify British ownership.

To consolidate the British position in Nova Scotia, a systematic program of deportation of the French Acadians was put into practice, and the only other British successes in 1755 and 1756 were on the high seas where the superior British Navy preyed on French shipping. On Sunday, June 8, 1755, British Admiral Boscowen captured the French 64-gun ship of the line *Alcide*, along with two fully laden troop transports that were bringing reinforcements to Canada.

All of these hostile activities occurred a year or so before war was actually declared. When Anglo-French hostilities ended with the Treaty of Paris in 1763, an estimated 900,000 to 1,400,000 people had died as direct or indirect casualties of the war. The conflict had spread across the globe, drawing Prussia, Hanover, Brunswick-Wolfenbüttel, Portugal, Hesse-Kassel, Schaumber-Lippe, and the Iroquois Confederacy in on the side of the British. France was supported by Austria, Russia, Spain, Sweden, Saxony, the Mughal Empire, and numerous Indian tribes from Canada and New France.

Some of the people who took part in the events leading up to the war continued to play significant roles, while others briefly came on scene and then exited the stage of history. The following are postscripts to many of those who participated in or influenced the events relating to George Washington and the half-king, Chief Tanacharison.

François Bigot (1703–1778)

On Tuesday, November 17, 1761, Intendant Bigot and several of his cronies were arrested, taken to France and imprisoned in the Bastille. He remained there until he was tried and judgment was passed on Saturday,

December 10, 1763. His prosecutor recommended that Bigot be tortured and decapitated. Instead, Bigot was banished from France forever and all of his property was confiscated. In addition, he was ordered to pay 1.5 million livres restitution. Stripped of most of his wealth except for what he had been able to keep hidden from the crown, Bigot was banished from France and lived the remainder of his life in Switzerland as François Bar (de Barre or Desbarres), which was the name of his brother-in-law. Bigot died at the age of 75 in Neuchâtel, Switzerland, on January 12, 1778.

Lieutenant Charles de Deschamps de Boishébert et de Raffetot (1727–1797)

Boishébert was regarded as a promising officer from the time he entered military service in about 1739. During King George's War, he participated in several operations along the New York frontier, led a contingent of Micmac Indians on a reconnaissance to Prince Edward Island, and was wounded in action during an engagement with the British near Grand Pré in Acadia. He was promoted to Lieutenant in February 1748 and was sent to Fort Detroit, where he participated in the skirmishes against the Wyandot chief Nicolas Orontony. In 1752, after leading the advance party of Marin's expeditionary force to fortify the Allegheny and Ohio Rivers, Boishébert was briefly placed in command of Fort Le Bœuf, but by the autumn of 1753, he returned to Québec, where he received orders to take part in the defense of Acadia against the British. In 1755 the British captured Fort Beauséjour near present Aulac, New Brunswick. The fort was situated near the present border between New Brunswick and Nova Scotia. With the fall of Fort Beauséjour, Boishébert sought refuge among the civilian populace and continued a partisan type of warfare against the British. In September of 1755, he engaged and defeated a British detachment at Petitcodiac, New Bruswick, losing only one man. In March 1756, Boishébert was promoted to captain. He continued his energetic and mostly successful guerrilla operations against British troops in Acadia and New Brunswick until the fall of Fortress Louisbourg in July 1758. He led a corps of Acadian volunteers in the defense of Québec in 1759, and also took part in the climactic battle on the Plains of Abraham. For some reason General Montcalm did not like him and made general accusations that Boishébert had amassed a considerable fortune through war profiteering. After the fall of Canada, Boishébert returned to France, where due to Montcalm's accusations, he was charged with the offense of being one of Bigot's profiteering cronies. He was arrested and imprisoned in the Bastille, but after 15 months in prison, Boishébert was summarily acquitted and released. In 1763, he was involved in a venture to resettle Acadians at Cayenne (present French Guiana), but was unable to obtain the required backing. He died on January 9, 1797, at his estate at Raffetot in France at the age of 70.

Pierre Joseph Céloron de Blainville (1693–1759)

After his lead plate burying expedition of 1749, Céloron was posted to command Fort Detroit. There Céloron's half-hearted planning and subsequent failure to follow Governor-General Jonquièr's orders to destroy the recalcitrant Miamis at Pickawillany earned him the governor-general's enmity. Céloron's rationale for noncompliance was his claim that the mission would likely be disastrous to the French in the long run. Although Céloron was unquestionably brave and loyal, there were other complaints regarding his conduct. He was accused of being haughty and injudicious and not a very good administrator. He was undoubtedly better suited for military operations than for administrative duties. When Duquesne became governor-general, he recalled Céloron and made him the town-major of Montréal. Later, however, Duquesne wrote that although Céloron was a very good officer, he was not suited for routine administrative work. Little else is known of Céloron's subsequent activities. He died in Montréal on April 12, 1759. He was 66 years old. Interestingly, his widow joined the Grey Nuns after his death and remained in Canada, thereby forfeiting the annual pension of 300 livres that the king had awarded her.

Claude-Pierre Pécaudy de Contrecœur (1705–1775)

Contrecœur remained as commander of Fort Duquesne until 1756, but after Braddock's defeat, he realized that it was only a matter of time before another expedition would be launched against the fort. He made repeated requests for significant numbers of troops and materiel with which to strengthen the post and to consolidate the gains the French had made in the Ohio territory. However, those requests were mostly futile. Citing poor health and fatigue, Contrecœur finally asked to be relieved of command of Fort Duquesne, rather than be responsible for the fort's eventual loss. He also petitioned the ministers that he be awarded the cross of the Order of Saint Louis, which he received in March 1756. At the same time, he asked for promotions for his two sons who were in the military, one an ensign and the other a cadet. Contrecœur's military career was essentially finished, although he did not officially retire until January 1759. After the war, Contrecœur remained in Canada, tended to his very large seigneury (estate) and was appointed to the legislative council in 1775. However, his legislative career was cut short by his death after having attended only one meeting. He died in 1775 at the age of 70.[5]

George Croghan (ca. 1718–1782)

With the start of hostilities in 1754, Croghan's trading enterprise in the Ohio territory was ruined and his employees in the Ohio territory were either killed or driven back over the mountains. Croghan moved his trading operation to Aughwick, and after Tanacharison, Queen Aliquippa and several other Indians who were friendly to the British sought refuge there, Croghan fortified his post and called it Fort Shirley. During the war, he built another three forts along the frontier. Croghan served as captain of scouts during the Braddock expedition and also assisted Washington's efforts to defend the Virginia frontier. In 1756, Croghan relocated to the New York frontier and was appointed by Sir William Johnson to be his Deputy Superintendent for Indian Affairs. Croghan accompanied General John Forbes's expedition to capture Fort Duquesne in 1758. Interestingly, Forbes assigned Croghan and Montour the perilous job of bringing the intractable Delaware Indians into the English fold. Croghan succeeded, which was something that even Sir William Johnson had been unable to accomplish. In 1760, Croghan went with Colonel Bouquet to occupy Detroit, where he conducted negotiations with the tribes who had supported the French. In 1764, he traveled to England to lobby for a strong Indian department and upon his return, Johnson sent him on a mission to open the Illinois territory, which was still occupied by the French. In 1768 he played an important role in the Treaty of Fort Stanwix, which designated Indian lands that essentially encompassed the area west and southwest of Fort Stanwix, and north of the Ohio River. It was hoped that implementation of the treaty provisions would ease the bloody and costly Indian wars by promising the Indians a permanent homeland that was free from white encroachment. Over the years, Croghan had amassed several thousand acres of land, and throughout this life he continued in land speculation. His greatest rival in land ownership was George Washington, who occasionally challenged Croghan's land titles when they conflicted with his own. He was associated with William Trent in the Indiana and Vandalia land speculation projects, investing heavily in trying to establish the "fourteenth" English colony. Benjamin Franklin and his son William were also involved in that land deal to a lesser extent. However, British policy prohibited Crown agents from being involved in such ventures, so Croghan resigned his government post in 1772 in order to continue with his land speculation. Lord Dunmore's War, which was fought in 1774, was a war between the colony of Virginia and primarily the Shawnee and Mingo Indians in the Ohio territory. That war and the outbreak of the Revolutionary War in 1775 destroyed all prospects of the Indiana and Vandalia ventures, and Croghan was wiped out financially. To make matters worse, he was unjustly accused of being a Tory even though he had served the patriot cause as chairman of the Pittsburgh Committee of Correspondence. He was finally able to clear his name in a trial held in November 1778. Croghan spent his final years in poverty and died at Passyunk, near Philadelphia, on Saturday, August 31, 1782. He was buried in the churchyard at St. Peter's Church in Philadelphia, but by that time he was so unknown that his death was not even reported in the newspapers. He was 64 years old when he died.

Lieutenant Governor Robert Dinwiddie (1693–1770)

Virginia Lieutenant Governor Dinwiddie refused to release the French captives taken in the fight with Jumonville, and as a result Robert Stobo and Jacob Van Braam remained hostages of the French until Stobo escaped from Québec in 1759 and Van Braam was released in 1760. After the defeat of Braddock, Dinwiddie criticized the fallen general for splitting his force and advancing with only about half his army. Dinwiddie maintained that Braddock should have marched to the Forks in strength rather than leave Dunbar and half the men 40 miles to the rear. Even so, Dinwiddie still hoped that Dunbar might retrieve the situation and oust the French from the Forks. Unfortunately, Dunbar also proved to be a disappointment when he retreated his force all the way back to Philadelphia, leaving Virginia and Pennsylvania open to attack by the French and Indians. Dinwiddie appointed Washington to command the forces for the defense of Virginia, and the lieutenant governor raised troops, including tough frontier rangers, for Washington's command. By 1757, Dinwiddie also gained the assistance of some 400 friendly Indians from Virginia and the Carolinas to augment Washington's defense force.

Dinwiddie waged a constant struggle with his own Virginia assembly over ways to generate funds to raise troops with which to defend the frontier. In desperation he appealed for intercolonial cooperation, and even suggested that the British Parliament impose a land tax and a poll tax to finance the war. All of these exertions took a toll on his health, and on Tuesday, March 22, 1757, Dinwiddie requested a leave of absence for a recuperative visit to Bath, England. He left Virginia on Sunday, January 8, 1758, and was succeeded by Francis Fauquier as lieutenant governor. Dinwiddie never returned to America. He died at Clifton, Bristol, England, on Friday, July 27, 1770. He was 77 years old.

Michel-Ange Duquesne de Menneville, Marquis Duquesne (ca. 1700–1778)

After the Battle of Fort Necessity in 1754, Duquesne was satisfied with Villiers's success, but the governor-general had reservations concerning the clause in the capitulation that barred the English from returning to the Ohio territory for only one year. His concerns were proven correct when he received intelligence that the British were preparing for a massive retaliation under Braddock. Duquesne took immediate steps to reinforce Fort Duquesne and the other Pennsylvania forts by concentrating his forces in the defense of the Ohio territory. This drained a significant portion of his regular army, and it left the Champlain–Richelieu route and Arcadia to be defended mostly by militia. Duquesne was aware of the steep odds of winning a war against England in the long run, so he chose to quit on a high note. He requested to be recalled in October 1754, and was replaced as governor-general by Pierre de Rigaud de Vaudreuil de Cavagnial on June 24, 1755. On taking office, Vaudreuil publicly criticized Duquesne's actions in putting most of the military might of New France in the Ohio region while neglecting the other sectors. Duquesne was enraged at Vaudreuil's comments, and he sailed for France to explain his actions to the ministers. Fortunately for Duquesne, the annihilation of Braddock's army seemed to justify Duquesne's policies, and it certainly satisfied the ministers. In fact, Duquesne was rewarded for his service in Canada and was often consulted on matters pertaining to New France. He resumed his naval career, and in 1756 was named inspector general of the coasts of France. In 1757, he assumed command of the fleet at Toulon and took part in minor actions until 1758, when he was defeated in an engagement with a British squadron and taken prisoner. Upon his return to France, he was granted a pension of 3,000 livres, and in 1763 the king made him a "Commander of the Order of Saint Louis." He finally retired in 1776, and spent his last days at his residences in Paris and Antony. He died in September 1778 at the age of 78.

George William Fairfax (1729–1787)

George William Fairfax was the son of Sir William Fairfax and Sarah Walker Fairfax. Sarah died in 1731, and Sir William remarried to Deborah Clarke and took up residence at Belvoir Plantation on the lower Potomac River, where they became one of the more influential families in Virginia. They were neighbors of George Washington, and from an early age, George Washington and George William Fairfax established a lifelong friendship. The families grew even closer when in 1743, George Fairfax's older sister Sally, who was 15 years of age, married George Washington's brother Lawrence, who was 25. Lawrence had just returned from serving with Admiral Edward Vernon in the Caribbean, fighting the Spanish in the so-called War of Jenkin's Ear.

George Washington's friendship and connection with the Fairfax family propelled him into a lucrative career as a surveyor, and also as a soldier and a politician. It also provided him access to Virginia society. Washington claimed his association with the Fairfax family included the happiest moments of his life. The Fairfax family became a rather extended family for George Washington, and George William was not only a close friend, but also became a mentor for young George Washington.

In 1748 George William married Sally Cary Fairfax, who came from one of Virginia's oldest and wealthiest families. The couple never had children. George Washington apparently became enamored with Sally Fairfax, and as surviving documents indicate, the feeling may have been somewhat mutual. Mount Vernon and Belvoir Plantation were approximately three miles apart, and after George Washington's 1759 marriage to Martha Dandridge Custis Washington, the two couples frequently hosted each other. In the 1770s, as the pre-Revolution patriotic movement grew, George William Fairfax remained a staunch Loyalist, but it never diminished the friendship that existed between he and George Washington.

In 1773, George William and Sally Fairfax travelled to England to deal with a complicated inheritance suit, and Fairfax gave George Washington power of attorney to look after his business and financial interests in Virginia. Washington represented Fairfax until Washington was appointed to command the American army in 1775. George and Sally Fairfax intended to return to Virginia after the Revolutionary War ended, but because of the American victory they never returned. The two men continued to correspond and remained friends until George William Fairfax died at his home in Bath, England, in 1787 at the age of 58.

Sally Cary Fairfax (ca. 1730–1811)

Sally Fairfax was the wife of George William Fairfax. Sally Cary, as she was born, came from one of the oldest and wealthiest families in Virginia. Sally was the oldest of four daughters and reportedly was considered by the young men of Virginia society the most eligible and sought after of the Cary daughters. She married George William Fairfax in 1748, and the couple moved into the family estate at Belvoir Plantation.

During his visits to Belvoir, George Washington became enamored with the beautiful, intelligent, and popular Sally Fairfax. To Washington, she represented the ideal of womanhood and reportedly inspired him to constantly strive to better himself culturally, socially, and intellectually. While accompanying the 1758 Forbes expedition against Fort Duquesne, Washington began to write letters to Sally that through allusions to literary romances hinted at his love for Sally. There is some evidence that the attraction was reciprocated, however, there is nothing to indicate that the affair ever progressed beyond flirtation to anything physical. Sally's husband was perhaps Washington's best friend, and it's thought that Washington would not violate the high ethical and moral standards that he had set for himself by engaging in an affair with the wife of his friend. Washington confessed his feelings to Sally when he wrote to her that he had never been able to eradicate from his mind the happiest moments in his life, when he was in her company. After Washington married Martha Dandridge Custis, the two couples frequently visited at each other's homes. They apparently enjoyed each other's company, and George William Fairfax and Martha Washington either had no knowledge of previous flirtations between George Washington and Sally Fairfax, or those particular circumstances were politely ignored.

The two couples separated in 1773, when the Fairfaxes moved to England, but they remained friends and corresponded. George William Fairfax died in 1787. The only hint of feelings Sally may have had for George Washington was in a melancholy letter she wrote to her sister in 1788, after her husband's death, that included the statement that is thought to allude to Washington. She wrote that the worthy man is to be preferred to the high-born. Sally died in 1811, at the age of 81.

John Fraser (1721–1773)

After the fight at Great Meadows, John Fraser was unable to maintain his trading venture at either the Venango or Turtle Creek locations. He moved farther east to present Bedford County, Pennsylvania, and in 1754, he married Jane McClain, nee Jane Bell. He continued in the military service both as a militia officer and as a lieutenant in the British army, serving in Braddock's ill-fated expedition. On Wednesday, October 1, 1755, Fraser's wife Jane was returning home from the trading post at Wills Creek, several miles away, when she was captured by Indians and taken over 300 miles to an Indian village near present Dayton, Ohio. Jane remained a captive of the Indians for over 18 months, but she eventually escaped and somehow made her way back home. However, after his wife disappeared, Fraser assumed she was dead, so he remarried. When Jane finally made her way back home, she found that her husband had taken another wife. To rectify the situation, Fraser welcomed his wife back and returned his second wife to her father.

In 1758 Fraser accompanied the successful Forbes expedition against Fort Duquesne. When he returned, he began to petition the government for restitution for his losses caused by the war, and in 1766 he was granted 300 acres along Forbes Road near present Latrobe, Pennsylvania. As a side note, in 1790 his 300 acres were sold to Father Theodore Bouwers O.F.M., and in 1846, St. Vincent College and Archabbey were established. It is now the oldest Benedictine monastery in the United States. Fraser continued to speculate in land, and in 1769, he purchased the land that encompassed the Braddock battlefield, where he built a cabin. Fraser's widow sold the land in 1774 for living expenses and to satisfy debts. In 1771, Governor Penn appointed John Fraser the justice of the peace for the newly formed Bedford County. John Fraser died suddenly two years later on April 16, 1773. He was 52 years old.

Christopher Gist (1706–ca. 1759)

After the Battle of Great Meadows, during his return to Fort Duquesne, Coulon de Villiers burnt Gist's plantation to the ground. There are no accounts of Gist's activities in the ensuing year, but in 1755, he accompanied Braddock's expedition as a guide. After Braddock's defeat, Gist was commissioned a lieutenant in the Virginia forces, and in October of 1755 he was promoted to Captain of Scouts. Early in 1756, Dinwiddie appointed Gist to be a deputy for Indian affairs in Virginia, and later that year he travelled to eastern Tennessee to seek Indian allies for the British. After that trip, there is no further information regarding Gist's whereabouts or activities. Even the time and place of his death are uncertain. Gist reportedly died in 1759 from smallpox, either in Virginia, South Carolina or Georgia. He was 53 years old.

Roland-Michel Barrin de La Galissonière (1693–1756)

After leaving the post of governor-general of New France, Galissonière was promoted to the rank of rear admiral in recognition for his service in New France. This promotion was in spite of the fact that he had never been tested as a military officer, much less a naval commander. His duties were to head the Dépôt de la Marine. In 1756, Galissonière was part of the Minorca invasion force, and he was engaged in a three-hour sea battle against British Admiral John Byng. Galissonière was very cautious in the engagement, but Byng was even more so and ordered a withdrawal from the fight. The surprised Galissonière was accorded a victory and lauded in France to the point where the king was planning to honor him with a marshal's baton upon his return. Byng, on the other hand, was considered a coward and was court-martialed for "failing to do his utmost," and he was executed by a firing squad as he knelt on the quarterdeck of HMS *Monarch*. Interestingly, Byng's execution was satirized by Voltaire in Candide: "In this country, it is good to kill an admiral from time to time, in order to encourage the others." Galissonière never received his marshal's baton. He died from illness at the age of 63, before he could be presented to the king.

James Innes (ca. 1700–1759)

In 1754, with the desertion of most of the troops in his command during their march to the Forks, Innes continued on to Wills Creek with his few remaining men, where he assumed command of the post. Innes was commander at Wills Creek during the construction of Fort Cumberland in 1755, but had a difficult time with the troops there, who were ill disposed toward him since he was a North Carolinian. Within five months, Lieutenant Governor Horatio Sharpe of Maryland relieved him of his position, but Innes stayed on as campmaster general. When General Edward Braddock arrived at Fort Cumberland, he again placed Innes in command, naming him governor of Fort Cumberland, and Innes was tasked with maintaining the fort and its reserve troops. After Braddock's defeat on the Monongahela, Innes was the first to forward news of the disaster to Dinwiddie. Fort Cumberland was used to treat the sick and wounded from Braddock's expedition. Innes stayed on at Fort Cumberland for about another year, and in the summer of 1756, he resigned his commission, and returned home to North Carolina.

He retired as a gentleman farmer on his plantation in North Carolina, where he died in 1759 at the age of 59. Innes left a bequest for a school, to be called the Innes Academy. It eventually became the Thalian Hall Center for the Performing Arts in Wilmington, North Carolina. Innes's wife married Innes's business associate, and after her death, she was buried between her two husbands.

René-Hippolyte LaForce (1728–1802)

It's unclear what role the enigmatic LaForce played in the French army during the time of Washington's encounters with him. Robert Stobo, who was a hostage of the French and who was in a good position to gather information about LaForce, said that it appeared that LaForce was an important personage in the French military. Dinwiddie released LaForce in 1756, and upon his return to Canada, LaForce was given command of a frigate on Lake Ontario. That same year, he was involved in a skirmish against the British near Fort Oswego. In 1758, he was stationed at Fort Niagara until it fell to the British in 1759. After the fall of Québec in 1759, LaForce moved to Kamouraska, about 82 miles northeast of Québec City, where he remained until 1767. In 1767, he moved to Québec City and started a shipping company that dealt primarily with the West Indies trade; LaForce captained one of his company's ships.

The start of the American Revolution halted LaForce's shipping venture. Governor Guy Carleton initially appointed LaForce as captain of the city's artillery company, but a few days later LaForce was ordered to take command of a British warship that was patrolling the Saint Lawrence River. In 1776, he was appointed captain of the armed schooner *Seneca,* which became his flagship when he was later appointed as commander of the British fleet operating on Lake Ontario. In 1778, he was given control of the shipyard at Pointe-au-Baril, and then named master and commander of "His Majesty's Naval Armament upon the Rivers and Lakes within the Province." In 1780, he was promoted to Commodore of the Fleet. In 1784, after the war, LaForce retired on half-pay and resumed his trading venture between Québec and the West Indies. In 1788, he sold his share of the business, but in 1794, he was appointed lieutenant colonel of militia of Québec. He died in 1802, just two months after his seventy-third birthday.[6]

Charles-Michel Mouet de Langlade (1729–ca. 1801)

Langlade did not participate in the battle at Great Meadows, but in 1755, he was at Fort Duquesne, where he took part in the defeat of Braddock on the Monongahela. In later years, Langlade claimed that he had actually planned the ambush of Braddock. After Braddock's defeat in 1755, Langlade traveled to present Grand Haven, Michigan, where he established a trading post at the mouth of the Grand River, but he returned to Fort Duquesne in 1756, where he and his Indians scouted for the French. In late 1756 Langlade took his Indians east to the northern New York frontier, and on Friday, January 21, 1757, Langlade was part of the French-Canadian force that defeated the celebrated Robert Rogers and his rangers in the famous Battle on Snowshoes. Later that year Langlade accompanied General Montcalm's army during the siege of Fort William Henry. While there, Langlade was instrumental in capturing a British flotilla on Lake George, and he was present when Fort William Henry surrendered on Tuesday, August 9, 1757. In September of 1757, Langlade returned to present Michigan where he was named second-in-command at Fort Michilimackinac.

In 1759 Langlade again traveled east and was with General Montcalm in Quebéc during the climactic battle on the Plains of Abraham that resulted in the fall of the city. After the surrender of Quebéc to the British, Langlade returned to Michilimackinac, but in 1760 he was back in Montréal. Langlade left Montréal before the city surrendered to the British on Monday, September 8, 1760. He returned to Michilimackinac, where he was in command until the British took it over in September 1761. After the French and Indian War ended, Langlade contented himself with his Grand River trading venture, and he continued to oversee its operation through 1790.

Immediately prior to Pontiac's War in 1763, Langlade warned George

Etherington, the commander of Fort Michilimackinac, about the imminent Indian uprising. However, Etherington did not take heed, and as a result the fort was captured and most of the garrison was killed. Langlade did, however, at great personal risk, save Etherington and a few other Englishmen from being taken and killed by the Indians. For the remainder of Pontiac's War, Langlade commanded Fort Michilimackinac until British control was reestablished the following year. He then moved to La Baye (present Green Bay, Wisconsin), where his father was living.

During the American Revolution, Langlade served as a captain in the Indian Department, and Governor Guy Carleton stated that Langlade's influence among the Indians was of great use to the British effort. Langlade and his Indians fought in defense of Montréal in 1776, and later joined Burgoyne's expedition in the summer of 1777. He remained with Burgoyne until the Battle of Bennington on Saturday, August 16, 1777, and then he returned to the west to assist Henry Hamilton, commander of Fort Detroit in his war against the American rebels under George Rogers Clark.

After the Revolutionary War, Langlade continued to serve in the Indian Department. In 1791, he was briefly implicated in an embezzling scandal at Michilimackinac. He managed to avoid punishment and retained his position, but his alleged co-conspirator was charged and dismissed from his post. Langlade remained active in the Indian Department until his death. He enjoyed relating tales of the supposed 99 battles in which he fought. A colleague of Langlade said that he had never seen a man so perfectly cool and fearless on the field of battle. Charles Langlade died during the winter of 1800–1801 at La Baye. He was about 71 years of age.

Jacques Legardeur de Saint-Pierre (1701–1755)

Shortly after receiving Washington at Fort Le Bœuf, Legardeur requested to be relieved as commander on the Ohio, ostensibly for health reasons. Turning over his command to Claude-Pierre Pécaudy de Contrecœur, Legardeur returned to Montréal for convalescence. In 1755, in response to the British thrust led by William Johnson to capture Fort Saint Frédéric at Crown Point, Legardeur led a large contingent of Canadian militia and Indians south to engage Johnson's army and to defend Lac Saint Sacrement and Lake Champlain. On September 8, 1755, Jacques Legardeur de Saint-Pierre was killed in the Battle of Lake George. He was 54 years old.

Captain James Mackay (ca. 1718–1785)

There is very little information concerning Captain James Mackay of the South Carolina independent company of regulars. He was born about 1718, making him about 14 years older than Washington. Early in the campaign, Mackay disputed Washington's authority as commander and refused to place himself or his men under Washington's command. However, when the fight started, Mackay and his men fought courageously, suffering a higher percentage of casualties than the Virginians. Reportedly, Washington and Mackay became friends during the campaign. During the retreat to Wills Creek, Mackay remarked that as a result of the capitulation, Washington was "not very gay company."[7] Mackay and the independent company remained at Wills Creek while Washington continued on to Williamsburg. For unknown reasons, Mackay sold his king's commission in 1755 and moved to Georgia, where he settled on an estate called White Hall. Mackay had three daughters, named Ann, Barbara, and Mary. Later he moved to Rhode Island for health reasons and transferred White Hall to his daughter Barbara. Sometime in 1785, Mackay travelled south, intending to visit Washington at Mount Vernon, but he died at Alexandria, Virginia, before seeing Washington, and before Washington learned of his presence in the area.[8] He was about 67 years old.

Jean-Baptiste Machault d'Arnouville (1701–1794)

Machault, born in Paris, was the son of Louis Charles Machault d'Arnouville, a lieutenant of police. In 1721, at the age of 20, he was made counsel to the parliament. He rose through the ranks, being promoted to president of the Great Council and in 1743 he was appointed Intendant of the Hainaut section of France. In 1745 he was appointed Controller-General of Finance. On taking office, he learned that because of the War of the Austrian Succession or King George's War (1740–1748), the French government was borrowing heavily and the French financial structure was on the verge of bankruptcy. After the war, in 1749, he attempted financial reform by abolishing the old one-tenth tax system (dîme) that exempted the clergy and was easily evaded by most of the nobility. He proposed a new system of direct taxes of one-twentieth (vingtième) that would be levied on everyone. His plan to require the church and the clergy to also pay taxes made the proposal popular with the general public, but the clergy insisted on their historical privileges and railed loudly from the pulpit against the new tax. Supported by the nobility, and also by the religiously devout members of Louis XV's court, the proposal was rejected. Many historians believe that if Machault's tax reforms had been enacted, it would likely have done much to prevent the bloody French Revolution. Machault retained his post as Controller of Finance until July 1754, when he became Minister of the Navy. Machault opposed an alliance with Austria and other schemes backed by Madame de Pompadour, the mistress of Louis XV, and it gained him her bitter enmity and ill will. On February 1,

1757, the king acquiesced to Madame Pompadour's demands for Machault's removal. Machault retired to his estate at Arnouville, where he remained until the French Revolution broke out in 1789. He went into hiding for a period, but was arrested by the revolutionaries in 1794 and imprisoned in the Prison des Madelonnettes, a former Paris convent. Machault died there a few weeks later. He was 93 years old.

Captain François-Marc-Antoine Le Mercier (1722–ca. 1798)

Captain François-Marc-Antoine Le Mercier was a career soldier from a military family. Some sources indicate that he was a militia lieutenant when he was 14 years of age. In 1744, during King George's War, Le Mercier was in sole charge of the artillery that was part of the defense of Québec, during which time he supervised over 500 workmen in constructing defenses and placing batteries. In 1745, he served under Marin in the Acadian campaign, but returned to Québec after the fall of Fort Louisbourg. In 1746, he was at Fort Saint-Frédéric to bolster its defenses and to inventory its munitions and supplies. In February 1747, he was part of the force of 300 Canadians and Indians that force-marched through the bitter cold and successfully attacked the New Englanders at Grand Pré in Acadia. At the end of King George's War in 1748, Le Mercier went to France to study artillery and military engineering. In 1750 he was back in Canada where, because of the discipline and professionalism of his artillery unit, he made a strong impression on the governor-general. In 1753, he was assigned to Marin's expedition as an engineer to fortify the Allegheny and Ohio Rivers. He was instrumental in constructing Fort Presque Isle and the other forts along the Allegheny. He was promoted to captain that year, and Duquesne recommended Le Mercier for the Order of Saint Louis. However, the request was turned down. Governor-General Duquesne did, however, place Le Mercier in charge of artillery and military engineering. He took part in the capture of Fort Prince George at the Forks of the Ohio in the spring of 1754 and was second-in-command at the Battle of Great Meadows. That autumn, he sailed for France to report on the operations along the Allegheny and Ohio Rivers, and he returned to Québec in the spring of 1755. In September of that year, he took part in the Battle of Lac Saint-Sacrament that ended in a defeat for the French and the capture of the French commander, Baron de Dieskau. General Montcalm, who frequently showed a streak of pettiness, made the statement that Le Mercier was likely the cause of Dieskau's defeat and capture. The following summer, Le Mercier commanded the artillery at the capture of Fort Oswego. While it was Montcalm's first victory in New France, he was miffed by Le Mercier's insistence on the placement of the artillery. Le Mercier was correct in his insistence, and his nine guns forced a surrender of the fort in six hours, but Montcalm never forgave Le Mercier, and characterized him as a weak and ignorant man. Le Mercier was active in the Champlain and Lake George arena and took part in the siege of Fort William Henry, and also in Montcalm's victory over Abercrombie at Fort Ticonderoga. He spent the winter of 1758 in Québec in the company of Intendant Bigot and his cronies, where they spent a great deal of time gambling. After the fall of Québec, Le Mercier was sent to France in November 1759 to inform the court of the situation in New France. While in Paris he was arrested and accused of being party to Bigot's criminal activities. He was imprisoned in the Bastille, but in 1763, he was acquitted and released. He took up residence in Lisieux, where he was living comfortably in 1798 at the age of 76. No date has been found regarding his death.

Lieutenant Colonel George Muse (1720–1791)

Accused of cowardice for unilaterally withdrawing his company during the fight at Great Meadows, Muse resigned his commission in late October 1754. This caused Dinwiddie to remark, "As he is not very agreeable to the other Officers, I am well pleas'd at his resignatn."[9] However, in 1756, Muse was appointed colonel of militia involved in the defense of the Virginia frontier. As such, he attended the military councils at Winchester, once again under Washington's command.

After the war, Muse was pointedly excluded from the land bounty that Dinwiddie had promised in 1754 to the recruits that joined Washington's expedition to the Forks of the Ohio. Muse had been omitted from receiving his share of the land bounty because of the taint of his supposed cowardice during the Battle of Great Meadows, but the 1754 resignation of his lieutenant colonel's commission was used to support his exclusion. Muse reckoned that his share of the land would have amounted to some 15,000 acres, and he was not willing to give up on that so easily. Apparently there was no real animosity between Muse and Washington, because Washington's papers indicate that in January 1768, Muse made a social visit to Mount Vernon in the company of Washington's brother Charles and a Mr. Charles Dick. During that visit, they spent much of the time playing cards.

In 1770, Muse once again approached George Washington, this time to ask his assistance in obtaining a share of the land bounty. Muse agreed to give Washington one-third of the land if Washington would pay all the costs of obtaining it for Muse. Washington used his influence and was successful in obtaining a share of the land bounty for Muse, but it initially was not as large as Muse had reckoned. Muse was issued a patent for 3,323 acres in November 1770, to which Washington was entitled to a third. Muse concluded that he had been cheated out of the land owed him, and felt that Washington was to blame. Unknown to Muse, Washington continued to work to get a larger share of land for the disgraced officer. Unfortunately, before he learned of Washington's efforts, Muse wrote to Washington in December 1773, apparently accusing Washington of short-changing him in the land deal. That letter did not survive, but Washington's answer, written in January 1774, does.

> Sir, Your impertinent letter was delivered to me yesterday. As I am not accustomed to receive such from any man, nor would have taken the same language from you personally, without letting you feel some marks of my resentment, I would advise you to be cautious in writing me a second of the same tenor. But for your stupidity and sottishness you might have known, by attending to the public gazette, that you had your full quantity of ten thousand acres of land allowed you, that is, nine thousand and seventy-three acres in the great tract, and the remainder in the small tract. But suppose you had really fallen short, do you think your superlative merit entitles you to greater indulgence than others? Or, if it did, that I was to make it good to you, when it was at the option of the Governor and Council to allow but five hundred acres in the whole, if they had been so inclined? If either of these should happen to be your opinion, I am very well convinced that you will be singular in it; and all my concern is, that I ever engaged in behalf of so ungrateful a fellow as you are. But you may still be in need of my assistance, as I can inform you, that your affairs, in respect to these lands, do not stand upon so solid a basis as you imagine, and this you may take by way of hint. I wrote to you a few days ago concerning the other distribution, proposing an easy method of dividing our lands; but since I find in what temper you are, I am sorry I took the trouble of mentioning the land or your name in a letter, as I do not think you merit the least assistance from me.[10]

Despite Muse's unfounded accusations and Washington's vitriolic response, both men apparently made peace and concluded their agreed upon land arrangement. In the 1780s, Washington retained Muses's son Battaile as the rental agent for Washington's western lands. Little more is known of George Muse. He died in 1791 at the age of 69.

Michel-Jean-Hughes Péan (1723–1782)

Son of a prominent officer, Péan joined the colonial regulars at an early age and progressed rapidly through the ranks. He possessed high military aptitudes, but his chief talent was obtaining favors from those holding high office. Through his position as Adjutant of the Town and Government of Québec, and his connections through marriage, Péan associated himself with Intendant Bigot and profited greatly through Bigot's corrupt profiteering ventures. Péan became Bigot's middleman and helped facilitate the Intendant's schemes by recommending them and influencing their adoption. In 1750, Péan became involved in the wheat trade. Using his government associations, he was able to buy large quantities of grain at low prices. Intendant Bigot then fixed the resale price of wheat high, which resulted in immense profits for the two. In 1756, Bigot recommended Péan for the very prestigious Cross of Saint Louis, which Péan received that year. Also in 1756, Péan joined a group of profiteering entrepreneurs, known as the Grand Société, who were able to obtain a monopoly on the sale of supplies to the king's stores, and also a virtual monopoly on furnishing supplies of all types to the colony. Péan, who primarily protected the venture from government scrutiny, did not have any expenses associated with it, but was able to pocket immense profits. After the fall of Québec, Péan was arrested in 1761 along with Bigot, and both were imprisoned in the Bastille. While Péan was among the more corrupt of the profiteers, he was able to extricate himself from most of the accusations, with the help of his wife's family connections. He was released after paying a relatively lenient restitution of 600,000 livres. Unbelievably, there was never any hint of dishonor attached to his name. He lived as a seigneur at his domain of Orzain, not far from Blois, and in 1771 he obtained permission for his old crony Bigot to visit with him. He died in 1782 at the age of 59.

William Chevalier La Peyronie (?–1755)

William Chevalier La Peyronie was a Protestant native of France who emigrated to Virginia between 1750 and 1752. He was an esteemed and popular person in the colony, where among other things, he served as a fencing and dancing master for the Randolph family. Peyronie obtained an ensign's commission in the Virginia Regiment, presumably as a result of his prior military experience in France. He was a brave and efficient officer who was gravely wounded at Great Meadows. After recovering from the injuries he received at Fort Necessity, he petitioned the Assembly at Williamsburg for recompense for personal losses including the loss of his clothes at Great Meadows. On Friday, August 30, 1754, the Burgesses voted him their thanks, and recommended that Lieutenant Governor Dinwiddie promote him. He was promoted to Captain with his commission pre-dated to Sunday, August 25, 1754. The following summer Peyronie was killed at the Battle of the Monongahela while serving with Braddock's expedition.

Queen Aliquippa (ca. 1670s–1754)

Queen Aliquippa and her band of Mingos left Great Meadows with Tanacharison and the other Indians just prior to the arrival of the French force. She, along with the half-king, sought refuge at Aughwick, Pennsylvania, near Croghan's trading post. By this time she was around 80 years old and rather frail from her constant moves. Her poor health was likely exacerbated by the continued stress of worrying for her people. She lived about six months at Aughwick, dying there on Monday, December 23, 1754. George Croghan noted her passing in his journal: "Alequeapy, ye old quine is dead."[11] She was close to 80 years old.

Scarouady (?–ca. 1757 or 1758)

Scarouady traveled with Tanacharison to Aughwick in 1754, and he succeeded Tanacharison as the principal half-king after Tanacharison's death. Frustrated with their life in Aughwick, most of the Indians who accompanied the half-kings there abandoned Scarouady and returned to Fort Duquesne, where they made peace with the French. Scarouady, on the other hand, joined up with Braddock's expedition. During Braddock's march, Scarouady's son was shot and killed by a nervous sentry who mistook him for a hostile Indian. In spite of his loss, Scarouady stayed with the expedition and survived the devastating defeat on the Monongahela. In 1756, documents indicate that Scarouady attended councils in which he gave speeches that advocated peaceful measures. After 1756 there is no extant record of his activities. Some sources indicate he died in 1757 or 1758. Scarouady's age when he died is not known.

Shikellamy also known as Swatana (?–1748)

The Oneida half-king Shikellamy supervised the Pennsylvania Shawnee and Delaware tribes for the Iroquois but did not live long enough to witness or take part in the opening events leading to the French and Indian War. He allowed the Moravian missionaries to remain at Shamokin, Shikellamy's village, because he believed they had the best interests of the Indians at heart. Although there is a present town nearby named Shamokin, Shikellamy's village was located along the Susquehanna River near present Sunbury, Pennsylvania. In November 1748, he converted to Christianity at the Moravian city of Bethlehem, Pennsylvania, but on the return to his home village of Shamokin, he became ill. In spite of the best efforts of his Moravian friends and Indian healers, he died at Shamokin on December 6, 1748. Shikellamy's age when he died is not known.

Major Adam Stephen (1718–1791)

Adam Stephen continued to serve with his friend George Washington during the French and Indian War. Stephen remained a major of the Virginia Regiment and was part of Braddock's expedition during the disastrous march to the Monongahela in 1755. In 1758, Stephen was promoted to lieutenant colonel, and in that year was involved in actions against the Creek Indians.

During the French and Indian War, he was also active in the defense of the Virginia frontier. He was promoted to colonel, and at war's end, Stephen took over command of the Virginia Regiment from Washington. As commander of the Virginia Regiment, Stephen fought in Pontiac's Rebellion in 1763. When the Revolutionary War broke out, Stephen again offered his services to his friend George Washington, who was now Commander-in-Chief of the American Army. Stephen was appointed major general and served in the campaigns of 1776–1777, including commanding a division during the defense of Philadelphia in September 1777. During the Saturday, October 4, 1777, Battle of Germantown, Stephen's force advanced through heavy fog and came up on Anthony Wayne's troops ahead. Thinking they were the enemy, Stephen's men fired repeated volleys into the backs of Wayne's division, causing several casualties. The court martial that resulted from that incident found that Stephen was drunk at the time, and he was stripped of his command and cashiered out of the army. He returned home, and in 1778 laid out the plan for Martinsburg in what is now West Virginia, naming it after his friend Colonel Thomas Martin. He later became the sheriff of Berkeley County, and in 1788 was elected to the Virginia convention that ratified the U.S. Constitution. Stephen died in Martinsburg in 1791 at the age of 73.

Captain Robert Stobo (1726–1770)

As hostages after the surrender of Fort Necessity, Captains Robert Stobo and Jacob Van Braam were kept at Fort Duquesne for about a year. Shortly after Braddock's defeat on Wednesday, July 9, 1755, the French discovered a detailed map of Fort Duquesne among Braddock's captured documents. While Van Braam fully enjoyed a comradely association with French officers in drinking, carousing, and card playing, Stobo was learning French. At the same time, Stobo was painstakingly collecting every available bit of military intelligence, which he incorporated on his secret hand-drawn map of the French fortifications. Somehow, he was able to smuggle the map out of Fort Duquesne by way of a friendly Indian, and it eventually came into the possession of Lieutenant Governor Dinwiddie. Dinwiddie subsequently gave the map to Major General Braddock to assist him in the expedition against Fort Duquesne, but in an incredible breech of military intelligence, neither Dinwiddie nor Braddock redacted Stobo's name from the incriminating document. Worse yet, Braddock carried the original to the Monongahela, and after the battle, the French captured his papers. When the French examined Braddock's captured documents, they found the detailed map with Stobo's name on it.

Both Stobo and Van Braam were accused of violating their parole by spying for the British, and they were sent to Montréal for trial. After a two-and-a-half-week trial, Van Braam was acquitted, but Stobo, who admitted making the map, was sentenced to death by beheading. He was sent to Québec to await confirmation of the death sentence by the king. That confirmation never came. The court at Versailles secretly decided to do nothing, because they were not certain of the technical legality of executing someone for spying during a time when war was not officially declared. In Stobo's favor was the fact that he had an endearing Scottish personality, and he was someone whom everyone seemed to genuinely like. He was given a fair amount of freedom in his personal movements, which he used to attempt to escape. During two of his attempted escapes he was recaptured, but his third and most daring attempt in May 1759 was successful. He led a group of escapees, consisting of four men, a woman, and her three children, by canoe down the Saint Lawrence River. They subsequently captured a French schooner, and with its crew as captives, they sailed all the way to British-held Fort Louisbourg, arriving there 36 days after leaving Québec. At Louisbourg, Stobo joined General Wolfe's staff, and according to Stobo's memoirs, he showed Wolfe the hidden pathway from Anse au Foulon up to the Plains of Abraham, which made possible Wolfe's capture of Québec in September 1759. Stobo remained in the British army and was wounded in the head during a fight against the Spanish. He seemed to have made a full recovery, but later, he frequently became depressed and his behavior was somewhat erratic, possibly due to his head injury. On Tuesday, June 19, 1770, Stobo killed himself with his pistol in the military barracks at Chatham, England.[12] He was not quite 44 years old when he died.

Captain William Trent (1715–1787)

Captain Trent and John Fraser stood trial for leaving their post when the French captured the Forks, but they both were exonerated. In 1758, Trent took part in Forbes's successful expedition that recaptured the Forks of the Ohio. Since 1749, he had been in a trading partnership with George Croghan, but the venture suffered heavy losses during the war. About 1760, he joined another trading firm called Simon, Trent, Levy & Franks out of Fort Pitt, but they also suffered heavy losses as a result of Pontiac's War in 1763. Trent and his partners spent several years trying to get restitution for their losses that were incurred as a result of the wars. At the Treaty of Fort Stanwix in 1768, he was one of the people awarded compensation in the form of a vast tract of land southwest of Fort Pitt that became known as "Indiana." It should not be confused with the state of Indiana. The awarded tract was southwest of Fort Pitt between the Monongahela and Ohio Rivers, stopping short of the Kanawah River. Trent tried to merge his land grant with the larger "Vandalia" land speculation project, which abutted his "Indiana" tract on three sides. However, Trent and his partners were unable to receive royal authorization for title to the land, and the project stalled out. They continued to press their claim, but the Revolutionary War overtook their efforts. Trent then tried to obtain recognition of his claim from the American Congress both during and after the Revolution, but he was unsuccessful. Unable to receive authorization of any kind, his land speculation venture failed. In 1784, William Trent moved to Philadelphia, where he died in 1787 at the age of 72.

Captain Jacob Van Braam (1727–?)

As hostages of the French at Fort Duquesne, Van Braam and Captain Robert Stobo were accused of spying and were sent to Montréal for trial. Van Braam was found not guilty, but he remained a hostage in Montréal. As he did at Fort Duquesne, Van Braam availed himself of French hospitality to the maximum. He was quartered in the home of Lieutenant Louis Herbin, a distinguished French officer and a Knight of Saint Louis, who was at the time being held as a prisoner of war in England. Lieutenant Herbin's wife and daughter remained in the home and during the time Van Braam lived there, Herbin's daughter became pregnant. Van Braam was accused of being responsible, but he asserted that he could not have been the father, because at the time he was engaged in an affair with Madame Herbin, the girl's mother. Shortly thereafter, in September 1760, Van Braam was released, and he returned to Williamsburg, where despite his earlier censure regarding the Fort Necessity capitulation agreement, he was cordially welcomed. The Burgesses voted to give him his back pay and also an added compensation of £500 for his "sufferings." He joined the British regular army as a captain in the Royal American Regiment and served until the end of the war, after which he was placed on half pay. He spent the next years trying to get back on active duty and was called up at the outbreak of the American Revolution. He was promoted to major and served at St. Augustine, where he spent a good deal of his time unsuccessfully trying to convince the Royal Governor of Florida to give him a land grant. He resigned his commission in 1779 at the age of 50 and settled in France. His subsequent history is unknown.

Captain Sieur Louis Coulon de Villiers (1710–1757)

After defeating Washington in the Battle of Great Meadows, Villiers continued in the service of the French king. In 1755, Villiers was actively involved in the partisan warfare that raged along the Pennsylvania and western New York frontiers. He gained renown as part of Montcalm's force that captured Fort Oswego on Sunday, August 15, 1756, and Fort William Henry on Tuesday,

August 9, 1757. As a result of his distinguished and valorous service to the king, he was awarded the prestigious Cross of Saint Louis. Villiers went to Québec to receive the coveted award and there he contracted smallpox. "Les Grande" Villiers died of the disease on Wednesday, November 2, 1757, a few days after receiving his award. He was 47 years old.

Edward Ward (birth and death unknown)

In 1757, according to records in the Pennsylvania archives, Ward was promoted to captain in the First Battalion of the Pennsylvania Regiment, and in 1759, he was subsequently promoted to major. There is very little other information regarding his activities during the remainder of the French and Indian War. In 1775, Ward was appointed a justice for the district of West Augusta, Pennsylvania, and records indicate that he served at least into 1776. His son, John Ward, served as a lieutenant under Washington during the Revolutionary War.

Conrad Weiser (1696–1760)

While Washington was preparing to defend Great Meadows and Fort Necessity against the French, Weiser was in Albany meeting with the representatives of the colonies and the Iroquois. The British and colonial representatives were hoping to win the support of the Iroquois in the looming war against the French. Because of their differing perspectives, the colonies could not agree on a unified agreement, but rather each made their own deal with the Indian leaders. Weiser negotiated one of the more successful treaties, in which most of the Indian land in present day Pennsylvania was deeded to Pennsylvania, including the southwestern part that was claimed by Virginia. In 1756, after Braddock's defeat, the Pennsylvania government appointed Weiser a lieutenant colonel, and he along with Benjamin Franklin were tasked to construct a series of forts between the Delaware and Susquehanna Rivers for defense against the French. In 1758, Weiser participated in the Easton Council, which was attended by representatives of several Ohio tribes, and he was instrumental in negotiating an agreement with Ohio Indians for them to abandon their support for the French. The loss of the Ohio Indians was a major blow to the French and prompted them to destroy Fort Duquesne rather than attempt to defend it against Forbes's expedition.

In 1748, Weiser created the city plan for Reading, Pennsylvania, and he was a key figure in the creation of Berks County in 1752. Weiser served as the county's chief judge until his death. In addition, Weiser was active as a lay minister in the Lutheran Church, and was one of the founders of Trinity Church in Reading. Weiser died on his farm at Womelsdorf, Pennsylvania, on Sunday, July 13, 1760. He was about 64 years of age.

George Washington (1732–1799)

After the withdrawal from Great Meadows, Washington continued on to Williamsburg wondering what sort of a reception he would receive. Fortunately Dinwiddie, who was responsible for Washington's appointment as commander during the battle, was as eager as Washington to portray the actions of the Virginians as positively as possible. The governor forwarded Washington's accounts of the campaign to London, where they received mixed but generally favorable reviews by the crown. When King George II read Washington's remark that "I heard the bullets whistle, and believe me, there is something charming in the sound," the king, who was the last reigning monarch to lead troops into battle, remarked, "He would not say so, if he had been used to hear many."[13] However, within a week after the arrival of Dinwiddie's dispatches in England, the Duke of Newcastle and the Duke of Cumberland obtained permission from the king to send an army under General Braddock to remove the French encroachments in the Ohio territory, which they considered to be the domain of England. Near the end of 1754, when Washington learned that British regulars were arriving to fight the French, he resigned his commission as commander of the Virginia Regiment rather than face the possibility of being commanded by regular officers of a much lower rank. When Braddock arrived, however, he recognized that Washington had valuable knowledge of the area west of the Alleghenies, and the general offered the young Virginian a position as volunteer on his staff. In that capacity Washington accompanied Braddock on the march to the Forks of the Ohio and was present during the disastrous route of Braddock's army on Wednesday, July 9, 1755.

When Washington returned to Virginia, he resumed his adjutancy and issued a call for militia to prepare for the anticipated French and Indian invasion. In the autumn of 1755, Dinwiddie appointed Washington to head all Virginia forces, and gave the 23-year-old commander the responsibility of defending a 300-mile frontier. While serving as head of the Virginia forces, Washington ran for Burgess in 1755 and 1757, but was defeated both times. In 1758 Washington took his two Virginia regiments to support Forbes's expedition. Although he served effectively, Washington and Forbes had a disagreement over the route the army would travel. Washington pressed for the old Braddock route, because it would favor Virginia's claims to the Ohio territory. However, Forbes opted for a more northerly route that favored Pennsylvania's claims. Washington was bitterly disappointed over Forbes's choice of routes, and once they accomplished the objective of capturing Fort Duquesne, Washington once again resigned his commission.

On Saturday, January 6, 1759, Washington married the wealthy widow Martha Dandridge Custis, and later that year he was elected a Burgess. When he arrived in Williamsburg for the legislative session, the assembly thanked him for his meritorious military service. He spent the ensuing 15 years until the start of the Revolutionary War as a gentleman farmer and also involved himself in mundane legislative activities. Washington later stated that they were the most enjoyable years of his life. After Great Meadows, he never saw Tanacharison again. Washington died on December 14, 1799, at the age of 67.

Tanacharison (ca. 1700–1754)

After he left Great Meadows just prior to the July third battle, Tanacharison took no further part in the French and Indian War, and he never saw Washington again. He with his family and most of the Indians at Great Meadows went first to Wills Creek and then to Aughwick, Pennsylvania, where George Croghan had established his trading post. In August 1754, Tanacharison travelled to John Harris's Ferry (present Harrisburg, Pennsylvania), to meet with Conrad Weiser. The half-king had learned that Virginians were blaming the defeat at Great Meadows on the supposed treachery of the Indians, claiming they had secretly aided the French. Tanacharison protested this injustice, and publicly criticized Washington's performance and unwillingness to take the Indians' advice as the primary cause of the defeat. Weiser accompanied the half-king back to Aughwick, because the old chief had summoned Delaware and Shawnee leaders for a conference that was held on September 4 through 6, 1754. The conference was another attempt to gain the Ohio Indians' support for the British. The meeting was a failure, because the Indians did not want to leave their homes in Ohio, and they knew that the British could not protect them there.

After the conference, Tanacharison became increasingly ill, and he returned to the trading house of John Harris where he was treated by an Indian healer. The medicine man stated that the half-king had been bewitched by the French in revenge for the great blow he had struck against them in the death of Jumonville. Perhaps not so surprisingly, all the Indian acquaintances of the old chief concurred with the medicine man's assessment. However, based on what is known of his symptoms, it is believed that Tanacharison had contracted pneumonia. Tanacharison died at Harris's Ferry on Friday, October 4, 1754. He was about 54 years old.

The war that was started by the young Virginian and the Seneca half-king in the backwoods of America rapidly spread across the globe and became the French and Indian War or the Seven Years War, as it was referred to in Europe. Historians generally agree that it was, in fact, the real "First World War." It ended in 1763 with the British victorious. The French were evicted from most of New France, including the Ohio territory, which became the undisputed possessions of the British Crown. In that respect, Tanacharison's goal of removing French influence from the Ohio was achieved, but the Iroquois were never able to regain their suzerainty over the Ohio tribes. In reality, the age of the free and wild Indians in the northeast was coming to a close. Even the mighty Iroquois were forced to give way to rapacious white expansion into their traditional homeland. Tanacharison would probably have considered it fortunate that he did not live to see it.

Chapter Notes

Prologue

1. Tanacharison (ca. 1700–1754) was known by several names, including Tanaghrisson, Deanaghrison, Johonerissa, Tanahisson, Thanayieson and Tanareeco. Many writers commonly referred to him as "half-king," so he is often confused with the other half-kings in the Ohio territory, particularly with Scarouady, the Oneida Iroquois half-king. To further confuse readers, Scarouady is also occasionally referred to as Monacatootha, Scruniyatha, and Seruniyatha, names that some writers ascribe to Tanacharison. Tanacharison is described fully in the text, and especially in Chapter Four.

Chapter 1

1. Delaware Indians originally came from the Delaware River basin, hence the name given to them by white settlers. However, they referred to themselves as Lanape (the people) or Lenni-Lenape (the true people). In the early eighteenth century they were displaced westward across Pennsylvania and into the Ohio territory by encroaching white settlements and Iroquois enemies.

2. Venetian Zuan Chabotto, or more popularly Giovanni Caboto, was an Italian navigator and explorer commissioned by Henry VII of England to explore and discover new lands.

3. The Iroquois, also known as Haudenosaunee (People of the Longhouse), were an association of tribes that formed the Iroquois Confederacy, Iroquois League or the Five Nations of the Iroquois, and later, the Six Nations. The original five member nations were the Mohawk, Oneida, Onondaga, Cayuga, and Seneca. The Tuscarora joined the League in the eighteenth century, making it the Six Nations. The governing instrument was the Grand Council located at the central village of Onongada (near present Syracuse, New York), and it was composed of an assembly of 49 hereditary sachems.

4. Alfred Procter James and Charles Morse Stotz, *Drums in the Forest: Decision at the Forks, Defense in the Wilderness* (Pittsburgh: University of Pittsburgh Press, 2005), 21–22.

5. The Wea were a Miami-Illinois-speaking tribe originally located in western Indiana, closely related to the Miami. One French version of their name is Ouiatenon, and another Ouiateno; these were also their villages and are now known as Lafayette and Terre Haute, Indiana, respectively.

6. In 1722, the French built Fort Miamis at the present site of Fort Wayne, Indiana, to serve as a trading center. The Miami Indian central village of Quiskakon, or Kiskakon (cut tail), also referred to as Kekionga (blackberry patch), was located near the confluence of the St. Mary's and Maumee Rivers.

7. William W. Fowler Jr., *Empires at War* (New York: Walker, 2005), 9–10.

8. Randolph C. Downes, *Council Fires on the Upper Ohio* (Pittsburgh: University of Pittsburgh Press, 1940), 52.

9. Shikellamy (?–Dec. 6, 1748), also known as Swatana (enlightener), was an Oneida chief and half-king of the Iroquois who in 1727 was appointed to supervise the Shawnee and Delaware tribes in central Pennsylvania along the Susquehanna River. It was claimed by naturalist John Bartram, who met him in 1743, that Shikellamy was "a Frenchman born at Montréal, and adopted by the Oneidas after being taken prisoner." Contem-

porary accounts list him as able, intelligent, dignified and pleasant. Pennsylvania officials greatly relied on Shikellamy and Conrad Weiser to handle the colony's Indian affairs. Shikellamy was the father of the great chief Logan (Taghneghdorus).

10. Paul A. W. Wallace, *Indians in Pennsylvania* (Harrisburg: Commonwealth of Pennsylvania, 1961), 135.

11. Ibid., 96.

12. Simone Vincens, *Madame Montour and the Fur Trade (1667–1752)*, trans. and ed. Ruth Bernstein (Bloomington: Xlibris, 2011), 206.

13. No other information regarding the birth, death or details of the life of François Saguin has been located.

Chapter 2

1. C. B. Galbreath et al., eds., *Expedition of Celoron to the Ohio Country in 1749* (Columbus: F. J. Heer Printing, 1921), 13.

2. Céloron erroneously referred to Canewango Creek as the Chautauqua.

3. Galbreath et al., *Expedition of Celoron*, 16.

4. Ibid., 27–28.

5. Queen Aliquippa, a Seneca woman and a staunch ally of the British, born sometime between 1670 and 1700, died December 23, 1754, at Aughwick, Pennsylvania. Her name in Delaware means "hat" or "cap." She was a leader of a village of Mingo Seneca located near present McKees Rocks, Pennsylvania. Later she moved her village to present McKeesport, Pennsylvania, and in 1754, after Washington's defeat at Fort Necessity, she moved to Aughwick along with other Indians who favored the English colonies.

6. Galbreath et al., *Expedition of Celoron*, 28.

7. Ibid., 34–35.

8. Céloron's chaplain, Father Bonnecamp, calls it Sinhioto on his map. It was on the north bank of the Ohio, near the present site of Portsmouth, Ohio.

9. The English sometimes referred to the Miamis as Twightwees, which derived from a Delaware Indian term for the Miamis. Miami (Myaamia, plural Myaamiaki) apparently derives from the name for themselves meaning "downstream people."

10. Orontony was also known as Rontondi, Rondoenie, Wanduny, Orontondi, etc.

He is thought to have been born at the Jesuit-Huron village of St. Ignace, in present Michigan. He received the name Nicolas when he was baptized.

11. Wampum are traditional beaded belts of the eastern woodland tribes. The term is originally from the Wampanoag word Wampumpeag, which means "white shell beads." The white beads were generally fashioned from North Channel whelk shells and the purple beads from quahog or hard-shell clam. Woven belts of wampum were created and exchanged to commemorate treaties, historical events or social transactions.

12. Galbreath et al., *Expedition of Celoron*, 56.

13. Jonquière had been appointed governor-general of New France in 1746, but had been taken prisoner by the British that year, during King George's War. He did not arrive in Québec until the late summer or early fall of 1749.

14. A league was a common unit of distance in Europe and was usually reckoned as the distance a man or horse could walk in an hour. As expected, different countries interpreted that distance differently. The English-speaking world most often equated a league to be about 3 statute miles. In France, a league varied and was generally between 3.25 and 4.68 kilometers (approximately 2 to 3 statute miles). In the case of Jules Verne's novel *Twenty Thousand Leagues Under the Sea*, a league was meant to be 4 kilometers or about 2.5 statute miles.

15. Hurons or members of the Huron Confederacy were also referred to as Wyandot or Wynadotte (from Wendat, as they refer to themselves in their native language).

16. Galbreath et al., *Expedition of Celoron*, 57–58.

Chapter 3

1. Charles William Colby, *Canadian Types of the Old Régime, 1608–1698* (New York: Henry Holt, 1910), 51.

2. *The Complete Works of Voltaire*, ed. Theodore Besterman, tome 101 (Banbury, Oxfordshire: Voltaire Foundation, 1971), Correspondence XVII, 1968, letter D7215.

3. Voltaire, *Candide* (Mineola: Dover Publications, 1991), 64.

4. Fort Sandoski or Sandusky was the first fort built by whites in what is now Ohio. It was built on the Sandusky Bay side of

the Marblehead Peninsula in 1745 and remained in service until after 1754, when it was replaced by Fort Junundat at the Wyandot village of the same name across Sandusky bay.

5. Alfred A. Cave, *The French and Indian War* (Westport, CT: Greenwood Press, 2004), 126.

6. Lyman Copeland, ed., *Third Annual Report and Collections of the State Historical Society of Wisconsin for the Year 1856, Vol. III* (Madison, WI: Calkins & Webb Printers, 1857), 199.

7. Ibid., 230.

8. Some sources indicate July 30, 1752, as the date he took office.

9. Downes, *Council Fires on the Upper Ohio*, 60.

10. Ibid., 61.

11. Distances were calculated by customary water and portage routes. To reach the Forks of the Ohio, the route was from Lake Erie via portage to the Allegheny River and thence to the Forks of the Ohio.

12. Sylvester K. Stevens and Donald H. Kent, eds., *Wilderness Chronicles of Northwestern Pennsylvania* (Harrisburg: Pennsylvania Historical Commission, 1941), 41.

13. The French often referred to Lake Chautauqua as Lake Chatakoin.

14. Donald D. Kent, *The French Invasion of Western Pennsylvania 1753* (Harrisburg: Pennsylvania Historical and Museum Commission, 1954), 18.

15. Ibid.

Chapter 4

1. At the New York Council of 1753, a delegation of Mohawks insisted that an Iroquois alliance could only be accomplished by reinstating Johnson. He was reinstated as Indian Commissioner in 1755, and as Superintendent of Indian Affairs for the northern colonies in 1756.

2. Scarouady (side of the sky) (?–1757) was also referred to as Monacatuatha, Monakaduto, Monacatootha, Monacatoocha, etc., meaning "great arrow." He was an Oneida Iroquois and, like Tanacharison, was also a half-king. He was recognized by the Iroquois to provide oversight of the Shawnee in the Ohio territory. He was also known as a famous warrior and chief who participated in 31 battles, killed seven warriors, and took 11 captives. He sided with the British and attempted to sway the Delaware Indians to the British cause. He died in Lancaster, Pennsylvania, in 1757 while attending a treaty.

3. William A. Hunter, "Tanaghrisson," in *Dictionary of Canadian Biography, Vol. 3* (University of Toronto/Université Laval, 2003), accessed February 17, 2013, http://www.biographi.ca/en/bio/tanaghrisson_3E.html.

4. Washington Irving, *George Washington—A Biography* (New York: De Capo Press, 1995), 22.

5. Catawba means "river people," but they also called themselves Iyeye (people) or Nieye (real people). Their homeland was along the Catawba River in North and South Carolina. They were called Flatheads by the Iroquois, because of their practice of forehead flattening of male infants.

6. Wallace, *Indians in Pennsylvania*, 181.

7. Marin to Contrecœur, July 15, 1753, Archives du Séminaire de Québec, V-V, 1:65.

8. Marin, undated letter, Archives du Séminaire de Québec, V-V, 1:65.

9. Kent, *The French Invasion of Western Pennsylvania 1753*, 43.

10. Stevens and Kent, *Wilderness Chronicles of Northwestern Pennsylvania*, 50–51.

11. Ibid.

12. Wallace, *Indians in Pennsylvania*, 107.

13. Susan Katler, ed., *Benjamin Franklin, Pennsylvania, and the First Nations* (Champaign: University of Illinois Press, 2006), 162.

14. Wallace, *Indians in Pennsylvania*, 185.

15. Hugh Cleland, *George Washington in the Ohio Valley* (Pittsburgh: University of Pittsburgh Press, 1955), 10.

16. Charles H. Ambler, *George Washington and the West* (Chapel Hill: University of North Carolina Press, 1936), 41.

17. Cleland, *George Washington in the Ohio Valley*, 11.

18. C. Hale Sipe, *The Indian Chiefs of Pennsylvania* (Lewisburg, PA: Wennawoods, 1994), 186.

Chapter 5

1. Samuel Hazard, ed., *Hazards Register of Pennsylvania, Volume 4* (Philadelphia: Wm. F. Geddes, 1831), 236–237.

2. Severe dysentery; an intestinal inflammation or infection particularly of the colon with symptoms of severe diarrhea in which blood is mixed with the intestinal discharge.

3. Francis Parkman, *Montcalm and*

Wolf—The French & Indian War (New York: De Capo Press, 1995), 77.

4. Kent, *The French Invasion of Western Pennsylvania 1753*, 60.

5. Lawrence Washington had been the adjutant general of all of Virginia's militia units, but upon his death, Virginia was divided into four militia districts. Washington first was given responsibility for the southern district and later held the post for the northern neck and the eastern shore.

6. Joseph L. Peyser, *Jacques Legardeur de Saint-Pierre: Officer, Gentleman, Entrepreneur* (East Lansing: Michigan State University Press, 1996), 203–204.

7. Vernon was first appointed captain in the Royal Navy at the age of 21. He was appointed vice-admiral in 1739. In November 1739, Vernon captured Porto Bello (present Panama) from the Spanish. As a result, he was granted Freedom of the City of London and presented with commemorative medals. Thomas Arne composed "Rule Britannia" to commemorate Vernon's victory at Porto Bello. In 1740, Vernon ordered that the sailors' daily rum ration be diluted with water and that citrus juice be added to the mix. Since Vernon habitually wore a grogham coat, his sailors called him "Old Grog" and the watered down rum ration became known as "grog." It turned out that the vitamin C from the citrus prevented scurvy, which was not proven until 1747 (by James Lind). In 1741, with a much larger fleet of 186 ships and over 26,000 men, Vernon attacked Cartegena and was so certain of victory that before the attack, he sent a message to the king declaring that he had been victorious. His premature message caused a celebration in England larger than when he had conquered Porto Bello. Unfortunately, the garrison of less than 2,000 men and six ships commanded by one-eyed, one-legged, and one-armed Spanish Admiral Blas de Lezo repulsed his assault. In 1745, the British admiralty refused to grant him status as commander-in-chief, which prompted Vernon to resign from the navy the following year.

8. Nemacolin (ca. 1715–1767) was of the Delaware or Lenapi nation, Unami or turtle tribe and the fish clan. He was born along the Susquehanna River in Pennsylvania and died on Blennerhassett Island in the Ohio River. He succeeded his father as chief of a Delaware village located at present Brownsville, Pennsylvania. In 1751, he assisted Thomas Cresap in blazing a trail from Wills Creek (Cumberland, Maryland) to the mouth of Red Stone Creek on the Monongahela River (present Brownsville, Pennsylvania). The route became known as "Nemacolin's Trail" or "Nemacolin's Path," and it approximates present U.S. 40.

9. Allan Powell, *Christopher Gist, Frontier Scout* (Shippensburg, PA: Burd Street Press, 1992), 29.

10. Shingas (ca. 1740–1763) was an Ohio Delaware chief who tried to remain neutral, but eventually sided with the French during the French and Indian War. He became known as "Shingas the Terrible," because of his devastating raids against Anglo-American settlements. The colonial governments of Virginia and Pennsylvania offered a reward for his death. Though he was a very effective warrior, he was also a mild-mannered orator who was never known to treat prisoners with cruelty. He adopted several young white captives as his sons, and according to them, they were accorded equal treatment with his own offspring. It is assumed that he died in the winter of 1763–64, possibly from smallpox-infected blankets that were given to the Indians during Pontiac's War.

11. William A. Hunter, *Forts on the Pennsylvania Frontier, 1753–1758* (Lewisburg, PA: Wennawoods, 1999), 27.

12. Sipe, *The Indian Chiefs of Pennsylvania*, 190.

13. Custaloga was a member of the wolf clan of the Delaware nation. His principal town was located at the confluence of French Creek and North Deer Creek, approximately one mile southeast of Carlton, Pennsylvania. He built another village known as Cussewago, along French Creek at the present site of Meadville, Pennsylvania. He was first mentioned in Washington's journal in 1753. He was on friendly terms with the French until 1759, and then made peace with the English. He became a principal chief of the Delaware in Ohio, settling near present Coshocton, Ohio. He took part in Pontiac's War in 1763, and after Pontiac's War he resettled at Kuskusky near present New Castle, Pennsylvania. In 1770, on his invitation, the Moravians established a mission near present Moravia, Pennsylvania. He died in 1776 and was succeeded as tribal leader by his nephew, Captain Pipe.

14. Kaghswaghtaniunt (?–ca. 1762) was also known as Coswentannea, Gaghswaghtaniunt, Kachshwuchdanionty, and Tohaswuchdoniunty (Belt of Wampum, Old

Belt, Le Collier Pendu, White Thunder). He was a Seneca Indian living on the upper Ohio River.

15. L. H. Everts, *History of Allegheny County, Pennsylvania* (Philadelphia: L. H. Everts, 1876), 22.

16. A Delaware community of several small villages along the Connoquenessing Creek and Breakneck Creek near present day Harmony and Evans City, Pennsylvania. The town was located along the Logstown or Venango Path, which was a trail connecting the Forks of the Ohio, Fort Machault at Venango, Fort Le Bœuf, and Fort Presque Isle.

17. Joncaire to Marin, undated, Archives du Séminaire de Québec, V-V, 5:60:2.

18. Sipe, *The Indian Chiefs of Pennsylvania*, 191.

19. Cleland, *George Washington in the Ohio Valley*, 18.

20. John Marshall, *The Life of George Washington, Vol. I* (Philadelphia: James Crissy and Thomas, Cowperthwait, 1843), 7.

21. Cleland, *George Washington in the Ohio Valley*, 17–18.

22. LaForce (Dec. 4, 1728–Feb. 3, 1802) was the son of Pierre Pepin, also called LaForce, and Michelle Lebert. Some sources list his name as Michél Pepin. See "LaForce, René-Hippolyte," *Dictionary of Canadian Biography Online*, http://www.biographi.ca/009004-119.01-e.php?&id_nbr=2490, accessed February 18, 2013.

23. Cleland, *George Washington in the Ohio Valley*, 19–20.

24. Donald Chaput, "Legardeur de Saint-Pierre, Jacques," in *Dictionary of Canadian Biography, Vol. 3* (University of Toronto/Université Laval, 2003), accessed February 18, 2013, http://www.biographi.ca/en/bio/legardeur_de_saint_pierre_jacques_3E.html.

25. Cleland, *George Washington in the Ohio Valley*, 20.

26. Ibid., 21.

27. Ibid., 31–32.

28. Sipe, *The Indian Chiefs of Pennsylvania*, 193–194.

29. Hunter, *Forts on the Pennsylvania Frontier, 1753–1758*, 27.

30. Cleland, *George Washington in the Ohio Valley*, 25.

31. Hunter, *Forts on the Pennsylvania Frontier, 1753–1758*, 28.

32. Cleland, *George Washington in the Ohio Valley*, 25.

33. Ibid.

34. Ibid., 26.

35. Powell, *Christopher Gist, Frontier Scout*, 32–33.

36. William Darlington, *Christopher Gist's Journals* (Pittsburgh: J. R. Weldin, 1893), 84.

37. Ibid., 84.

38. Cleland, *George Washington in the Ohio Valley*, 26–27.

39. The island was later named Wainwrights Island, but it no longer exists.

40. Cleland, *George Washington in the Ohio Valley*, 27.

41. Darlington, *Christopher Gist's Journals*, 86.

42. Hunter, *Forts on the Pennsylvania Frontier, 1753–1758*, 28.

Chapter 6

1. Andrew Montour (ca. 1720–1772) was also known as Sattelihu and Eghnisera. He was an Indian of mixed blood. His father was Carondawanna, an Oneida war chief, and his mother was Catherine Montour, known as Madame Montour, a noted interpreter for New York Governor Robert Hunter. Andrew Montour was also gifted as a linguist and spoke several languages fluently, including French, English, Delaware, Shawnee, and several of the Iroquois dialects. He held a captain's commission from Virginia. Montour sided with the British throughout the French and Indian War, and his influence among the Indians was so great that the French put a bounty on his head. He was murdered by a Seneca Indian in 1772.

2. Alfred T. Goodman, ed., *Journal of Captain William Trent from Logstown to Pickawillany, A.D. 1752* (Cincinnati: Robert Clarke, 1871), 84.

3. Wilbur R. Jacobs, *Diplomacy and Indian Gifts: Anglo-French Rivalry along the Ohio and Northwest Frontiers, 1748–1763* (Lewisburg: Wennawoods, 2001), 117.

4. Hunter, *Forts on the Pennsylvania Frontier 1753–1758*, 39.

5. Goodman, *Journal of Captain William Trent from Logstown to Pickawillany, A.D. 1752*, 61.

6. Walter O'Meara, *Guns at the Forks* (Englewood Cliffs, NJ: Prentice Hall, 1965), 41.

7. Peyser, *Jacques Legardeur de Saint-Pierre: Officer, Gentleman, Entrepreneur*, 213.

8. Stevens and Kent, *Wilderness Chronicles of Northwestern Pennsylvania*, 31.

9. Israel Daniel Rupp, *Early History of Western Pennsylvania, and of the West, and of Western Expeditions and Campaigns, from MDCCLIV to MDCCCXXXIII* (Pittsburgh: Daniel W. Kauffman, 1847), Appendix VII.

10. Hunter, *Forts on the Pennsylvania Frontier 1753–1758*, 40.

11. An Indian Chief also known as "Old Days." No other information regarding him has been found.

12. Peyser, *Jacques Legardeur de Saint-Pierre: Officer, Gentleman, Entrepreneur*, 219–220.

13. Hunter, *Forts on the Pennsylvania Frontier 1753–1758*, 40–41.

14. O'Meara, *Guns at the Forks*, 41–42.

15. Peyser, *Jacques Legardeur de Saint-Pierre: Officer, Gentleman, Entrepreneur*, 192.

16. O'Meara, *Guns at the Forks*, 43.

17. Ibid.

18. Cleland, *George Washington in the Ohio Valley*, 61.

19. Ibid., 63.

20. George Washington to Robert Dinwiddie, March 9, 1754, Virginia Historical Society, Richmond, E312.72 1962 1:73.

21. Ambler, *George Washington and the West*, 58.

22. *Instant* refers to the current month, abbreviated *inst.*; *ultimo* refers to the previous month, abbreviated *ult.*; *proximo* refers to the next month, abbreviated *prox.*

23. Cleland, *George Washington in the Ohio Valley*, 67.

24. Peter Hog (pronounced with a long *o*, sometimes spelled Hogg or Hoge), was born in 1753 and came to Virginia from Scotland about 1745. He was commissioned captain in 1754 and served with the Virginia Regiment until the fall of Fort Duquesne; he died in 1782.

25. Carolus Gustavus de Spiltdorph was later killed with Braddock at the Battle of the Monongahela.

26. Cleland, *George Washington in the Ohio Valley*, 67–68.

27. Ward was also the half-brother of trader George Croghan. No other information regarding Ward's birth or death have been located.

28. O'Meara, *Guns at the Forks*, 49.

29. Fred Anderson, *Crucible of War* (New York: Vintage Books, 2001), 47.

30. O'Meara, *Guns at the Forks*, 49–50.

31. Linsey-woolsey was a coarse twill used on the frontier that was composed of linen and wool or sometimes of cotton and wool.

32. Vestal's Gap or Keye's Gap crosses the Blue Ridge Mountains at the border of Loudon County, Virginia, and Jefferson County, West Virginia. The gap, at 906 feet in elevation, is one of the lowest crossings of the Blue Ridge in Virginia. It is presently traversed by VA State Route 9 and WVA State Route 9. During the colonial period, it was the main route of travel between Alexandria and Winchester, Virginia.

33. Adam Stephen was a Scottish-born physician (ca. 1718–July 16, 1791). He graduated from King's College in Aberdeen and studied medicine in Edinburgh. He served in the Royal Navy as a medical doctor and immigrated to Virginia in the late 1730s or early 1740s.

34. Alan Axelrod, *Blooding at Great Meadows* (Philadelphia: Running Press Book Publishers, 2007), 155–156.

35. A discussion or conference, particularly between opposing sides to discuss terms of a truce or other matters. From the French word *parler*, which means "to speak," or specifically from *parlez*, meaning "you speak."

36. *Minutes of the Provincial Council of Pennsylvania, Vol. VI* (Harrisburg: Theo. Fenn & Co. Printer, 1851), 29–30.

37. O'Meara, *Guns at the Forks*, 52.

38. William W. Fowler, Jr., *Empires at War* (New York: Walker, 2005), 37.

39. Ibid. Fowler states that "Contrecœur offered rations for the tools, and the next morning as the Virginians were leaving, the French were already busy with their newly acquired hammers and saws." In addition, Francis Jennings reports that "the two gentlemen got along so well that Ward sold Contrecœur his carpentry tools, with which the French resumed the building of the fort." Jennings, *Empire of Fortune* (New York: W. W. Norton, 1988), 65.

40. Darlington, *Christopher Gist's Journals*, 276.

41. Sylvester K. Stevens et al., eds. *Travels in New France by J.-C. B.* (Harrisburg: Pennsylvania Historical Commission, 1941), 56.

Chapter 7

1. Stevens et al., *Travels in New France by J.-C. B.*, 56.

2. Hunter, *Forts on the Pennsylvania Frontier, 1753–1758*, 104.

3. Darlington, *Christopher Gist's Journals*, 278.

4. Ibid.

5. Present Oldtown, Maryland, was initially a Shawnee village abandoned in the early eighteenth century and was subsequently referred to as Shawnese Old Town. Thomas Cresap established a trading post there in 1741, and the place became known as Cresap's Old Town or simply Old Town.

6. George Washington, *Journal of Colonel George Washington: Commanding a Detachment of Virginia Troops*, ed. J. M. Toner, M.D. (Albany: Joel Munsell's Sons, Publishers, 1893), 30.

7. Ibid.

8. Ibid., 44.

9. Ibid., 49.

10. Ibid., 49–50.

11. Ibid., 50–51.

12. Ambler, *George Washington and the West*, 62.

13. Washington, *Journal of Colonel George Washington: Commanding a Detachment of Virginia Troops*, 51–52.

14. James Innes (ca. 1700–1759) was a personal friend of Dinwiddie. He was a native of Scotland and had some prior military experience.

15. Washington, *Journal of Colonel George Washington: Commanding a Detachment of Virginia Troops*, 55.

16. James Mackay also wrote his name as Mackaye. No details are known concerning his birth, other than he was a native of Scotland. He commanded the independent company of South Carolina that joined Washington at Great Meadows in June 1754. He died in 1785.

17. Washington, *Journal of Colonel George Washington: Commanding a Detachment of Virginia Troops*, 63.

18. George Washington, *The Papers of George Washington: 1748–August 1755*, ed. W. W. Abbot (Charlottesville: University of Virginia Press, 1983), 105.

19. Ye is an older spelling of the definite article *the*. The "y" in *ye* was pronounced "th." In Old English and Middle English, the sound "th" was represented by the letter "thorn" (þ). When English printing presses were first established in the 1470s, the type came from continental Europe, where the letter "thorn" was not in use. Instead, typesetters used the letter "y" for "þ" because in the handwriting of the day, the two were similar. This practice was carried over into handwritten documents. The modern revival of the archaic spelling of *the* has not been accompanied with an understanding of how it was pronounced, with the result that the usual pronunciation is "yee."

20. Robert Dinwiddie, *The Official Records of Robert Dinwiddie, Lieutenant-Governor of the Colony of Virginia 1751–1758*, ed. R. A. Brock (Richmond: Virginia Historical Society, 1883), 175.

21. Washington, *Journal of Colonel George Washington: Commanding a Detachment of Virginia Troops*, 74.

22. Ibid., 77.

23. Ibid., 78.

24. No other information regarding Silverheels has been found.

25. Washington, *Journal of Colonel George Washington: Commanding a Detachment of Virginia Troops*, 88.

26. Ibid., 88.

27. Stevens et al., *Travels in New France by J.-C. B.*, 57–58.

28. Ibid., 58.

29. James Veech, *The Monongahela of Old; or, Historical Sketches of Southwestern Pennsylvania to the Year 1800* (Baltimore: Genealogical Publishing, 1975), 46–47.

30. Ambler, *George Washington and the West*, 65.

31. Anderson, *Crucible of War*, 6.

32. Some accounts list his name as Monceau or Marceau, but no other information regarding his full name or biographical data has been found.

33. Stevens et al., *Travels in New France by J.-C. B.*, 57–58.

Chapter 8

1. Washington, *Journal of Colonel George Washington: Commanding a Detachment of Virginia Troops*, 89–90.

2. George Washington, *The Writings of George Washington, Vol. 3*, ed. Jared Sparks (Boston: Russell, Odiorne, & Metcalf and Hilliard, Gray, 1834), 26.

3. Ibid., 32.

4. Washington, *Journal of Colonel George Washington: Commanding a Detachment of Virginia Troops*, 91–94.

5. Ibid., 90.

6. Washington, *The Writings of George Washington, Vol. 3*, 32–34.

7. Caroline Matilda Kirkland, *The Memoirs of Washington* (New York: D. Appleton, 1857), 139.

8. Washington, *The Writings of George Washington, Vol. 3*, 38–39.
9. Ibid., 38–39.
10. Ibid.
11. Ibid., 35.

Chapter 9

1. Washington, *Journal of Colonel George Washington: Commanding a Detachment of Virginia Troops*, 98.
2. George Washington to John Augustine Washington, May 31, 1754, *The Writings of George Washington from the Original Manuscript Sources, Vol. 1* (Washington: U.S. Government Printing Office, 1931), Electronic Text Center, University of Virginia Library.
3. Washington, *Journal of Colonel George Washington: Commanding a Detachment of Virginia Troops*, 99.
4. This is conjecture since there is no surviving evidence of the actual height of the palisade. The archeological details are described in the book *New Light on Washington's Fort Necessity* by J. C. Harrington (Richmond: Eastern National Park and Monument Association, 1957).
5. Washington, *Journal of Colonel George Washington: Commanding a Detachment of Virginia Troops*, 102.
6. It's difficult to determine with any accuracy the number of reinforcements that arrived with Muse, Stobo, and Lewis. In his journal Washington states that "one hundred men and upwards" were with Fry at Winchester. Before the arrival of reinforcements in June 1754, Washington had about 165 men. Some historians place the number of reinforcements with Muse, Stobo, and Lewis from 80 to 180 men. On or about June 14, the independent company under Captain James Mackay arrived with about 100 men. Dinwiddie, is his account of the Battle of Fort Necessity, lists the number of troops under Washington as "few more than 300 besides officers," however most accounts number Washington's force during the defense of Fort Necessity as approximately 400 men. That would indicate that Muse, Stobo, and Lewis arrived with approximately 140 troops.
7. The arrival of Mackay's company of regulars was not recorded in Washington's journal or in other documents. June 14, 1754, is the generally accepted date of their arrival at Great Meadows.

8. Ambler, *George Washington and the West*, 76.
9. Ibid.
10. O'Meara, *Guns at the Forks*, 91.
11. There are several different spellings of Connotaucarious, depending on the source. Washington spelled it "Conotocarious" in his April 1754 letter to Tanacharison.
12. Ambler, *George Washington and the West*, 75.
13. William Polson (?–July 9, 1755) was a native of Scotland who was killed with Braddock at the Battle of the Monongahela.
14. Cleland, *George Washington in the Ohio Valley*, 91–93.
15. Pistole is the name for the last Scottish gold coin. It was minted in Scotland in 1701 under William II. Scottish pistoles were valued at 12 Scottish pounds (£12 Scots) and were the equivalent to one British pound sterling (£1 sterling).
16. Four pistoles or £4 sterling in the mid-eighteenth century is the equivalent of approximately £333 or $600 at today's (2013) rate. However, at the time, the weekly wage for a journeyman tradesman was approximately £1 per week or about £52 per annum. A pound is comprised of 20 shillings (s). The following is a list of the cost of various items in the mid-eighteenth century: dinner in a steakhouse = 1s; sign-on bonus for army enlistment = 1s; postage of one-page letter from London to New York = 1s; weekly rent of a furnished room = 2s; a bottle of claret = 5s; stays for a working woman = 6s; a dozen rabbits = 7s; a stout pair of shoes = 7s; a bottle of Champagne = 8s; 14 1/2 yards of Indian sprigged muslin = 9s; silver-hilted sword = £5; silver watch = £5 5s; a night out, including supper, a bath, and a fashionable courtesan = £6.
17. Washington, *Journal of Colonel George Washington: Commanding a Detachment of Virginia Troops*, 139–140.

Chapter 10

1. O'Meara, *Guns at the Forks*, 93.
2. It is difficult to determine the precise size of Villiers's force. His own journal states that Contrecœur detailed 500 French and 1,100 Indians. Historians generally agree that this is a gross overestimation of the Indian force. Other sources list the French and Canadian force as around 500 to 650 men, plus anywhere from 100 to 300 Indians. J.-C. B.,

who accompanied the expedition, does not give a number of French troops other than to say it was originally intended to be 100 men; he says it was "augmented by 300 savages." However, it is safe to say that the force greatly outnumbered Washington's defenders.

3. O'Meara, *Guns at the Forks*, 95.

4. J. C. Harrington, *New Light on Washington's Fort Necessity* (Richmond: Eastern National Park and Monument Association, 1957), 64.

5. Ibid., 65.

6. A screw tool that attaches to the end of a ramrod, used to withdraw fouled loads from a musket.

7. Cleland, *George Washington in the Ohio Valley*, 99.

8. Harrington, *New Light on Washington's Fort Necessity*, 64.

9. Ibid.

10. Louis Coulon de Villiers, "Articles of Capitulation," transcribed and translated by the National Park Service, Fort Necessity National Battlefield, from *The Papers of George Washington, Vol. 1*, ed. by W. W. Abott (Charlottesville: University Press of Virginia, 1983), http://www.nps.gov/fone/historyculture/capitulation.htm, accessed Feb. 27, 2013. The original document is in the Archives of the District of Montréal.

11. Cleland, *George Washington in the Ohio Valley*, 99–100.

12. Sipe, *The Indian Chiefs of Pennsylvania*, 208.

13. Cleland, *George Washington in the Ohio Valley*, 99–100.

14. Ibid., 111.

15. Ibid., 103–104.

Epilogue

1. Sipe, *The Indian Chiefs of Pennsylvania*, 209–210.

2. Cleland, *George Washington in the Ohio Valley*, 110.

3. Ibid., 112.

4. There were several fortifications constructed on both sides of the Oswego River during the eighteenth and nineteenth centuries. The British outpost constructed in 1727 and destroyed by the French in 1756 was located on the west side of the mouth of the Oswego River, near the present intersection of West 1st Street and Lake Street in Oswego, New York. It was called Fort Oswego; a stone blockhouse was called Fort Burnett; and to further confuse historians, a triangular stone wall, added in 1741, was called Fort Peperrell.

5. Fernand Grenier, "Pécaudy de Contrecœur, Claude-Pierre," in *Dictionary of Canadian Biography, Vol. 4* (University of Toronto/Université Laval, 2003), accessed March 4, 2013, http://www.biographi.ca/en/bio/pecaudy_de_contrecoeur_claude_pierre_4E.html.

6. Pierre Pouchot, *Memoirs on the Late War in North America between France and England*, trans. Michael Cardy and Brian Leigh Dunnigan (Youngstown, NY: Old Niagara Publications, 1994), 141–238.

7. O'Meara, *Guns at the Forks*, 41.

8. Robert C. Alberts, *The Most Extraordinary Adventures of Major Robert Stobo* (Boston: Houghton Mifflin, 1965), 329.

9. Frank E. Grizzard, *George! A Guide to All Things Washington* (Buena Vista, VA: Mariner Publishing, 2005), 231.

10. George Washington, *The Writings of George Washington, 1758–1775, Vol. 2*, ed. Worthington Chauncey Ford (New York: Putnam's, 1889), 343, note 1.

11. Robert Hilliard, "Queen Aliquippa: A History," *Milestones* 21, Autumn 1996, http://www.bchistory.org/beavercounty/BeaverCountyTopical/NativeAmerican/QueenAliquippMA96.html, accessed March 3, 2013.

12. For a full biography of Stobo, see Robert C. Alberts, *The Most Extraordinary Adventures of Major Robert Stobo* (Boston: Houghton Mifflin, 1965).

13. Horace Walpole, *Memoirs of the Reign of King George the Second, Vol. I* (London: Henry Colburn Publisher, 1847), 400.

Bibliography

Albert, G. D. *Report of the Commission to Locate the Site of the Frontier Forts of Pennsylvania: The Frontier Forts of Western Pennsylvania*. Harrisburg: Wm. Stanley Ray, 1916.

Alberts, Robert C. *A Charming Field for an Encounter*. Washington, DC: National Park Service, 1975.

———. *The Most Extraordinary Adventures of Major Robert Stobo*. Boston: Houghton Mifflin, 1965.

Ambler, Charles H. *George Washington and the West*. Chapel Hill: University of North Carolina Press, 1936.

Anderson, Fred. *Crucible of War*. New York: Vintage Books, 2001.

Anonymous. *The Militia-Man: Containing Necessary Rules for Both Officer and Soldier*. Schenectady: United States Historical Research, 1995. Originally published in London circa 1740.

Anson, Bert. *The Miami Indians*. Norman: University of Oklahoma Press, 1970.

Axelrod, Alan. *Blooding at Great Meadows*. Philadelphia: Running Press, 2007.

Baker, Norman L. *Fort Loudon: Washington's Fort in Virginia*. Winchester: French and Indian War Foundation, 2006.

———. *French & Indian War in Frederick County Virginia*. Winchester: Winchester-Frederick County Historical Society, 2000.

Baker-Crothers, Hayes. *Virginia and the French and Indian War*. Chicago: University of Chicago Press, 1928.

Bearor, Bob. *The Battle on Snowshoes*. Bowie, MD: Heritage Books, 1997.

———. *French and Indian War Battlesites: A Controversy*. Bowie, MD: Heritage Books, 2000.

———. *Leading By Example: Partisan Fighters & Leaders of New France, 1660–1760, Vol. 1*. Bowie, MD: Heritage Books, 2002.

———. *Leading By Example, Vol. 3*. Bowie, MD: Heritage Books, 2004.

Berleth, Richard. *Bloody Mohawk: The French and Indian War and American Revolution on New York's Frontier*. Hensonville, NY: Black Dome Press, 2010.

Cave, Alfred A. *The French and Indian War*. Westport, CT: Greenwood, 2004.

Céloron, Pierre-Joseph, and Father Bonnecamps. *The Céloron Expedition to the Ohio Country 1749: The Reports of Pierre-Joseph Céloron and Father Bonnecamps*. Edited by Andrew Gallup. Bowie, MD: Heritage Books, 1997.

Chafe, Wallace L. *Handbook of the Seneca Language*. Albany: University of the State of New York, 1963.

Chaput, Donald. "Legardeur de Saint-Pierre, Jacques." *Dictionary of Canadian Biography, Vol. 3*. University of Toronto/Université Laval, 2003. Accessed February 18, 2013. http://www.biographi.ca/en/bio/legardeur_de_saint_pierre_jacques_3E.html.

Chartarand, René. *The Forts of New France in Northeast America, 1600–1763*. Oxford: Osprey, 2008.

_____. *Monongahela 1754–55: Washington's Defeat, Braddock's Disaster.* Oxford: Osprey, 2004.

Clay, Glen M. *History of Harrison Township.* Harrison Township, PA: Bicentennial Commission, 2010.

Cleland, Hugh. *George Washington in the Ohio Valley.* Pittsburgh: University of Pittsburgh Press, 1955.

Colby, Charles William. *Canadian Types of the Old Régime, 1608–1698.* New York: Henry Holt, 1910.

Copeland, Lyman, ed. *Third Annual Report and Collections of the State Historical Society of Wisconsin for the Year 1856, Vol. III.* Madison, WI: Calkins & Webb Printers, 1857.

Corzier, William Armstrong, ed. *Virginia Colonial Muster: 1651–1776.* New York: Genealogical Association, 1905.

Craig, Neville B. *The Olden Time.* Lewisburg, PA: Wennawoods, 2003.

Custis, George Washington Parke. *Recollections and Private Memoirs of Washington.* Washington, DC: William H. Moore, 1859.

Dale, Ronald J. *The Fall of New France.* Toronto: James Lorimer, 2004.

Darlington, William. *Christopher Gist's Journals.* Pittsburgh: J. R. Weldin, 1893.

Denny, Ebenezer. *Denny's Vocabulary of Wyandot.* Merchantville, NJ: Arx, 2005.

Desloges, Yvon. "LaForce, René-Hippolyte." *Dictionary of Canadian Biography, Vol. 5.* University of Toronto/Université Laval, 2003. Accessed February 18, 2013. http://www.biographi.ca/en/bio/laforce_rene_hippolyte_5E.html.

Dinwiddie, Robert. *The Official Records of Robert Dinwiddie, Lieutenant-Governor of the Colony of Virginia 1751–1758.* Edited by R. A. Brock. Richmond: Virginia Historical Society, 1883.

Downes, Randolph C. *Council Fires on the Upper Ohio.* Pittsburgh: University of Pittsburgh Press, 1940.

Eccles, W. J. *The Canadian Frontier, 1534–1760.* Albuquerque: University of New Mexico Press, 1983.

Eckenrode, H. J. *List of Colonial Soldiers of Virginia.* Richmond: Virginia State Library, 1917.

Everts, L. H. *History of Allegheny County, Pennsylvania.* Philadelphia: L. H. Everts, 1876.

Fowler, William W., Jr. *Empires at War.* New York: Walker, 2005.

Galbreath, C. B., A. A. Lambing, J.-P. de Bonnecamps, and O. H. Marshall, eds. *Expedition of Celoron to the Ohio Country in 1749.* Columbus: F. J. Heer Printing, 1921.

Gallatin, Albert. *A Vocabulary of Seneca.* Merchantville, NJ: Arx, 2009.

Galloway, Colin G. *The Scratch of a Pen.* Oxford: Oxford University Press, 2006.

Gillman, Carolyn. *Where Two Worlds Meet: The Great Lakes Fur Trade.* St. Paul: Minnesota Historical Society, 1982.

Gipson, Lawrence Henry. *The British Empire before the American Revolution.* New York: Alfred A. Knopf, 1970.

Goodman, Alfred T., ed. *Journal of Captain William Trent from Logstown to Pickawillany, A.D. 1752.* Cincinnati: Robert Clarke, 1871.

Grenier, Fernand. "Pécaudy de Contrecœur, Claude-Pierre." *Dictionary of Canadian Biography, Vol. 4.* University of Toronto/Université Laval, 2003. Accessed March 4, 2013. http://www.biographi.ca/en/bio/pecaudy_de_contrecoeur_claude_pierre_4E.html.

Grizzard, Frank E. *George! A Guide to All Things Washington.* Buena Vista, VA: Mariner, 2005.

Hamilton, Edward P. *Fort Ticonderoga: Key to a Continent.* Boston: Little, Brown, 1964.

Harrington, J. C. *New Light on Washington's Fort Necessity.* Richmond, VA: Eastern National Park and Monument Association, 1957.

Hazard, Samuel, ed.. *Hazards Register of Pennsylvania, Vol. 4.* Philadelphia: Wm. F. Geddes, 1831.

Hilliard, Robert. "Queen Aliquippa: A History." *Milestones* 21, Autumn 1996. http://www.bchistory.org/beavercoun

ty/BeaverCountyTopical/NativeAmerican/QueenAliquippMA96.html, accessed March 3, 2013.

Hintzen, William, and Joseph Roxby. *The Heroic Age: Tales of Wheeling's Frontier Era*. Freetown, IN: William Hintzen, 2000.

Hodge, Frederick Webb, ed. *Handbook of American Indians North of Mexico, in Two Parts*. New York: Rowman and Littlefield, 1965.

Hunter, William A. *Forts on the Pennsylvania Frontier, 1753–1758*. Lewisburg, PA: Wennawoods, 1999.

———. "Tanaghrisson." *Dictionary of Canadian Biography, Vol. 3*. University of Toronto/Université Laval, 2003. Accessed February 17, 2013. http://www.biographi.ca/en/bio/tanaghrisson_3E.html.

Hurt, R. Douglas. *The Ohio Frontier: Crucible of the Old Northwest, 1720–1830*. Bloomington: Indiana University Press, 1996.

Irving, Washington. *George Washington—A Biography*. New York: De Capo Press, 1995.

Jacobs, Wilbur R. *Diplomacy and Indian Gifts: Anglo-French Rivalry along the Ohio and Northwest Frontiers, 1748–1763*. Lewisburg, PA: Wennawoods, 2001.

———. *Dispossessing the American Indian*. New York: Scribner's, 1972.

James, Alfred Procter, and Charles Morse Stotz. *Drums in the Forest: Decision at the Forks, Defense in the Wilderness*. Pittsburgh: University of Pittsburgh Press, 2005.

Jennings, Francis. *Empire of Fortune*. New York: W. W. Norton, 1988.

Johnston, John. *Specimen of Shawanoese & Wyandott, or Huron Language*. Waterville: Smoke and Fire, undated.

———. *A Vocabulary of Wyandot*. Merchantville, NJ: Arx, 2009.

Joncaire to Marin, undated. Archives du Séminaire de Québec, V-V, 5:60:2.

Jones, Elizabeth. *Gentlemen and Jesuits: Quests for Glory and Adventure in the Early Days of New France*. Toronto: University of Toronto Press, 1986.

Katler, Susan, ed. *Benjamin Franklin, Pennsylvania, and the First Nations*. Champaign: University of Illinois Press, 2006.

Keeler, Lucy E. *Old Fort Sandoski of 1745 and the Sandusky Country*. Columbus, OH: F. J. Heer, 1912.

Kemmer, Brenton C. *Redcoats, Yankees and Allies: A History of Uniforms, Clothing and Gear of the British Army in the Lake George–Lake Champlain Corridor, 1755–1760*. Bowie, MD: Heritage Books, 1998.

Kent, Donald D. *The French Invasion of Western Pennsylvania 1753*. Harrisburg: Pennsylvania Historical and Museum Commission, 1954.

Kingsford, William. *The History of Canada: Canada under French Rule, Vol. III*. Toronto: Rowsell and Hutchinson, 1889.

Kirkland, Caroline Matilda. *The Memoirs of Washington*. New York: D. Appleton, 1857.

Knepper, George W. *Ohio and its People*. Kent, OH: Kent State University Press, 1989.

Kopperman, Paul E. *Braddock at the Monongahela*. Pittsburgh: University of Pittsburgh Press, 1977.

Leach, Douglas Edward. *Arms for Empire*. New York: Macmillan, 1973.

———. *Roots of Conflict: A Military History of the British Armed Forces and Colonial Americans, 1677–1763*. Chapel Hill: University of North Carolina Press, 1986.

Leckie, Robert. *A Few Acres of Snow*. New York: John Wiley & Sons, 1999.

Lengel, Edward G. *General George Washington: A Military Life*. New York: Random House, 2005.

Lowdermilk, Will H. *History of Cumberland County (Maryland)*. Washington DC: Clearfield, 1878.

Maracle, David Kanatawakhon. *One Thousand Useful Mohawk Words*. London: University of Western Ontario, 1992.

Marin de la Malgue, Paul. Letters. Archives du Séminaire de Québec, V-V, 1:65.

Marshall, John. *The Life of George Washington, Vol. I.* Philadelphia: James Crissy and Thomas, Cowperthwait, 1843.

McCardell, Lee. *Ill-Starred General: Braddock of the Coldstream Guards.* Pittsburgh: University of Pittsburgh Press, 1958.

Miller, Larry L. *Ohio Place Names.* Bloomington: Indiana University Press, 1996.

Moorehead, Warren King. *The Indian Tribes of Ohio.* Edited by Arthur W. McGraw. The Ohio Archaeological and Historical Publications Vol. VII, 1899.

Netherton, Ross. *Braddock's Campaign and the Potomac Route to the West.* Falls Church: Higher Education Publications, 1989.

O'Donnell, James H., III. *Ohio's First Peoples.* Athens: Ohio University Press, 2004.

O'Meara, Walter. *Guns at the Forks.* Englewood Cliffs, NJ: Prentice Hall, 1965.

Parker, Gilbert. *The Seats of the Mighty: Being the Memoirs of Captain Robert Moray, Sometime an Officer in the Virginia Regiment, and Afterward of Amherst's Regiment.* New York: D. Appleton, 1896. EBook available from Project Gutenberg (http://www.gutenberg.org), last updated 2009.

Parkman, Francis. *Montcalm and Wolf: The French & Indian War.* New York: De Capo Press, 1995.

Peckham, Howard H. *The Colonial Wars, 1689–1762.* Chicago: University of Chicago Press, 1964.

_____. *Pontiac and the Indian Uprising.* Chicago: University of Chicago Press, 1961.

Pennsylvania. *Minutes of the Provincial Council of Pennsylvania, Vol. VI.* Harrisburg: Theo. Fenn & Co. Printer, 1851.

Pennsylvania Historical and Museum Commission. *War for Empire in Western Pennsylvania.* Edited by J. Martin West. Harrisburg: Fort Ligonier Association, 1993.

Peyser, Joseph L. *Ambush and Revenge.* Dunbar, PA: Stefano's Printing, 1999.

_____. *Jacques Legardeur de Saint-Pierre: Officer, Gentleman, Entrepreneur.* East Lansing: Michigan State University Press, 1996.

Pouchot, Pierre. *Memoirs on the Late War in North America between France and England.* Translated by Michael Cardy and Brian Leigh Dunnigan. Youngstown, NY: Old Niagara Publications, 1994.

Powell, Allan. *Christopher Gist, Frontier Scout.* Shippensburg, PA: Burd Street Press, 1992.

Quarles, Garland R. *George Washington and Winchester, Virginia 1748–1758.* Winchester: Winchester-Frederic County Historical Society, 1974.

Remington, Frederic. *Goodenough of the Rangers.* Ticonderoga: Fort Ticonderoga, 1997.

Ross, John F. *War on the Run: The Epic Story of Robert Rogers and the Conquest of America's First Frontier.* New York: Bantam Books, 2009.

Roxby, Joseph. *Lost Legends of Fort Henry.* Freetown, IN: William Hintzen, 2001.

Rupp, Israel Daniel. *Early History of Western Pennsylvania, and of the West, and of Western Expeditions and Campaigns, from MDCCLIV to MDCCCXXXIII.* Pittsburgh: Daniel W. Kauffman, 1847.

Sargent, Winthrop. *The History of an Expedition Against Fort Du Quesne in 1755.* Lewisburg, PA: Wennawoods, 1997.

Schutt, Amy C. *The Lands Would Be Entirely Theirs Again: Indians and the Seven Years' War in the Ohio Valley.* Fort Washington, PA: Eastern National, 2009.

Schwartz, Seymour I. *The French and Indian War, 1754–1763: The Imperial Struggle for North America.* New York: Simon & Schuster, 1994.

Sipe, C. Hale. *The Indian Chiefs of Pennsylvania.* Lewisburg, PA: Wennawoods, 1994.

Smith, Carter, ed. *Battles in a New Land: A Sourcebook on Colonial America.* Brookfield, CT: Millbrook Press, 1991.

Steele, Ian K. *Betrayals: Fort William Henry & the "Massacre."* New York: Oxford University Press, 1990.
Stevens, Sylvester K., and Donald H. Kent, eds. *Wilderness Chronicles of Northwestern Pennsylvania*. Harrisburg: Pennsylvania Historical Commission, 1941.
_____, Donald H. Kent, Emma E. Woods, H. R. Casgrain, and J.-C. B., eds. *Travels in New France by J.-C. B.* Harrisburg: Pennsylvania Historical Commission, 1941.
Stotz, Charles Morris. *Outposts of the War for Empire*. Pittsburgh: Historical Society of Western Pennsylvania, 1985.
_____. *Point of Empire: Conflict at the Forks of the Ohio*. Pittsburgh: Historical Society of Western Pennsylvania, 1970.
Todish, Timothy J. *America's 'First' World War: The French and Indian War, 1754–1763*. Ogden: Eagle's View Publishing, 1988.
Tottle, Edward Loring. *War in the Woods*. Windham, ME: Educational Materials, 1991.
Trudel, Marcel. *The Jumonville Affair*. Translated by Donald H. Kent. Fort Washington, PA: Eastern National Park & Monument Association, 1989.
Veech, James. *The Monongahela of Old; or, Historical Sketches of Southwestern Pennsylvania to the Year 1800*. Baltimore: Genealogical Publishing, 1975.
Villiers, Louis Coulon de. "Articles of Capitulation." Transcribed and translated by the National Park Service, Fort Necessity National Battlefield, from *The Papers of George Washington, Vol. 1*, edited by W. W. Abbott (Charlottesville: University Press of Virginia, 1983). http://www.nps.gov/fone/historyculture/capitulation.htm, accessed Feb. 27, 2013.
Vincens, Simone. *Madame Montour and the Fur Trade (1667–1752)*. Translated and edited by Ruth Bernstein. Bloomington, IN: Xlibris, 2011.
Voltaire. *Candide*. 1759. Mineola: Dover Publications, 1991.
Voltaire. *The Complete Works of Voltaire*. Edited by Theodore Besterman. Banbury, Oxfordshire: Voltaire Foundation, 1971.
Wahll, Andrew, J. *Braddock Road Chronicles, 1755*. Bowie, MD: Heritage Books, 1999.
Wallace, Paul A. W. *Conrad Weiser, Friend of Colonist and Mohawk*. Lewisburg, PA: Wennawoods, 1996.
_____. *Indians in Pennsylvania*. Harrisburg: Commonwealth of Pennsylvania, 1961.
Walpole, Horace. *Memoirs of the Reign of King George the Second, Vol. I*. London: Henry Colburn, 1847.
Washington, George. *Journal of Colonel George Washington: Commanding a Detachment of Virginia Troops*. Edited by J. M. Toner, M.D. Albany: Joel Munsell's Sons, 1893.
_____. *The Papers of George Washington: 1748–August 1755*. Edited by W. W. Abbot. Charlottesville: University of Virginia Press, 1983.
_____, to Robert Dinwiddie, March 9, 1754. Virginia Historical Society, Richmond, E312.72 1962 1:73.
_____. *The Writings of George Washington, 1758–1775, Vol. 2*. Edited by Worthington Chauncey Ford. New York: Putnam's, 1889.
_____. *The Writings of George Washington from the Original Manuscript Sources, Vol. 1*. Edited by John C. Fitzpatrick. Washington: U.S. Government Printing Office, 1931. University of Virginia Library, Electronic Text Center.
_____. *The Writings of George Washington, Vol. 3*. Edited by Jared Sparks. Boston: Russell, Odiorne, & Metcalf and Hilliard, Gray, 1834.
West, Martin. *Fort Ligonier*. Pittsburgh: Knepper Press, 2009.
White, Richard. *The Middle Ground: Indians, Empires, and Republics in the Great Lakes Region, 1650–1815*. Cambridge: Cambridge University Press, 1991.
Wilcox, Frank. *Ohio Indian Trails*. Cleveland: Gates Press, 1934.
Williams, Noel St. John. *Redcoats Along the*

Hudson: The Struggle for North America, 1754–63. London: Brassey's, 1997.

Winchester-Frederic County Historical Society. *Winchester-Frederick County Historical Society Journal, Vol. XII 2000*. Winchester, VA: Winchester-Frederic County Historical Society, 2000.

Works Project Administration (WPA) Writers Program. *The Ohio Guide*. Minneapolis: Somerset Publishers, 1940.

Index

Numbers in ***bold italics*** indicate pages with maps.

à la façon du pays 12
Abercrombie, James 168
Abraham 46
Acadians 154, 155, 167
Adirondak Indians 35
adoption 46, 49, 179, 182
Agathe 139
agent 47, 80, 153, 157, 169
Albany, New York 51, 80, 175
Albemarle, Lord 83
Alexandria, Virginia 62, 63, 89, 91, 136, 166, 184
Allegheny River 2, 12, 15, 23–24, ***37***, ***42***, 43–45, 47, 52–53, 57–58, 60, 62, ***63***, 64, 67, 78, 80, 82–87, 90, 92, 154–155, 167, 181
ambush 116, 140, 164
ammunition 47, 85, 90, 99–100, 106, 108, 128, 143, 149
Anse au Foulon 173
Appalachian Mountains 12, 20, 33, 36
Arkansas River 12
arquebus 50; see also matchlock
artillery 36, 47, 73, 82, 84, 90, 92–96, 98–99, 103, 106, 123, 125, 134, 141, 144, 145, 153, 164, 167; see also cannon
Ashland, Wisconsin 71
assassination 139, 144–147, 153
Aughwick, Pennsylvania 157, 170–171, 177, 180
Austria 7, 154, 166

Baltimore, Maryland 13, 18
Bar, François 43, 154–155, 168–170; see also Bigot, François
Barcelona, New York 23
Bastille 154–155, 168, 170
bateau 18, 21, 23, 30–31, 44, 53, 85, 92, 98, 103
Bath, England 158, 160, 186
Battle of Lake George 154, 165
Battle of the Monogahela 147, 153–154, 156–159, 161–164, 170–172, 175–176, 184, 190
Battle on Snowshoes 164
La Baye 39, 165; see also Green Bay, Wisconsin
Beauharnois, Charles de la Boische, Marquis de 71

Beaver, Pennsylvania 49
Beaver River ***42***, 49, 55, ***63***, ***64***
beaver wars 50–51
Belestre, François-Marie 35
la Belle Rivière 12, 15, ***22***, 23, 33, ***42***, 45; see also Ohio River
Belvoir 63, 79, 159–160
Benedictine 162
Berkeley County, West Virginia 172
Berks County, Pennsylvania 175
besieged 102, 143, 164, 168
Bethlehem, Pennsylvania 171
bewitched 177
Bigot, François 43, 154–155, 168–169; see also Bar, François
bison 15
bivouac 10, 85, 92, 108–110, 113, 152
Blois, France 170
bloody flux 60
Blue Ridge Mountains 90, 184
Boishébert, Charles de Deschamps de et de Raffetot 45, 155–156
bonus 87, 186; see also bounties
Boscowen, Edward 154
bounties 8, 15, 168, 183; see also bonus
Bouquet, Henry 157
Braddock, Edward V. 133, 147, 153–154, 156–159, 161–164, 170–172, 175–176, 184, 186, 190
Braddock, Pennsylvania 63
Brant, Joseph 46; see also Thayendanegea
Brant, Molly 46
Bristol, England 158
British Navy 62, 154, 182, 184
Broken Straw Creek 24
Brownsville, Pennsylvania 36, 182
Brunswick-Wolfenbüttel 154
Buckaloons 24; see also Kachinodiagon; Paille Coupe
Buffalo, New York 48
burgesses 87, 136, 146, 170, 174, 176–177
Burgoyne, John 165
Byng, John 162

195

Index

Cabot, John 13, 179
Callender, Robert 101
Canachquasy 131
Canada 4, 10, 12, 15, 21, 28, 33–34, 38–039, 61, 73, 80, 94, 114, 140, 145, 151, 153–156, 159, 163–165, 167
Candide 34, 162
cannon 36, 47, 73, 82, 84, 90, 92–96, 98–99, 103, 123, 125, 141, 144–145, 153, 164, 167; *see also* artillery
canoe 18, 21, 23, 25, 30–31, 35, 64, 73–76, 92, 98, 103, 173
capitulation 97, 139, 144, 146–149, 151–152, 159, 166, 174
Carleton, Guy 163, 165
Carlton, Pennsylvania 71, 182
Carolina 13, 27–28, 46, 48, 87–88, 94, 101–102, 125–126, 130–131, 142, 162–163, 165, 185
Cartier, Jacques 11
cartridges 142
casualties 28, 113, 142–143, 152, 154, 166, 172
Catawba Indian 48, 88, 181
Cayenne 155; *see also* French Guiana
Céloron, Pierre Joseph, de Blainville 21–36, 22, 38–40, 44, 53, 57, 68, 85, 156, 189
Chagouamigon 71
Champlain, Samuel de 11, 50
Chapman, Nathaniel 20
Charlevoix, Fr. Pierre François-Xavier de 11
Charlottesville, Virginia 88
"charming field for and encounter" 106, 121, 137
Charter of 1609 13
Chartier, Peter 25
Chartier's Creek 64
Chartier's Old Town 22, 25
Chatakoin 22, 23, 42, 43–45, 181
Chatham, England 173
Chauvignerie, Michel Maray de La 83
Cherokee Indians 88
Chestnut Ridge 37, 103–105, 108, 131, 132, 133, 135
Chickasaw 39
La Chine 21, 53
Chiningué 11, 16, 22, 27, 35, 37, 41, 43–44, 48–49, 54–56, 64, 67–68, 71, 75–66, 80–81, 83–85, 88, 122, 183; *see also* Logstown; Shenango
Chippewa Indians 35, 39, 99
Cincinnati, Ohio 28
Clements, William F. Library 4
Cleveland, Ohio 15, 19
Cold Foot 31, 34–35, 38; *see also* Pied Froid
College of William and Mary 88
Columbus, Christopher 4
Committee of Correspondence 158
company (military) 81–82, 88–91, 102–103, 117, 124–125, 128, 130, 134–136, 139, 142, 149, 152, 164–166, 186
Conchaké 3, 22, 29

Conewango 23, 42
Congress 4, 174
Connellsville, Pennsylvania 101
Conotocarious or Connotaucarious 100, 131, 186
Contrecœur, Claude-Pierre Pécaudy de 44, 156, 165, 187
Cooper, James Fenimore 2
copper plate 21, 23; *see also* tin plate
Corlear 54
corruption 15, 18, 24, 27–28, 41, 43, 155, 169, 170; *see also* profiteering
Coshocton, Ohio 29, 182
council 9, 11, 16, 2426, 28, 31, 34, 41, 47–50, 52–54, 64–65, 68, 70, 75, 80–81, 83, 88, 100, 109, 118, 131–132, 134, 156, 166, 168–169, 171, 175, 179
coureurs de bois 12, 151
court martial 102, 162, 172
cowardice 39, 90, 142, 146, 151, 162, 168
Creek Indians 171
Cresap, Thomas 36, 63, 81, 97–98, 182, 185
Croghan, George 3, 14–16, 19, 35, 47, 80, 82, 83, 84, 157, 158, 170–171, 173, 177, 184
Crown Point 4, 153, 165
Cumberland 36, 163, 176, 182; *see also* Fort Cumberland; Wills Creek
Curran, Barnaby 62, 69
Cussewago 42, 71, 95, 182
Custaloga 42, 67, 71, 84, 182
Cuyahoga River 15, 18–19, 22

damn the capitulation 149
Darcy, Robert, 4th Earl of Holderness 58
Davidson, John 64, 69–70, 105
Dayton, Ohio 161
Deer Creek 71, 182
Dejiqueque 84
Delaware (colony) 13
Delaware Indians 11, 13–17, 24–26, 36, 47, 49, 51, 54, 63–64, 66–68, 71, 83–84, 128, 134, 157, 171, 177, 180–181, 183
Delaware River 175, 179
le demi roi 47; *see also* half-king
La Demoiselle 29, 31; *see also* Old Briton, Memeskia
deserter 35, 84, 102, 104, 118–119, 128, 134, 137, 140, 152, 163
Dick, Charles 168
Dieskau, Baron de 154, 167
Dinwiddie, Robert 9, 20, 41, 47, 57–59, 61–62, 65–66, 71, 73–74, 76, 79, 80–82, 86–89, 91, 95, 99, 101–103, 106–107, 116–121, 124, 130, 136, 158, 162–163, 168, 170, 172, 176, 185–186
diplomacy 2, 8, 10, 16–17, 37, 39, 48, 51, 54–56, 64–66, 68, 83, 109–110, 114, 116, 134, 146
Domitilde 39
Drouillon, Pierre Jacques de Macé 104, 116
drums 89, 93, 143–145, 150, 179, 191

Index

drunk 83, 143, 172
Duke of Bedford 120
Dunbar, Thomas 158, 192
Dunlap, William 36
Duquesne, Michel-Ange 33, 36, 38, 40–41, 43–45, 54, 60, 73, 74, 85–86, 97, 140, 156, 158–159, 167
Dutch 50–51, 143, 146

earthworks 36, 81, 126–127, 131, 136; *see also* entrenchments
Easton, Pennsylvania 175
Easton Council 175
emissary 10, 53–54, 58, 65, 83, 101, 115, 116, 118, 146
entrenchments 106, 122, 126, 131, 136, 153; *see also* earthworks
Erie, Pennsylvania 45
Erie Indians 50
Etherington, George 164–165
Etna, Pennsylvania 47
Evans City, Pennsylvania 67, 183
exhaustion 52–53, 60, 76, 85–86, 104, 135

factor 80; *see also* agent
Fairfax, Deborah Clarke 159
Fairfax, George William 79, 159–161
Fairfax, Sally Cary 79, 160–161
Fairfax, Sarah Walker 159
Fairfax, Sir William 159
Fairfax County 4
falls 15, 37, 44, 99, 104
Falls of the Ohio 37; *see also* Louisville, Kentucky
Farmington, Pennsylvania 105
First Virginia Regiment of the Continental Line 4
First World War 10, 178
flag 22, 27, 92, 96, 144, 145, 150
fleur-de-lis 96
fools 151
Forbes, John 157, 160–161, 173, 175–176
Forks of the Ohio 9, 11, 20, *22*, 25–26, 36, *37*, 41, 43–44, 47, 49, 55, 57–58, *63*, 64–65, 76–93, 95–99, 101–107, 116, 140, 153–154, 158, 173, 167, 173, 176, 183
fort 1, 3–4, 9, 12, 14, 18–20, 28–31, 33, 35–38, 40–41, 43–46, 49, 52–55, 57–62, 64, 66–71, 73–77, 79–86, 90–93, 95–104, 106, 110, 114, 116, 121–129, 131–132, 134–137, 139–142, 144–145, 148, 151–165, 167–168, 170–175, 177, 179–180, 183–184, 186–187; *see also* strong house
Fort Beauséjour 155
Fort Bedford 4
Fort Crown Point 4
Fort Cumberland 163; *see also* Cumberland; Wills Creek
Fort Detroit 18–19, *22*, 29, 31, 35, 38, 40, 43, 57, 83, 86, 155–157, 165
Fort du Portage 44, *42*, *63*

Fort Duquesne 103–104, 106, 110, 114, 116, 122–123, 128, 140, 145, 148, 152–153, 157–162, 164, 167, 171–172, 174–175, 177, 184
Fort Edward 4
Fort Frontenac 153
Fort Junundat 3, *22*, 28, 31, 181; *see also* Junundat
Fort Le Bœuf 4, 15, *42*, 52–53, 55, 60, *63*, 69–71, 73, 75, 80–81, 84, 86, 154–155, 165, 183
Fort Ligonier 4, 91, 93
Fort Machault *42*, 54, 60, *63*, 67–71, 75–77, 80–81, 83–84, 86, 154, 183
Fort Miamis 14, *22*, 28, 30–32, 38, 139, 179
Fort Michilimackinac 39, 164–165
Fort Necessity 4, 122, 125–129, 132, 135–136, 140, 141, 142, 144, 148, 153, 158, 170, 172, 174–175, 186–187
Fort Niagara *22*, 41, *42*, 43–44, 53, 57, *63*, 68, 85, 153, 163
Fort Oswego 153, 163, 174, 187
Fort Pitt 173
Fort Presque Isle *42*, 45–47, 53–55, 60, *63*, 85–86, 98, 154, 167, 183
Fort Prince George 80, 82–83, 83, 86, 90, 92, 97–98, 167; *see also* Trent's Fort
Fort Roberdeau 4
Fort St. Frédéric 153–154, 165, 167
Fort Sandoski 3, *22*, 28, 35, 56, 180
Fort Shirley 157
Fort Stanwix 157, 173
Fort Ticonderoga 168
Fort Wayne, Indiana 14, 30, 179
Fort William Henry 154, 164, 168, 174
40th degree north latitude 11
Fortress Louisbourg 155, 167, 173
fossil 38
Franklin, Benjamin 175, 181, 191
Franklin, William 157
Fraser, Jane Bell McClain 161–162
Fraser, John 14–15, 25, 47, 69, 78–79, 89–90, 93, 95, 102, 161–162, 173
Fredericksburg, Virginia 62, *63*
French Creek 15, *42*, 45, 52, 54, 60, *63*, 70–73, 75, 86; *see also* Rivière aux Bœufs
French Guiana 155; *see also* Cayenne
French Revolution 167
Fry, Joshua 9, 88–89, 91, 98–99, 101, 107, 117, 122–124, 186
fur trade 12–14, 18–20, 25, 30, 39, 50, 89

Galissonière, Marquis Roland-Michel Barrin de La 21, 23, 25, 31, 33–34, 162
George II (king) 14, 16, 25, 33, 44, 80, 155, 166–167
George III (king) 82
Georgia 162, 166
Germantown, Pennsylvania 172
gifts 24, 29–30, 35, 40, 48, 58, 69, 75, 81, 131, 183

Gist, Christopher 35, *37*, 37–38, *63*, 68–69, 76–79, 81–82, 89, 92, 101, 105–108, 110, 124, 131–132, *132*, 134–135, 140, 153, 162
Glen, James 88
Goochland County, Virginia 88
governor-general 21, 23, 25–26, 31, 34, 38, 40, 43, 60, 68, 71, 73, 85–86, 94, 97, 139, 153, 156, 158–159, 162, 167, 180
Grand Haven, Michigan 164
Grand Pré 155, 157
Grand River 164
Grand Société 170
Great Crossing *37*, 102, 105
Great Lakes *22*, 30
Great Meadows *37*, *63*, 102, 105–110, 118, 121–132, *132*, 134–143, *141*, 145–153, 161–162, 164, 170, 174–177
Great Miami River 15, *22*, 28; *see also* Miami River
greed 18–19, 43, 65
Green Bay Wisconsin 39, 165; *see also* La Baye
Grey Nuns 156
la Guerre de la Conquéte 10; *see also* War of Conquest
gunpowder 19, 149
Guyasuta 67, 69; *see also* Hunter

Half-King 2, 4, 9, 41, 44, 47–52, 54, 56, 58, 60, 62, 64–70, 74–76, 78, 82–83, 92, 96–100, 103, 105, 107–110, 113–115, 117–118, 120, 122–123, 131, 136–137, 147, 151, 154, 170–171, 177–179, 181; *see also* Scarouady; Tanacharison
Hamilton, James 47
Hanbury, John 20
Hanover 154
Harmony, Pennsylvania 67, 183
Harris, John 177
Harrisburg, Pennsylvania 177
Harris's Ferry 177
hatchet 54, 78, 94, 108, 118, 128
Hendrick (king) 46; *see also* Tiyanoga
Hendrick, Caroline 46
Herbin, Louis 174
Hesse-Kassel 154
Historical Society of Pennsylvania 4
Hog, Peter 89, 108, 184
honors of war 144–145
hostage 145, 148–150, 158, 163, 172, 174
hub, trading 18, 27, 29, 57
Hunter 67; *see also* Guyasuta
Huron 2, 28, 32, 50, 180; *see also* Junundat; Wendat; Wyandot; Wyandotte,

"I heard the bullets whistle..." 122, 176
Illinois 13, 34, 44, 157, 179
Independent Company of Regulars 87, 102–103, 125, 128, 134–136, 139, 142, 152, 165–166, 185–186
Indian healer 177; *see also* medicine man

Indian Run 105, *132*, 141
Indian walking dress 17
Indiana 13–14, 28, 30, 38, 62, 179; land speculation 157, 173–174
industrial revolution 14, 17
infantry 89, 138, 140, 144
Innes, James 101–102, 124, 163, 185
Innes Academy 163; *see also* Thalian Hall
intelligence 9, 70, 84, 92, 95, 98, 107, 110, 119, 152, 159, 172
interpreter 15, 29, 64, 69, 81, 95, 104, 114, 146, 183
Iroquois 2, 8–9, 11, 13–14, 16–17, 34–35, 41, 46–56, 58–59, 64–68, 88, 94, 153–154, 171, 175, 178, 179, 181, 183; protests 54–56; women delegation 54; *see also* Six Nations
Irvine, Pennsylvania 24

J.C.B. 152
Jefferson, Peter 88
Jefferson, Thomas 88
Jenkins, William 62, 69
Jeskakake 67, 69
Jesuit 8, 39, 180
Johnson, William 16, 46–47, 153–154, 157, 165, 181; *see also* Warraghiyagey
Joliet, Louis 11
Joncaire, Phillipe-Thomas Chaubert de 35, 44, 68–70, 75–77, 83–84
Jonquière, Jacques-Pierre de Taffanel Marquis de la Jonquière 31–35, 38, 68, 156, 180
Jumonville, Ensign Joseph Coulon de Villiers de 1, 97, 104, 107, 109–110, 113–121, 123–124, 139–140, 143, 145–148, 150, 158, 177
Jumonville Glen 1, 7, 9, 109–113, *111*, 117, 119, *132*, 139–140
Junundat 3, *22*, 28, 31, 181

Kachinodiagon *22*, 24, *42*, 182; *see also* Buckaloons; Paille Coupe
Kaghswaghtaniunt 67, 69, 76, 182; *see also* White Thunder
Kamouraska, Québec 163
Kan-es-ta-ke 68–69
Kanawha River *22*, 173
Kentucky 13, 15, 62
King George's War 14, 16, 25, 33, 44, 80, 155, 166–167; *see also* War of the Austrian Succession
"king of the Pennsylvania traders" 14, 83
King William's War 7–8, ;*see also* War of the League of Augsburg
Kiskakon *22*, 29, 179; *see also* Kekionga; Quiskakon
Kittanning *22*, 25, *42*

Lac Saint Sacrement 154, 165; *see also* Lake George
LaForce, René-Hippolyte 70, 89, 100–101, 104, 107, 109, 116–117, 119–120, 163–164, 183

Index

Lake Champlain 50, 153, 159, 168
Lake Chautauqua 23, *42*, 44–45, 180, 181
Lake Erie *22*, 31, *42*, 44–45, 52, *63*, 85, 181
Lake George 154, 164–165, 168; *see also* Lac Saint Sacrement
Lake of the Two Mountains 68–69, 94
Lake Ontario *22*, 23, *42*, 70, 153, 163–164
Lake Superior 12
Lancaster, Pennsylvania 34, 41, 57, 80, 181
land bounty 87, 168, 183
land grant 20, 161, 173–174
land speculation 13, 20, 41, 57–59, 157, 162, 173–174
Langlade, Augustin 39
Langlade, Charles, Jr. 39
Langlade, Charles Michel 39–40, 81, 1645–165
La Salle, René-Robert Cavelier, Sieur de 11, 70
The Last of the Mohicans 2
Latrobe, Pennsylvania 161
Laurel Ridge 104
lead plate 22–25, 28, 57, 156; inscription 23–24
Lee, Thomas 8
Legardeur, Jacques de Saint-Pierre 69–76, 82, 84–86, 165
legislature 59, 87, 102–103, 156, 177
Lewis, Andrew 91, 124, 134, 186
Library of Congress 4
lieutenant governor 1, 9, 20, 41, 47, 57–58, 60–61, 71, 74, 76, 80–81, 86–87, 103, 107, 117, 119–121, 136, 158, 163, 170, 172
liquor 69, 74–75, 83, 148; *see also* rum
Lisieux, France 168
livre 155–156, 159, 170
Logstown 11, 16, *22*, 26–27, 35, 37, 41, *42*, 43–44, 48–49, 54–56, *63*, 64, 67–68, 71, 75–76, 80–85, 88, 122, 183; *see also* Chiningué; Shenango
London, England 20, 58, 176, 186
Longueuil, Charles Le Moyne de 36, 38–39
Lord Dunmore's War 157
Louis XIV, King 11, 60
Louis XV, King 23, 33, 166
Louisville, Kentucky 15; *see also* Falls of the Ohio
Lower Shawnee Town 3, 27; *see also* St. Yotoc; Scioto Town
Loyalist 160

Machault, Jean-Baptiste d'Arnouville 60, 166–167
Mackay, Ann 166
Mackay, James 102, 128–132, 134–135, 137, 146, 152, 165, 166, 185, 186
mammoth 38
Marin, Paul de la Malgue 44–46, 51–56, 58, 60, 66, 68–71, 85–86, 155, 167
Markleysburg, Pennsylvania 102
Marquette, Fr. Jacques 11

Martin, Thomas 172
Martinsburg, West Virginia 172
Maryland 13, 36, 47, 54, 58–59, 97, 99, 101, 163, 182, 185
Massachusetts 8, 153
match coat 77
matchlock 50; *see also* arquebus
Maumee River *22*, 30–31, 179
Mayville, New York 23
McGuire, John 62, 69
McKay, Barbara 166
McKay, Mary 166
McKee's Rocks 26, 44, 79, 180
McKeesport, Pennsylvania 180
Meadville, Pennsylvania 71, 182
medals 131, 182
medicine man 177; *see also* Indian healer
Memeskia 29–31, 34–35, 38–40, 49, 51; *see also* La Demoiselle; Old Briton
Mercer, George 20
Mercer, John 20
Mercier, François-Marc-Antoine Le 45, 53, 86, 93–95, 143, 167, 168
Miami Indians 28–32, 34–35, 38–40, 49, 51, 83, 156, 179, 180
Miami River 15, *22*, 28; *see also* Great Miami River
Michigan 13, *22*, 39, 164, 180
Michilimackinac 39, 164–165
Micmac 155
militia 39, 61, 81, 85, 87–88, 91, 123, 128, 137, 143, 159, 161, 164–165, 167–168, 176, 182
Mingo 9, 47–48, 66, 98–99, 108, 122, 134, 157, 170, 180
Minnesota 13
Minorca 162
Misencik, Karen 4
Misencik, Paul, Jr. 4
Misencik, Sally 4–5, 128
Mississippi River 11–12, 16
Missouri River 12
Mohawk 15, 34, 46, 68, 179, 181
Monacatootha 49, 117, 179, 181; *see also* Scarouday; Scruniyatha; Seruniyatha, HMS *Monarch* 162
Moncrif, François-Augustin Paradis de 34
Monongahela River *22*, 36, *37*, *42*, 43, *63*, 63–64, 78–79, 81, 84, 99, 103, *132*, 163–164, 170–173, 182, 184, 186
Montcalm, Louis-Joseph de 155, 164, 167–168, 174
Montour, Andrew 81–83, 157
Montour, Madame Catherine 183
Montréal 12, 17–18, 21, 31, 33, 36, 38–39, 44–45, 51, 55, 60, 68, 85, 94, 153, 156, 164–165, 173–174, 179, 187
Montréal Treaty 51
Moravian 171, 182
Mouceau 114, 123
mound builder 36
Mount Vernon 4, *63*, 160, 166, 168

Muddy Creek 71
Mughal Empire 154
murder 10, 15, 113, 115, 147, 183
Murdering Town *63*, 67, 77; *see also* Murthering Town
Murthering Town *63*, 67; *see also* Murdering Town
Muse, Battaile 169
Muse, George 124–125, 127, 142, 146, 168–169, 186
musket 7, 27, 50, 77, 82, 85, 112–113, 123, 125–126, 136, 139, 141–142, 187
musketry 1, 139–140, 142

National Museum of the American Indian 4
Native Americans 3–4, 11; *see also* First Nation
Nemacolin, Nemacolin Trail 36, *37*, 63, 100, 131, *132*, *141*, 182
Neuchâtel, Switzerland 155
New France 8, 12–13, 17, 19, 21, 23, 25, 31, 33, 43, 151, 153–154, 159, 162, 167–168, 178, 180
New Jersey 13
New York 4, 8, 13, 15, 18, 23, 41–44, 47–48, 50–51, 54, 59, 68, 87, 102, 136, 155, 157, 164, 174, 179, 181, 183, 186–187
Niagara, Fort Niagara, Niagara Falls 22, 41, *42*, 43–44, 53, 57, *63*, 68, 85, 153–154, 163
Nicollet, Jean 11
Nippissing Indians 35
Nissowaquet 39; *see also* La Fourche
North Carolina 13, 27–28, 48, 88, 94, 101, 163
Le Nouvelle Orlans 12; *see also* New Orléans
Nova Scotia 154–155

Oglethorpe, James 130
Ohio 2–4, 14–15, 18–21, *22*, 24–25, 27–29, 31–41, 43–45, 47–52, 55–59, 61–62, 64–68, 72, 75, 80–83, 88–89, 96–97, 99, 128, 130–132, 134, 140, 153, 156–157, 161, 175–182
Ohio Company of Virginia 20–21, 36–38, 41, 57–59, 61, 64, 79–82, 84, 87, 99
Ohio Historical Society 4
Ohio Indian Trails 3; *see also* Wilcox, Frank
Ohio Indians 2–4, 9, 11, 14–21, 27–32, 34–38, 40–41, 44, 48–53, 56–57, 65–68, 75, 80–81, 88–89, 96–97, 99, 118, 128, 130–132, 134, 157, 161, 175, 177–181
Ohio River 11–13, 15–17, 23, 26–28, 33, 36, *27*, *42*, 43–45, 49, 60–61, *63*, 64, 70, 73, 79, 81, 84, 87, 103, 155, 157, 167, 173, 181–183; *see also* la Belle Rivère
Ohiopyle 104
Oka 68
Old Bedford Village 4
Old Briton 29, 39–40, 81; *see also* La Demoiselle; Memeskia
Old Town, Maryland 97, 185
Onas 54
"110 Rules of Civility & Decent Behavior" 8

Oneida 4, 34, 64, 171, 179, 181, 183
Onondaga 47–48, 52, 53, 179
Orontony, Nicolas 28–29, 31, 34, 38, 49, 155
Ottawa Indians 35, 39, 77, 81, 99
Ottawa River 68

Paille Coupe 22, 24, *42*, 44; *see also* Buckaloons; Kachinodiagon
palisade 84, 90, 97, 121–124, 128, 131–132, 136, 140
Paris, France 83, 154, 159, 166, 167–168
parley 93, 143
parliament 158, 166
parole 143, 147–148, 172
Passyunk, Pennsylvania 158
Patten, John 82–83
pay 8, 12, 14, 87, 101–103, 136, 149, 155, 164, 166, 168, 170, 174
Péan, Michel-Jean-Hughes 86, 169–170
pence 102
Penn 13, 162
Pennsylvania 4, 9, 11, 13–17, 20, *22*, 23–26, 34, 36, 41, 44–45, 47–50, 52, 58–59, 62–63, 67, 71, 79–80, 82–83, 91, 93, 99, 101, 102, 105, 158–159, 161, 170–171, 174–177, 179–182
Petitcodiac, New Brunswick 155
Peyronie, William Chevalier La 101, 143–144, 170
Philadelphia 13, 16, 25, 158, 172, 174
Pickawillany 3, 15, *22*, 28–31, 34–35, 38–40, 51, 57, 81, 156
picket 108, 110, 123, 136–137, 140
Pied Froid 31, 34–35, 38; *see also* Cold Foot
Pine Creek 47
Piqua, Ohio 4, 15, 29
pistole 135, 186
Pittsburgh, Pennsylvania 9, 16, 20, 26, 158
Plains of Abraham 155, 164, 173
pneumonia 60, 177
Polson, William 134, 186
Pompadour, Jeanne Antoinette Poisson Marquise de 166–167
Pontiac 39, 81, 164–165, 172–173, 182
Pontiac's War 164–165, 172–173, 182
population 8, 19, 34
Port Clinton, Ohio 35
portage 18, 23, 44–45, 52, 75, 85–86, 103, 181
portmanteau 149
Portsmouth, Ohio 27, 44, 180
Portugal 154
Potomac River 36, *37*, *63*, 118–119, 159
pound (£) 15, 41, 87, 149, 174, 186
Presque Isle 42, 45–47, 52–55, 60, 85–86, 98, 154, 167, 183
Presque Isle Portage *42*, 45, 52–53, 60, 86
Prince Edward Island 155
profiteering 15, 18, 24, 27–28, 41, 43, 155, 169, 170; *see also* corruption
provincial governor 47
Prussia 154

Que, Isle of 17
Québec 12, 17, 31, 34, 73, 83, 85–86, 155, 158, 163–164, 167–170, 173, 175, 180
Queen Aliquippa 22, 26, **63**, 79, 122, 131, 157, 170–171, 180
Queen Anne's War 7; *see also* War of the Spanish Succession
Quiskakon 22, 29–31, 34–35, 38, 40, 83, 179; *see also* Kekionga; Kiskakon

Radisson, Pierre-Esprit 11
rapids 103–104
rations 53, 95–96, 102, 122, 135, 184
Reading, Pennsylvania 175–176
Red Stone 36, **37**, 79, 81, 84, 98–99, 101–105, 132, *132*, 134, 140, 153, 182
regiment 4, 76, 87–91, 99, 114, 143, 149, 153, 170–172, 174–176
Revolutionary War 157, 160, 163, 165, 167, 172, 174, 174–175, 177
Richelieu River 159
rifle 17, 82
Rivière aux Bœufs 15, 52–53, 71; *see also* French Creek
Rogers, Robert 64, 192
Royal American Regiment 174
royal coat of arms 21, 23–24, 28
royal governor 54, 68, 82, 88, 174
rum 69, 142, 182; *see also* liquor
Russia 154

Saguin, François 3, 18–19, 180
St. Augustine, Florida 174
St. Joseph River 22, 30
St. Lawrence River 17, 21, 153, 164, 173
St. Louis, Military Order of 60, 156, 159, 170, 175
St. Mary's River 22, 30, 179
St. Yotoc 22, 27, 29; *see also* Lower Shawnee Town; Scioto Town
Sandusky Bay 28, 180–181
Saratoga 8, 44
Sauconk 48; *see also* Shingas's Town
Sauk Indians 139
Saxony 154
scalp 8, 35, 40, 113, 117, 122, 140, 152
Scarouday 4, 47–49, 51, 64, 66, 82–83, 100, 109, 117, 122, 171, 179, 181; *see also* Monacatootha; Scruniyatha; Seruniyatha
Schaumber-Lippe 154
Schoharie, New York 15
Schuylerville, New York 44
Scioto River 22, 99
Scioto Town 22, 27, 44; *see also* Lower Shawnee Town; St. Yotoc
Scotland 130, 184–186
Scottsville, Virginia 88
scout 62, 84, 90, 104–109, 123, 127, 134, 136–137, 140–141, 151, 157, 162, 164
screws (musket tool) 143, 187

Scruniyatha 100, 179; *see also* Monacatootha; Scarouday; Seruniyatha
sea to sea 13, 20, 41
Selinsgrove, Pennsylvania 17
Seneca 2, 9, 15, 24, 25, 34, 49, 64, 68, 164, 176, 178–180, 183
HMS *Seneca* 164
Seruniyatha 179; *see also* Monacatootha; Scarouday; Scruniyatha
Seven Years' War 10, 178
shadow pay 103
Shamokin 171
Shanopin's Town 22, 26, **42**, **63**
Sharpe, Horatio 47, 54, 99, 163
Shaw, John 114
Shawnee 3, 15–16, 25, 27, 34, 47, 49, 66, 128, 134, 157, 171, 177, 179, 181, 183, 185
Shenandoah River **63**, 91
Shenango 16, 22, 44; *see also* Chiningué; Logstown
Shikellamy 16–17, 171, 179–180
shilling 90, 102, 130, 186
Shingas 64, 67, 83, 182
Shingas's Town 49, **63**, 64; *see also* Sauconk
siege 102, 143, 164, 168
Silverheels 108
Six Nations 16, 50–52, 65, 88, 179; *see also* Iroquois
smallpox 29, 35, 38, 162, 175, 182
South Carolina 48, 87, 102, 125–126, 130–131, 142, 162, 165, 181, 185
Spain, Spanish 7, 154, 159, 173, 182
speech belts 66–67, 70, 75; *see also* wampum
spies 92, 110, 116, 118–120, 134, 172–174
Spiltdorph, Carolus Gustavus de 121, 184
starvation 123
Stephan, Adam 91, 101, 111–113, 124, 143, 146, 149–150, 171–172, 184
Stewart, Henry 62, 69
Stobo, Robert 91, 98, 124–126, 145, 149–150, 152, 158, 163, 173–174, 186
stockade 84, 90, 92, 122
storehouse 36, 44, 47, 73, 79, 81, 84, 98–99, 101, 126, 153
strategy 69–70, 74, 108, 134, 152–153
strong house 41, 57–58, 80–81, 85, 90; *see also* fort
Sulpician 68
Sunbury, Pennsylvania 171
surrender 10, 95, 98, 144–145, 147, 152, 164, 168, 172
Susquehanna River 17, **63**, 171, 175, 179, 182
Suver, Peter 103
Sweden 89, 154
swivel gun 84, 90, 91, 96, 98, 125, 127, 139–141, 144
Syracuse, New York 47, 179

Tanacharison 2, 9, 10, 35, 41, 47–49, 51–52, 54–56, 58, 64–70, 74, 80, 82–85, 89–90, 92–93, 95–100, 103, 105–110, 112–115, 118,

Index

120, 122–123, 130–132, 134, 136–137, 147, 151, 154, 157, 170–171, 175, 177–179, 181, 186
Tarentum, Pennsylvania 25
tax 43, 158, 186
Tennessee 162
Tennessee River 12
Thalian Hall 163; *see also* Innes Academy
"that little thing on the meadow" 123, 137, 151
Thayendanegea 46; *see also* Brant, Joseph
theft 43
Thomas, George 49
tin plate 21, 23; *see also* copper plate
Tinkers Creek 18
Tiyanoga 46; *see also* King Hendrick
tobacco 87
tomahawk 50, 113–114, 147
tools 50, 79, 82, 95–96, 184, 187
torture 152, 155
Tory 158
Toulon, France 159
trade goods, European 2–3, 14, 17–20, 24, 28, 30, 32, 35, 41, 53, 57, 75, 81, 83, 89
trading post 3, 12, 14, 18–19, 25, 28, 35, 47, 64, 68, 89, 97, 101, 161, 164–165, 170, 177, 185
translator 62, 73, 105, 114, 143–144, 146–147
Treaty of Aix-la-Chapelle 11, 24, 94
Treaty of Fort Stanwix 157, 173
Treaty of Lancaster 34, 41, 57, 181
Treaty of Logstown 11, 16, *22*, 41, *42*, 48, 54, *63*, 80, 88
Treaty of Montréal 51
Treaty of Paris 154
Treaty of Philadelphia 16
Treaty of Ryswick 11, 24
Treaty of Utrecht 13
Trent, William 79–86, 89–90, 92–93, 95, 97–98, 102, 157, 173–174
Trent's Fort 83–84
Trois-Rivières 38
Tulpehocken, Pennsylvania 16
Turtle Creek *37*, 63, *63*, 78, 89–90, 95, 161
Tuscarawas Indians 179
Tuscarawas River *22*, 29

Uniontown, Pennsylvania 37, 62, 101

Valley View, Ohio 18
Van Braam, Jacob 62, 69, 73, 77, 124, 143–150, 158, 172–174
Vandalia land speculation 157, 173
Vaudreuil, Pierre de Rigaud de Cavagnial de 150
Venango 15, *22*, 24–26, *42*, 47, 55, 60, *63*, 64, 47–68, 71, 75–77, 80, 98, 161, 183
Vérendrye, Pierre Gaultier de Varness, Sieur de la 11
Vermillion River 38
Vernon, Adm. Edward 62, 159, 182
Versailles, France 33, 173
Vestal's Gap 90, 184
Villeneuve, Daniel 39
Villiers, Sieur Louis Coulon de 104, 139–146, 148, 151–153, 158, 162, 174–175, 186
Virginia 2, 4, 7, 9–11, 13, 20–21, 36–38, 41, 47–48, 57–59, 61–62, 64–65, 67, 71, 75–76, 79–84, 86–89, 91–92, 95–100, 102–106, 108–110, 112–115, 118, 122–124, 130–132, 135–137, 140, 143, 146, 149, 150, 152–153, 157–160, 162, 166, 168, 170–172, 175–178, 182–184
volley 7, 113, 139–142, 172
Voltaire 33–34, 162

Wabash Indians 34
Wabash River 12
Waggoner, Thomas 117, 122
wagons 36, 52, 89–91, 103, 106, 131, 135, 148
Walhonding River *22*, 29
walking purchase 17
Walpole, Horace 7
wampum 29, 46, 55–56, 66, 98, 100, 122, 131, 180, 182; *see also* speech belts
War of Conquest 10, 50; *see also* la Guerre de la Conquéte
War of Jenkin's Ear 159
War of the Austrian Succession 7, 166; *see also* King George's War
War of the League of Augsburg 7; *see also* King William's War
War of the Spanish Succession 7; *see also* Queen Anne's War
Ward, Edward 80, 90, 92–93, 94–98, 102–175, 184
Warraghiyahey 46; *see also* Johnson, William
Warren, Pennsylvania 23
warriors 24, 26–28, 35, 38–39, 50, 54, 67, 82–84, 88, 98–100, 109, 115, 122, 124, 126, 131, 139, 181–182
Washington, Anne Fairfax 79
Washington, Augustine, Jr. 20
Washington, Charles 168
Washington, George 1–2, 4, 7–10, 20, 49, 57, 61–62, 64–67, 69–81, 82, 86–92, 97–125, 127–128, 130–132, 134–154, 157–161, 163, 165–166, 168–169, 172, 174–177, 180
Washington, John Augustine 121
Washington, Lawrence 20, 79, 159, 182, 186–187
Washington, Martha Dandridge Custis 160–161, 177
Wayne, Anthony 172
Wea Indians 14, 179
Weems, Parson Mason Locke 147
Weisenberg, Catherine 46
Weiser, Conrad 14–17, 175–177, 180
West, John 121–122, 124
West Augusta, Pennsylvania 175
West Indies 163–164
West Virginia 13, 62, 172

White Thunder 67, 183; *see also* Kaghswaghtaniunt
Wilcox, Frank 3; *see also* Ohio Indian Trails
Williamsburg, Virginia 3, 58, 61–62, *63*, 71, 74, 79, 87–88, 92, 102, 120, 148, 166, 170, 174, 176–177
Wills Creek 36, *37*, 62, *63*, 79, 81, 89–90, 92, 95, 97–98, 100, 102, 104–105, 107, 124–125, 135–137, 143, 148, 152, 161, 163, 166, 177, 182; *see also* Cumberland; Fort Cumberland
Wilmington, North Carolina 163
Winchester, Virginia 4, 62, *63*, 91–92, 101–102, 107, 118, 121, 123–124, 168, 184, 186, 189
Wis-e-kau-kau-tshe 31; *see also* Cold Foot; Pied Froid
Wisconsin 13, 39, 71, 165
Wolfe, James 173
Womelsdorf, Pennsylvania 176
wounded 39, 113, 117, 122, 136, 139, 142–144, 148, 150, 152, 154–155, 163, 170, 173

Youghiogheny River 22, *37*, *42*, *63*, 79, 102–105, *132*
Youngstown, New York 41

www.ingramcontent.com/pod-product-compliance
Ingram Content Group UK Ltd.
Pitfield, Milton Keynes, MK11 3LW, UK
UKHW042005140426
5217PUK000158/995